Punishment in Latin America

PERSPECTIVES ON CRIME, LAW AND JUSTICE IN THE GLOBAL SOUTH

Series editors: Prof. Kerry Carrington and Prof. Máximo Sozzo

Scholarly perspectives on crime, law and justice have generally been sourced from a select number of countries from the Global North, whose journals, conferences, publishers and universities dominate the intellectual landscape. As a consequence, research about these matters in the Global South has tended to uncritically reproduce concepts and arguments developed in the Global North to understand local problems and processes. In recent times, there have been substantial efforts to uno this colonized way of thinking leading to a burgeoning body of new work. Southern theories, subaltern knowledges and border epistemologies are challenging the social science to open up new ways of thinking about society, crime, law and justice.

This book series aims to publish and promote innovative new scholarship with a long-term view of enhancing cognitive justice and democratizing the production of knowledge. Topics of interest from the perspective of the global south include – environmental and ecological plunder; gendered violence; religion, war and terror drug wars; the historical and contemporary legacies of slavery; the contemporary legacies of injustice arising from dispossession and colonialization; systems of punishment and forms of customary or transitional justice; human rights abuses and struggles for justice – all of which threaten the security of peoples who inhabit the global south.

Previous Volumes:

Southern Green Criminology: A Science to End Ecological Discrimination
Authored by David Rodríguez Goyes

Transforming State Responses to Feminicide: Women's Movements, Law and Criminal Justice Institutions in Brazil
Authored by Fiona Macaulay

Histories of Punishment and Social Control in Ireland: Perspectives from a Periphery
Edited by Lynsey Black, Louise Brangan and Deirdre Healy

INTERNATIONAL EDITORIAL ADVISORY BOARD

Elena Azaola Garrido	*Centre for Study and Investigation Social Anthropology, Mexico*
G. S. Bajpai	*National Law University, India*
Rosemary Barberet	*John Jay College of Criminal Justice, USA*
Jarrett Blaustein	*Monash University, Australia*
Avi Brisman	*University of Kentucky, USA*
Meda Chesney-Lind	*University of Hawaii, USA*
Elliott Currie	*University of California, USA*
Patricia Faraldo Cabana	*University of A Coruna, Spain*
Kate Fitzgibbon	*Monash University, Australia*
Manuel Iturralde	*Universidad de Andes, Colombia*
Jianhong Liu	*University of Macau, China*
Vera Malaguti	*State University of Rio de Janeiro, Brazil*
Leon Moosavi	*University of Liverpool, Singapore*
Camila Prando	*University of Brazil, Brazil*
David Rodriguez Goyes	*Antonio Nariño University, Colombia*
Clifford Shearing	*University of South Africa, South Africa*
Chuen-Jim Sheu	*National Taipei University, Hong Kong*
Ragnhild Sollund	*University of Oslo, Norway*
Nigel South	*University of Essex, UK*
Richard Sparks	*University of Edinburgh, UK*
Elizabeth Stanley	*Victoria University of Wellington, New Zealand*
Sandra Walklate	*University of Liverpool, UK*
Robert White	*University of Tasmania, Australia*
Eugenio R. Zaffaroni	*University of Buenos Aires, Argentina*
Diego Zyman	*University of Buenos Aries, Argentina*

Punishment in Latin America: Explorations from the Margins

EDITED BY

LUIZ DAL SANTO
University of Oxford, UK

AND

MÁXIMO SOZZO
National University of Litoral, Argentina

United Kingdom – North America – Japan – India – Malaysia – China

Emerald Publishing Limited

Emerald Publishing, Floor 5, Northspring, 21-23 Wellington Street, Leeds LS1 4DL.
First edition 2025

Editorial matter and selection © 2025 Luiz Dal Santo and Máximo Sozzo.
Individual chapters © 2025 The authors.
Published under exclusive licence by Emerald Publishing Limited.

Reprints and permissions service
Contact: www.copyright.com

No part of this book may be reproduced, stored in a retrieval system, transmitted in any form or by any means electronic, mechanical, photocopying, recording or otherwise without either the prior written permission of the publisher or a licence permitting restricted copying issued in the UK by The Copyright Licensing Agency and in the USA by The Copyright Clearance Center. Any opinions expressed in the chapters are those of the authors. Whilst Emerald makes every effort to ensure the quality and accuracy of its content, Emerald makes no representation implied or otherwise, as to the chapters' suitability and application and disclaims any warranties, express or implied, to their use.

British Library Cataloguing in Publication Data
A catalogue record for this book is available from the British Library

ISBN: 978-1-83797-329-3 (Print)
ISBN: 978-1-83797-328-6 (Online)
ISBN: 978-1-83797-330-9 (Epub)

Printed and bound by CPI Group (UK) Ltd, Croydon, CR0 4YY

INVESTOR IN PEOPLE

Contents

About the Editors   *ix*

About the Contributors   *xi*

Introduction   Punishment in Latin America: Explorations from the Margins
Luiz Dal Santo and Máximo Sozzo   *1*

Section 1: Penal Trajectories

Chapter 1   From *Senzalas* to Dungeons: The Constitution of the Penitentiary System in Brazil
André R. Giamberardino   *19*

Chapter 2   Punitive Turn or Punitive Imperialism? Analyzing the Transformation in the Ecuadorian Penal Realm
Martha Vargas Aguirre   *39*

Chapter 3   Criminal Justice Reform, Americanization, and Conviction without Trial in Argentina
Máximo Sozzo   *59*

Section 2: Prison Order and Prison Life

Chapter 4   Contemporary Prison Management in Chile: Disputes About Order
Olga Espinoza M.   *89*

Chapter 5   In/Out: Revisiting the Relationships Between Prisons and Slums in Latin America
Andrés Antillano   *109*

Chapter 6 The Arrival of the Risk Paradigm to Prison Management in Uruguay
Ana Vigna and Santiago Sosa Barón   *131*

Chapter 7 The Inca's Two Bodies: The Prison Condition in Latin America
Libardo José Ariza and Fernando León Tamayo Arboleda   *145*

Section 3: Theoretical Exchanges

Chapter 8 Actuarial and Managerial Justice: Theoretical and Empirical Impacts on Latin-American Criminological Realm
Mariano Sicardi and Claudio González Guarda   *163*

Chapter 9 Is Vigilantism an "Extralegal" Phenomenon?
Diego Tuesta   *183*

Chapter 10 Southern Green Victimology: A Look at the Cycle of Environmental Harms, Resistance and Over-criminalisation
Valeria Vegh Weis   *201*

Index   *219*

About the Editors

Luiz Dal Santo is a DPhil candidate at the Oxford Centre for Criminology and a Tutor in Criminology at Hertford College and St Catherine's College. He also teaches in Graduate Programs in Criminology and Law in Brazil. He previously taught at the University of Oxford, Oxford Brookes University, University of Law, and University of Roehampton. He has recently published a monograph titled *A punição no Brasil: crítica do giro punitive* (Tirant Lo Blanch, 2024) and co-edited the edited volume *Southernising Criminology: Challenges, Horizons and Praxis* (Routledge, 2024). He has also published journal articles and book chapters on punishment, penal populism, prison, police lethality, racism and criminal justice, Southern Criminology, and Criminal Law. His work has been published in English, Portuguese, Italian, and Spanish.

Máximo Sozzo is a Professor of Sociology of Law and Criminology at the National University of Litoral (Argentina) and Leverhulme Visiting Professor at the School of Law of the University of Edinburgh (United Kingdom) during 2024/2025. His research is focused on punishment and society in Latin America. His latest books are: Aliverti, H. Carvalho, A. Chamberlain, & M. Sozzo (Eds.) *Decolonising the Criminal Question* (Oxford University Press, 2023); M. Langer & M. Sozzo (Eds.) *Justicia penal y mecanismos de condena sin juicio. Estudios sobre América Latina* (Marcial Pons, 2023), and M. Sozzo (Ed.) *Prisons, Inmates and Governance in Latin America* (Palgrave, 2022).

About the Contributors

Martha Vargas Aguirre is a PhD candidate at the University of Ottawa. A lawyer by training with a Master's degree in Criminology, her research interests revolve around government practices in both criminal law and human mobility regulation, as well as the intersections between these two areas. A member of the academic commission of the Observatory of Criminology, Criminal Policy and Penal Execution of Ecuador, she develops constant evaluations in the area of criminal policy in this country as well as analysis of the use of these instruments as tools for the criminalization of immigration.

Andrés Antillano is Professor of Criminology at the Law School and Researcher at the Institute of Penal Sciences of the Universidad Central de Venezuela. He has written about prison, gangs, and crime.

Libardo José Ariza is a Lawyer from Universidad de los Andes. He holds a Master's degree in Legal Sociology from the Oñati International Institute of Legal Philosophy and PhD in Law from the University of Deusto. He is currently a Professor at the Universidad de los Andes. His lines of research focus on the sociology of law, sociology of punishment, and prisons. His most recent publications are the book *Tres décadas de encierro: el constitucionalismo liminal y la prisión en la era del populismo punitivo* published by Siglo del Hombre Editores and the papers "Tales from La Catedral: The Narco and the Reconfiguration of Prison Social Order in Colombia" in the book *Prisons, Inmates and Governance in Latin America* and "Locked in the Home: A Critique of House Arrest as an Alternative to Imprisonment for Women Sentenced for Drug-Related Crimes" (2021) in *The Prison Journal*.

André R. Giamberardino is Professor of the Postgraduate Programs in Law and Sociology of the Federal University of Paranà (UFPR) and Public Defender of the Public Defender's Office of Paraná, Brazil. He is also a Visiting Professor at the Università degli Studi di Bari Aldo Moro, Italy (2024). Previously, he was Visiting Scholar at Columbia Law School (2019–2020) and Chief of Staff of the Ministry of Public Security of Brazil (2018). He received his PhD in Law from UFPR (2014), and his Master's degree in Law from UFPR (2007) and in Criminology from the Università degli Studi di Padova, Italy (2009). His research and publications focus on prison, punishment, and criminal justice topics. He has recently published the books *Penal Abolitionism and Transformative Justice in Brazil* (Routledge, 2023), *Sociocriminologia*, and *Comentários à Lei de Execução Penal* (in Portuguese).

Claudio González Guarda holds a PhD in Law and Social Sciences from the University of Malaga, Spain. He also works as assistant professor in the Faculty of Government at the University of Chile and is currently the director of the Centro de Estudios en Seguridad Ciudadana (CESC) at the same university. Dr. Gonzalez is also currently president of the Chilean Society of Criminology.

Olga Espinoza M. is a Professor at the Faculty of Government at the University of Chile. She holds a PhD in Social Science from the University of Chile, and a Master's degree in Law from the University of Sao Paulo. She is a founder member of the Chilean Society of Criminology (SoChiCrim). Her research and publications are focused on prison policies, female prisoners, and criminal justice topics.

Mariano Sicardi is a PhD student at the Faculty of Social Sciences of the University of Buenos Aires. He holds a BA in Law (Faculty of Law, UBA) and an MA in Criminology (Faculty of Law & Social Sciences, National University of Litoral). Currently, he serves as jefe de trabajos prácticos at the UNPaz School of Law (Argentina).

Santiago Sosa Barón is a Sociologist and has a Postgraduate Diploma in Public Policies, Crime and Insecurity (University of the Republic). He is a Master's student in Human Sciences and Contemporary Philosophy. He is an Advisor at the Office of the Parliamentary Commissioner for Prisons in Uruguay, where he works in the area of statistics and monitoring, helping to verify compliance with human rights in Uruguayan prisons. He works on research on prison policies and the development of tools to address human rights violations. He has participated in several research projects on living conditions, rehabilitation opportunities, institutional violence, and deaths in custody, among other aspects of the prison system. He has also worked as a consultant at the Social Security Institute, researching various aspects of the social security system in Uruguay.

Fernando León Tamayo Arboleda is a Lawyer from Universidad de Antioquia. He holds a Master's degree in Criminal Law from Universidad Eafit and PhD in Law from Universidad de los Andes. He is currently a Professor at the Universidad de los Andes. His lines of research focus on criminology, sociology of law, sociology of punishment, and criminal law. His most recent publications are the book *Del Estado al parque: el gobierno del crimen en las ciudades contemporáneas* published by Siglo del Hombre Editores; and the papers "Understanding Contradictory Styles of Punishment" in *Theoretical Criminology*, "Urban Surveillance and Crime Governance in Bogotá" in *City, Culture and Society*; and "Building a Secure City: Urban Governance, Crime Control and Segregation in Bogotá" (2022) in *City*.

Diego Tuesta is a PhD candidate at the Centre for Criminology and Sociolegal Studies at the University of Toronto. His dissertation examines the relationship between prosecutorial discretion and racial disparities in the province of Ontario,

Canada. He has conducted multiple qualitative research projects that investigate prosecutorial discretion and police governance in cases of femicide, human trafficking and mining protests in his native Peru. Before his Doctoral studies, he worked as an advisor, consultant and data analyst for criminal justice agencies in Peru, as well as civil society organizations both nationally and internationally. He has been a Course Instructor of criminology courses at Pontificia Universidad Católica del Perú and Universidad del Pacífico. Currently, in addition to his academic work, he often participates as an expert witness for asylum-related cases in the United States.

Valeria Vegh Weis, LLM (NYU), PhD (UBA), is a Research Fellow at the Zukunftskolleg of the University of Konstanz, where she researches the role of human rights and victims' organizations in confronting state crimes in the Global South. She is also an Associate Professor at the Universidad de Buenos Aires, Universidad Nacional de Quilmes, and Universidad Madres de Plaza de Mayo in Argentina. She has held several fellowships, including the Alexander von Humboldt, Fulbright and Hauser Global. Her book *Marxism and Criminology: A History of Criminal Selectivity* (Brill, 2017; Haymarket Books, 2018) won the Choice Award and the Outstanding Book Award. She is also co-author of *Lawfare: The Criminalisation of Politics in the Global South* (2023) and Editor of *Criminalisation of Activism* (2021). She has 15 years' of experience in criminal courts and international organizations and is the winner of the ASC Critical Criminology of the Year Award (2021).

Ana Vigna is a Professor at the School of Social Sciences, University of the Republic (Uruguay), and holds a PhD in Sociology (University of the Republic). She has worked on several research projects on prison policy, desistance from crime, recidivism, punishment, and gender and crime. She has written several articles and contributed to books on the subject. She has also worked as a consultant for various national and international agencies on issues such as prison reform, prison ombudsman, and gender in the criminal justice system.

Introduction

Punishment in Latin America: Explorations from the Margins

Luiz Dal Santo and Máximo Sozzo

[a] *University of Oxford, UK*
[b] *National University of Litoral, Argentina*

Abstract

This introduction sets the scene for the book. It touches upon the recent growth of a literature on punishment in global peripheries within the wider punishment and society scholarship. It then briefly develops on two topics that constitute key elements of the whole book: knowledge production and exchange and peripheral punishment. In highlighting some common aspects, trends, and features of punishment in Latin America, it prepares the ground for the specific chapter contributions that are based on local experiences of different Latin American countries. In so doing, we also acknowledge the works of scholars who have initially advanced a movement for the understanding of punishment and the criminal question our marginalised Latin American realities.

Keywords: Punishment; Latin America; knowledge production; Global South; global peripheries; prison; punishment and society; marginalisation;. criminal question; criminal justice

Punishment and society scholarship have been growing and consolidating over the last few decades. This considerable growth has first and foremost been boosted by the exploration of certain English-speaking national contexts. Considering relations of inequality and power on a global scale – from the economic, political, and cultural domains, to the production and circulation of scientific knowledge in social sciences – these contexts are usually framed as central or as 'the core'. Among them, the United States of America and the United Kingdom are particularly privileged (Carrington et al., 2019, pp. 99–141; Faraldo-Cabana & Lamela, 2021).

Elsewhere, we have highlighted how the centrality of these contexts is reflected in the first handbook published on this field (Dal Santo & Sozzo, 2023). Published more than a decade ago, The *SAGE Handbook of Punishment and Society* (Simon & Sparks, 2013) comprises 22 chapters of which only one is written by an author who was not based at a university in an English-speaking country at that time. The author is Dario Melossi, whose chapter actually compares Europe and the United States. Only five authors were not based in the United States and the United Kingdom – two being in Australia, two in Canada and one in New Zealand. In this vein, what this Handbook presents as 'punishment and society' scholarship mostly corresponds to 'punishment and society in core countries'. And why does it matter? Most of the penal processes, policies, institutions, discourses and practices analysed throughout the Handbook are unsurprisingly those that have occurred in the United Kingdom and the United States, and occasionally in other national, central settings. Similarly, the problems, concepts and arguments discussed are those emerged in those particular scenarios, although the theoretical literature from other core settings has some relevance too, as the case of France, including the classical works of Durkheim, Foucault, and Bourdieu. The presence of penality in the global peripheries – as well as of the intellectual production on it – is rather scarce throughout the Handbook. On the one hand, this reflects the fact that the Handbook was planned for English-speaking audiences. On the other hand, this also evidences structures and relations of inequality and subordination in the production and circulation of knowledge both in criminology (Carrington et al., 2016, 2019) and the wider social sciences (Connell, 2007).

In more recent years, there has been a noticeable rise in works on penality in peripheral contexts in English-speaking international debates, following the increasing appeals and efforts to southernise and decolonise criminology. This rise often stems from individual contributions on specific peripheral countries, usually in formats of journal articles, but also – less frequently – as monographies (in the latter case, see, e.g., Anaraki, 2020; Bracco Bruce, 2022; Bonner, 2019; Brown, 2014; Bruce-Lockhart, 2022; Darke, 2018; Konaté, 2018; Li, 2018; Super, 2013). But there are also growing contributions on wider peripheral regions, usually taking shape as collaborative work in the format of special issues in scientific journals and edited collections. In recent years, there have been several such efforts on penality in Latin America (Bergman & Fondevilla, 2021; Darke et al., 2021; Darke & Garces, 2017; Hathazy & Müller, 2016; Sozzo, 2022), Africa (Alexander & Kynoch, 2011; Braatz et al., 2022; Morelle et al., 2021) and Asia (Ganapathy & Balachandran, 2016; Lee & Karen, 2013), as well as in global peripheries more generally (Dal Santo & Sozzo, 2023).

This edited volume *Punishment in Latin America: Explorations from the margins* contributes to the development of the punishment and society scholarship towards this wider and more collaborative direction, while being also part of those contemporary efforts to decolonise and southernise criminology. This work is itself a product of a collective project coming out from the international conferences *Punishment in Global Peripheries,* organised by the Oxford University Centre for Criminology (United Kingdom) and the Crime & Society Program of the National University of Litoral (Argentina). We organised the first edition of this conference in 2021. Since then, we have been annually gathering together researchers interested in punishment and society studies in different contexts and regions of the world, beyond the central scenarios. These conferences have been venues for expanding the international debate, where scholars have shed light on historical and contemporary dynamics affecting historically marginalised settings. In so doing, not only have we questioned concepts and arguments that are usually taken for granted, but we have also advanced theoretical and methodological issues through innovative perspectives and approaches.

This book reflects this spirit. Its contributions shed light on the complexities of penal dynamic, institutions and practices in Latin America, describing and explaining them from different methodological and theoretical perspectives. The chapters are in-depth case studies comprising the realities of eight countries – Argentina, Brazil, Chile, Colombia, Ecuador, Peru, Uruguay and Venezuela. In addition to being analyses of penality in Latin American countries, the chapters share a critical emphasis on the insufficiency, in some aspects and dimensions, of Northern concepts and arguments to make sense of punishment beyond core countries, despite some of those theoretical productions possessing – explicitly or implicitly – features of being universal, timeless and placeless. The authors of the different chapters engage in a critical dialogue with these Northern concepts and arguments. A dialogue that seeks to avoid subordination and dependency, considers their own contexts and problems, and develops different forms of adaptation and innovations, so to deal with their embedded and peculiar features.

This edited collection is organised in three main sections. The first section comprises chapters that engage with historical trajectories, trying to make sense of different types of penal changes. These changes have taken place in distinct moments in history, some that go back to colonial times, while others are more contemporary. Different conditions of possibility and mechanisms are identified and analysed in these chapters. The second section is made of chapters that deal more closely with prison order and prison life, identifying specific dynamics and features of this central institution of legal punishment in the region. Finally, the third section provides contributions that engage with theoretical discussions on significant topics in Latin America – from actuarial justice to vigilantism – enriching these debates from the very Latin American contexts and processes.

In addition to these three main sub-topics explored in the book, the reader will realise that there are two elements that, to some extent, are relevant in each and all chapters of this edited volume. The book is not a mere combination of random studies on punishment in Latin American countries put together, with the only common element being their geographical location. The two elements that bring all chapters together in a cohesive way are the underlying discussion on knowledge production and exchange, and the consideration of peripherality as a key point of analysis – being certain that these two elements relate to each other. On the one hand, the authors do not simply disregard knowledge originally produced in core countries, but nor do they assume knowledge based on other social realities can be merely transported elsewhere. On the other hand, each Latin American social reality and its dynamics are analysed from their feature of being peripheral or marginal. The authors are not merely analysing punishment in a given peripheral region, but they analyse punishment in that specific peripheral region as being precisely the product of its location in the periphery. And to do so, they bring to their analytical framework historical and contemporary events, forces, powers, and relations, such as colonialism, slavery, imperialism, dependency, subalternity and so on. Considering the centrality of these two elements throughout the book, we now touch upon them in order to establish some premises before the reader explores the book.

Knowledge Production and Exchange

The recent rise of southern and decolonial perspectives has been reshaping the field of criminology. Not only have these perspectives looked at different geographical realities and focussed on the interconnectedness between the centre and the peripheries to make sense of criminological issues around the world. They have also drawn attention to wider power imbalances and inequalities in the domain of knowledge production, dissemination and exchange. In fact, mirroring dynamics in other domains of social reality, there has been a more or less established flow of knowledge, theories, concepts, and arguments about crime and punishment from the core to the peripheries. But what does that mean? Does it mean that knowledge produced in the centre is better developed? Does it mean that there is no relevant production of knowledge in the peripheries? By highlighting this issue of knowledge production, dissemination, and exchange, are we implying that knowledge produced in the core should be completely and automatically disregarded if one is trying to make sense of realities in the peripheries? We have discussed these and other similar questions in more detail elsewhere (Aliverti et al., 2021, 2023; Carrington et al., 2016, 2018, 2019; Dal Santo & Sepúlveda Penna, 2024; Garcia & Sozzo, 2023; Sozzo, 2023). However, it is worthy retaking this discussion here, even if shortly.

Whereas this topic has assumed a more significant position in contemporary discussions on criminology, this is not at all a new debate. In the birth of critical visions in the criminological field in Latin America, the relations of inequality and subordination in the production and circulation of knowledge on the criminal question were a specific object of problematisation and debate (Aniyar de Castro, 1987; Del Olmo, 1975, 1981, 1987, 1990; Zaffaroni, 1984, 1988, 1989; see Alagia & Codino, 2019; Goyes & Sozzo, 2023).

On several occasions, critical authors like Raul Zaffaroni or Lola Aniyar de Castro pointed out that Northern theories were simply imported and reproduced in Latin America. This was particularly sustained in relation to the long history of positivist criminology in the region, from the 1880s until the 1960s. But around four decades ago, Del Olmo (1987, 1990; see also Sozzo, 2006) emphasised that not only mainstream criminology was reproducing 'Northern' concepts and arguments in Latin America, but even critical criminologists were uncritically importing the critiques of their European and North American colleagues, overlooking the particularities of the criminal question in Latin America. Some traces of this dynamic could also be seen nowadays (for some examples of that, see Dal Santo, 2020; Sozzo, 2018). This, however, is not a trend particularly limited to Latin America (see Agozino, 2003, 2004; Alemika, 2020; Cain, 2000; Igbinovia, 1989; Lee & Laidler, 2013; Liu et al., 2013).

As a matter of fact, a number of issues have significantly favoured a more uncritical reproduction of Northern theories on the criminal question in peripheral regions – and particularly in Latin America. These issues operate in different domains, from the material to the ideological, also going through matters such as the institutionalisation of academic fields. At the ideological level, these uncritical reproductions often take place in a more nuanced, involuntary and non-malicious way. We can here relate this to the reproduction of colonial knowledge and perspectives by the colonised – or the oppressor's ideology by oppressed people – which have been thoroughly analysed in broader terms by different authors. It is worth mentioning, among others, the internalisation of the colonial mentality and the production of colonised subjects (Fanon, 1952/2000), cultural hegemony (Gramsci, 1977), and mental colonialism (Unger, 2018), for example. In a different direction, in a more intentional way, there is also the figure of a 'castrated master who castrates his disciples' (Dussel, 1977). This may be the one that goes abroad, from the peripheral to central contexts, in the pursue of a badge and authority, that can only be attained, they believe, in the academic institutions of those central scenarios. These are the ones who go abroad – physically or virtually – and come back willing to show they are all up to date with the most recent developments in criminological thought, from the newest textbooks to the newest influential scholars. So they use a 'Northern' credential for personal purposes, and end up uncritically reproducing those Northern perspectives.

Ideological relations and processes have downplayed the development of more innovative knowledge production on the criminal question in the global peripheries, but so have the material conditions (Carrington et al., 2019; Dal Santo & Sepúlveda Penna, 2024; Moosavi, 2019; Sozzo, 2021; Travers, 2019). Profound economic inequalities across the world affect the academic fields and, in turn, the production of knowledge, which undeniably faces more limitations in contexts of scarcity of material infrastructure and funding. Faraldo-Cabana and Lamela (2021, p. 168) observed from UNESCO data that

> the US accounts for 33% of the world's research funding (55 countries surveyed), employs 24% of the world's researchers in terms of fulltime equivalent (53 countries surveyed) and produces around 26% of the world's PhDs in social sciences (48 countries surveyed) and 30–40% of all social science research articles.

World inequalities are also reflected in the investment in research and development as exposed in the latest UNESCO (2021) science report. Regions such as North America and European Union invest 2.73% and 2.02% as a share of their

GDP in research and development, whereas Latin America invests 0.66% – for comparison, these are the percentages in other peripheral regions: 0.09% in the Caribbean, 0.51% in Sub-Saharan Africa, 0.12% in Central Asia, and 0.60% in South Asia. If this disparity between core and periphery in relative terms is already striking, imagine how this translates in absolute numbers. Such disproportionality also reflects in the number of researchers (in full-time equivalent) per million inhabitants: this ratio is 4,432 in North America; 4,069 in the European Union; and 593 in Latin America. If ideological elements – with all its colonial facets – frame the periphery as backward and not as capable as the core, one cannot ignore the precarious material conditions in which research is conducted in the margins, which has significant implications to its volume and (lack of) possibilities.

Finally, considering criminology more specifically, there are also some significant problems with this academic field that are specific to most parts of the Global South. One of the issues Medina (2011) highlights, in his exploration about doing criminology in the periphery and semiperiphery, is the degree of academic institutionalisation, which in turn leads to problems such as lack of recognition and stable careers. Although massively expanding and presenting increasing levels of institutionalisation in many parts of the core countries (see Sparks & Loader, 2011, 2012) criminology has not acquired the appearance and paraphernalia of a 'discipline' (Garland, 2011) in the academic world of most of the peripheries.

In Latin America, criminology had an incipient institutionalisation in some countries since the last years of the 19th century, strongly associated with the academic worlds of law and medicine, in connection with the local translation of positivist vocabularies imported from European contexts, especially Italy and France (Caimari, 2004; Creazzo, 2007; Del Olmo, 1981, 1992, 1999; Huertas García-Alejo, 1991; Marteau, 2003; Salessi, 1995; Salvatore, 1992, 1996, 2001; Sozzo, 2006, 2011, 2015, 2017, forthcoming; Salvatore & Sozzo, 2009). This institutionalisation was extremely weak, as it was not articulated in the generation of faculties or departments and specific undergraduate and postgraduate degrees, but rather in the presence of professors (often part-time), courses, research projects and centres, and scientific journals, mainly based in law and medicine faculties. It is only from the 1970s that a new moment has opened up. A slow and gradual institutionalisation of a field in the academic world, defined as criminology, is taking place. This has included the creation of postgraduate degrees – specialisations and master's, but not doctoral degree – and, to a lesser extent, even the creation of undergraduate degrees. There has also been a significant growth in degrees linked to 'public security' and 'citizen security', although predominantly related to the training of police and prison officers and not strongly connected with the international criminological debate. There has also been a slight increase in the number of specialised scientific journals, research projects and centres and full-time professors and researchers, particularly in some countries, such as Brazil and Argentina. But there are still no specific faculties or departments of Criminology (Goyes & Sozzo, 2023; Sozzo, 2020, 2021). This increasing institutionalisation was initially connected to the regional dissemination of critical criminology perspectives, also linked to the translation of central theoretical vocabularies (Alagia & Codino, 2019; Andrade, 2012; Anitua, 2005; Carvalho & Matos, 2021a, 2021b; Garcia, 2021; Garcia & Sozzo, 2023; Giamberardino, 2012; Goyes, 2019, 2023; Malaguti-Batista, 2011, 2012; Souza Cordeiro, 2020; Sozzo, 2006, 2020;Vasconcelos, 2014, 2017). In parallel, however, there is also a vast and growing intellectual production from the social sciences – especially from sociology, but also from anthropology and political science – on different aspects of the criminal question that has grown significantly in recent decades and whose protagonists do not define themselves as 'criminologists' (Sozzo, 2020, 2021).

In anyway, this is all to illustrate that the development of a well-elaborated and established scholarship is not only held back by ideological dynamics and relations, but also by material conditions, and particularly by the level of institutionalisation that a field of knowledge possesses in most of peripheral regions – in our concrete case, in Latin America.

Even in the peripheries, scholars have often read punishment – as a set of institutions, discourses, and practices – 'from the centre' (Connell, 2007, p. 44; Sozzo, 2023). The problems, concepts, and arguments generated in core contexts have been presented as universal, giving rise to broad generalisations, which in turn conceal the fact that they have themselves arisen in specific places and times, and as a product of particular dynamics, processes, and relationships (Aas, 2012; Aliverti et al., 2021, 2023; Carrington et al., 2016, Carrington et al., 2019; Lee & Laidler, 2013). But researchers in the Global South often uncritically import this knowledge and apply it to their own settings as a transferable recipe, sometimes producing empirical data, and ratifying the purported universal character of that knowledge (Aas, 2012; Aliverti et al., 2021, 2023; Carrington et al., 2019; Lee & Laidler, 2013; Moosavi, 2019).

However, as one of us has recently argued (Sozzo, 2023), the history of knowledge on punishment in the peripheries also contains episodes of resistance to this inequality, dependence, and subordination in knowledge production and circulation. These episodes articulate different degrees of innovation, which involve operations of rejection and adaptation of what is produced in the Global North, always in relation to the exploration of local dynamics and processes, giving rise to a sort of 'metamorphosis' of theoretical vocabularies (Sozzo, 2006). Reconstructing these different episodes is an important contribution not only to avoid falling into a kind of 'amnesia' (Goyes & South, 2017), but also to find in them sources of inspiration for our contemporary research work (Garcia & Sozzo, 2023).

When taking back Latin America as our case study, one can identify examples of such episodes in different times in history. This is the case, for example, of a more distant past, during the development of a positivist criminology between the 1880s and 1930s (Sozzo, 2011, 2017, forthcoming). More recently, in the framework of the birth of critical criminology since the 1970s, such episodes have become more frequent and radical (Sozzo, 2023). One illustration is the important work of Eugenio Raúl Zaffaroni (1984, 1988, 1989) and his 'marginal criminological realism' (Alagia & Codino, 2019; Garcia & Sozzo, 2023). For Zaffaroni, the massive violation of human rights produced by Latin American penal systems was not only quantitatively but qualitatively different from those produced in central contexts. These differences, he claims, are also the result of the extremely high levels of marginalisation that peripheral capitalism has generated in the region. The more intense and frequent human rights violation as the main characteristic of Latin American penalty is also linked to the various forms of colonialism that have run through the history of the region. They are an undeniable phenomenon that constitutes a true 'genocide in action' (Zaffaroni, 1989, p. 127), which implies that 'the colonialist and neo-colonialist genocide has not ended on our margin, our penal systems continue to carry it out' (Zaffaroni, 1989, p. 129). In light of this extremely dramatic characteristic, Zaffaroni raises the imperative of acting publicly and politically, including as an operator of the penal system, in order to moderate the exercise of the power to punish (Sozzo, 2020). His position has been very influential in both the academic and penal fields in Latin America from that time to the present day (Alagia & Codino, 2019; Garcia & Sozzo, 2023).

More recently, other original and innovative intellectual contributions are emerging directly from Latin American realities and enriching the global criminological literature in many different topics. It is this type of work – and the critical dialogue with Northern theories, concepts and arguments – that composes this book. Throughout the chapters, the reader will notice that the authors do not a priori despise or reject knowledge originally developed in core countries, as in a nativist approach. However, nor do they uncritically reproduce Northern knowledge as if it represented the most advanced stage of knowledge valid across all times and places. The real compromise of the authors is to better understand their own realities, departing from a close encounter with them (Carrington et al., 2016, 2019; Dal Santo & Sepúlveda Penna, 2024; Sozzo, 2021, 2023). These realities are, however, also implicated in transnational relations, both from the past and in the present, which in turn may produce different outcomes locally. And, it is exactly this interconnectedness of these social realities, more precisely in the context of core and peripheries, that is, briefly explored in the section below.

Peripheral Punishment

The authors of the chapters of this book analyse various aspects of punishment - defined in broad terms – in different national contexts which form part of Latin America and which can be considered peripheral or marginal in the light of relations of inequality and domination of different kinds at the global level. As anticipated, one of the distinctive features of the analyses contained in this book is to address these different aspects of punishment by making their peripheral or marginal character a specific object of interrogation and exploration. Punishment in the peripheries is to a certain extent different from punishment in the centre because it is, precisely, a peripheral punishment. And this is the case in several senses that we clarify here.

Rescuing and emphasising the reference to 'peripheral punishment' does not imply assuming a kind of homogeneity of these diverse contexts addressed in this book. We do acknowledge that these contexts are crossed by important economic, social, political, institutional, and cultural differences, and so these distinctions are also reflected on the penal field. There are different ways of being peripheral in the contemporary global context and this has different consequences for penality and its analysis in these scenarios (Sozzo, 2023). However, this does not prevent us from affirming that, beyond all these differences, it is possible to identify common components, features, and trends of punishment in these contexts, which are linked precisely to their peripheral character.

Peripheral penality has been shaped by the relations of inequality and dependency between regions of the world that have in turn been intricated but hierarchised by different global relations throughout history, from colonialism to dependency. Penal institutions, discourses, and practices constructed in central contexts have incessantly influenced those generated in peripheral contexts. Borrowing and mutating for our purposes a widespread notion among Latin American decolonial theorists (Lander, 2000), the peripheral character of penality in the region reveals a facet that could be defined as the 'coloniality of penality' in these national contexts (Aliverti et al., 2021; Carrington et al., 2019; Sozzo, 2023).

In Latin America, it is interesting to note that in most contexts, it was only after the end of the era of 'original colonialism' (Zaffaroni, 2022, pp. 37–62) that the process of construction of 'modern' criminal law and penal institutions – police, criminal justice, prison – began. Despite the formal independence of its former imperial metropolises, the importation of models generated in central contexts was crucial in this construction. In many cases, the sources of influence ceased to be the Portuguese and Spanish scenarios, which were replaced by other contexts associated by Latin American elites with the advancement of 'civilisation' and 'modernity', such as France, the United Kingdom, and the United States of America. With a high degree of variation in terms of intensity and speed across countries – and even across different regions of the same country – this implied displacing other practices of social control associated with the colonial or pre-colonial past, giving penality a halo of 'modernity' but on a 'neo-colonial' basis (Zaffaroni, 2022, pp. 63–108).

However, the fact that the history of the birth of a 'modern' penality in Latin America has been traversed by processes of importation from the 19th century onwards does not mean that what was generated in peripheral countries was a perfect reproduction of what had previously emerged in the central countries. Even when, in some cases, the Latin American elites launched initiatives of imitation in this field, they faced a series of obstacles to achieve their objectives, from the limitations of material resources available to carry out these enterprises to the resistance of the actors who sought to reproduce previous ways of thinking and acting or try to build new ones, but an alternative to those central models. At the same time, these attempts at imitation were faced with an array of problems that 'modern', 'civilized' penal institutions, discourses and practices had to respond to, which could differ widely from those that the central scenarios sought to confront, giving rise also to varying degrees of obstacles to this kind of operation of adoption. As it was the case with theoretical vocabularies on the penal question, penal institutions and practices also underwent forms of 'metamorphosis', which gave them peculiar characteristics connected with the past and present of peripheral contexts (Aliverti et al., 2021; Carrington et al., 2019; Sozzo, 2011, 2023).

The example of the prison is illustrative in this respect. From the first half of the 19th century, sectors of the Latin American elites promoted the importation of this then-new form of legal punishment that had been developing in some central scenarios. In some Latin American countries, some penitentiary institutions sought to embody the 'correctional model' proclaimed in the rhetoric that accompanied and justified this process of importation, achieving varying degrees of implementation – from the House of Correction in Rio de Janeiro, whose construction began in 1834 (Bretas, 1996, p. 104) or the Penitentiary of Santiago de Chile, which began to be built in 1844 (Leon, 2003, p. 429). But, in general, these islands of penal modernism coexisted with a vast number – greater or lesser in the different countries and across the different regions of the same country – of custodial institutions in which the absence of human and material resources translated into mere sequestration and abandonment in, what Caimari has aptly called for the Argentine case, 'punitive swamps' (Caimari, 2004, pp. 109–124; see also Aguirre, 2007; Bracco Bruce, 2022; Darke, 2018; Salvatore & Aguirre, 1996). It can be thought that from that moment a sort of 'mixed economy' (O' Malley & Meyer, 2005) of prison life in the region was built, which has remained a constant over time, alternating moments and places of greater weight of a 'correctional model' with moments and places of greater weight of an opposite 'incapacitating model' – although less linked to the high-tech versions developed in the last 40 years in certain contexts of the Global North, and more to a traditional version of state neglect (Sozzo, 2007, 2009). In this framework, a very important number of specific elements appear – some of which are raised in the chapters on the subject in this book (Espinosa, this book; Vigna & Sosa Baron, this book; Antillano, this book, Ariza and Tamayo, this book) – that can be considered to acquire peculiar expressions and degrees in Latin American prisons, from their high level of permeability to their strong degree of informality, from the widespread diffusion of self-governance and co-governance schemes to their strong doses of collectivism (Bergman & Fondevilla, 2021; Birkbeck, 2011; Darke, 2018; Darke & Garces, 2017; Darke & Karam, 2016; Macaulay, 2019; Sozzo, 2022).

These features of punishment in Latin America – the marked influence of the legal, institutional, and practical designs created in the central scenarios and, at the same time, its inevitable metamorphosis in these other scenarios in relation to local problems, obstacles, and struggles – constitute a long-lasting phenomenon which, despite persisting in the present, has also undergone mutations (Aliverti et al., 2023, pp. 352–354; Iturralde, 2023). Suffice it to think, as examples, of those attempts at importation produced in recent decades in the framework of the penal transformations in the region, which are specifically explored in some chapters of this book: from the 'war on drugs' paradigm and its multiple implications (Aguirre, this book), to 'plea bargaining' as a mechanism for imposing convictions without trial (Sozzo, this book), from managerial language reconfiguring the criminal justice organisations (Gonzalez and Sicardi, this book) to the techniques of calculating and managing risk in penitentiary institutions (Vigan and Sosa Baron, this book).

In this sense, the recognition of the peripheral nature of punishment in Latin America, with all its complexity, makes it necessary for its understanding to start from its 'embeddedness' (Melossi, 2001; see Melossi et al., 2011; Nelken, 2011) in the present and past of these scenarios. The chapters in this book have in common, therefore, to claim an approach that has as its starting point the immersion – with different methodological strategies – in our own scenarios, in order to proceed inductively, rather than deductively, constantly striving to decentre the intellectual production generated in the punishment and society studies in and for the central contexts (Brangan, 2020, 2023). This implies assuming that dialogue with that literature is inevitable but at the same time may be insufficient to account for Latin American penality (Sozzo, 2023).

Almost four decades ago, Eugenio R. Zaffaroni, one of the key intellectuals in the construction of critical thought on the criminal question in Latin America, referred to exactly what we are here problematising when he claimed the need to assume the 'marginal' character in order to build our understanding of penality in our region (Garcia, 2021; Garcia & Sozzo, 2023; Sozzo, 2020). For Zaffaroni (1988),

> assuming the marginal position … does not cost anything for our subaltern populations but it is relatively difficult for the researcher, not only because of their class origin but also because all the preparation and training condition them to produce a discourse in a 'universal' way, as if 'centre' and 'margin' of power did not exist. (p. 3)

According to Zaffaroni (1988, p. 3, 1993, p. 9), to assume the condition of 'marginal' is to transform the fact that 'we are located on the periphery of global power' into a central axis of our gaze. However, he opts for 'marginal' instead of 'peripheral' 'because it is more expressive', he claims. 'Marginal' implies accepting a point of view about 'our facts of power' in the context of a 'relationship of dependency with the central power' (Zaffaroni, 1989, p. 170). 'Marginal' embodies a culturally diffused definition of the marginalised Latin American population, which was conceived in the stages of colonialism and which Zaffaroni (1989) calls the 'marginal-syncretic originality of Latin America'. It can only be understood historically, that is, in the five hundred years of dependency of Latin America, as a colossal process of marginalisation (pp. 170–172).

Hence the subtitle of this book, which is intended to function not only as a description of the orientation that guides the authors throughout its chapters, but also as an appeal to multiply this kind of explorations in the future.

References

Aas, K. F. (2012). The earth is one but the world is not': Criminological theory and its geopolitical divisions. *Theoretical Criminology*, *16*(1), 5–20.

Agozino, B. (2003). *Counter colonial criminology: A critique of imperialist reason*. Pluto.

Agozino, B. (2004). Imperialism, crime and criminology: Towards the decolonization of criminology. *Crime, Law and Social Change*, *41*, 343–358.

Aguirre, C. (2007). Prisons and prisoners in modernising Latin America. In I. F. Dikköter, & I. Brown (Eds.), *Cultures of confinement. A history of the prison in Africa, Asia and Latin America* (pp. 14–54). Cornell University Press.

Alagia, A., & Codino, R. (2019). *La descolonización de la criminología en América*. Ediar.

Alemika, E. E. O. (2020). Reflections on criminology in Africa. *Acta Criminologica (Criminological Society of Southern Africa)*, *33*(2), 1–11.

Alexander, J., & Kynoch, G. (2011). Special issue. Histories and legacies of punishment in Southern Africa. *Journal of Southern African Studies 37*(3).

Aliverti, A., Carvalho, H., Chamberlen, A., & Sozzo, M. (2021). Decolonizing the criminal question. *Punishment and Society*, *23*(3), 297–316.

Aliverti, A., Carvalho, H., Chamberlen, A., & Sozzo, M. (Eds.). (2023). *Decolonizing the criminal question. Colonial legacies, contemporary problems.* Oxford University Press.

Anaraki, N. R. (2020). *Prison in Iran: A known unknown*. Palgrave Macmillan.

Andrade, V. R. P. (2012). *Pelas mãos da criminologia. O controle penal para além da (des) ilusão*. Revan.

Anitua, G. I. (2005). *Historias de los pensamientos criminológicos*. Editores del Puerto.

Aniyar de Castro, L. (1987). *Criminología de la Liberación*. Universidad del Zulia.

Bergman, M., & Fondevilla, G., (2021). *Prisons and crime in Latin America*. Cambridge University Press.

Birkbeck, C. (2011). Imprisonment and internment: Comparing penal institutions North and South. *Punishment & Society*, *13*(3), 307–332.

Black, L., Seal, L., Seemungal, F., Malkani, B., & Ball, R. (2021). Special issue. Legacies of empire. *Punishment & Society*, *23*(5).

Bonner, M. (2019). *The rise of punitive populism in Latin America*. University of Pittsburgh Press.

Bowling, B. (2011). Transnational criminology and the globalisation of harm production. In M. Bosworth & C. Hoyle (Eds.), *What is criminology?* (pp. 361–379). Oxford University Press.

Braatz, E., Bruce-Lockhart, K., & Hynd, S. (2022). Special issue. African penal histories in global perspective. *Punishment & Society*, *24*(5).

Bracco Bruce, L. (2022). *Prison in Peru. Ethnographic, feminist, decolonial perspectives*. Palgrave Macmillan.

Brangan, L. (2020). Exceptional states: The political geography of comparative penality. *Punishment and Society*, *22*(5), 596–616.

Brangan, L. (2023). Penality at the periphery. deficits, absences and negation. *Journal of Contemporary Criminal Justice*, *39*(1), 94–113.

Bretas, M. L. (1996). What the eyes can't see: Stories from Rio de Janeiro's Prisons. In R. Salvatore & C. Aguirre (Eds.), *The birth of the penitentiary in Latin America* (pp. 101–122). University of Texas Press.

Brown, M. (2014). *Penal power and colonial rule*. Routledge.

Bruce-Lockhart, K. (2022). *Carceral afterlives: Prisons, detention, and punishment in post-colonial Uganda*. Ohio University Press.

Caimari, L. (2004). *Apenas un delincuente. Crimen, cultura y castigo en la Argentina*. Siglo XXI.

Cain, M. (2000). Orientalism, occidentalism and the sociology of crime. *British Journal of Criminology*, *40*, 239–260.

Carrington, K., Hogg, R., & Sozzo, M. (2016). Southern criminology. *British Journal of Criminology*, *56*(1), 1–20.

Carrington, K., Hogg, R., Scott, J., & Sozzo, M. (2018). Criminology, southern theory and cognitive justice. In K. Carrington, R. Hogg, J. Scott, & M. Sozzo (Eds.), *The Palgrave handbook of criminology and the global south* (pp. 3–19). Palgrave Macmillan.

Carrington, K., Hogg, R., Scott, J., Sozzo, M., & Walters, R. (2019). *Southern criminology*. Routledge.
Carvalho, S., & Matos, L. (2021a). The crisis of the critical criminology crisis in Brazil: Epistemological, methodological and political challenges in authoritarian times. *The Howard Journal of Crime and Justice*, *60*(3), 430–448.
Carvalho, S., & Matos, L. (2021b). A criminologia socialista e a crítica anticarcerária em roberto lyra (fontes da Criminologia Crítica brasileira). *Revista Culturas Jurídicas*, *8*(19), 209–239.
Castel, R. (1997). *Las Metamorfosis de la Cuestión Social*. Paidos.
Connell, R. (2007). *Southern theory: The global dynamics of knowledge social science*. Allen & Unwin.
Creazzo, G. (2007). *El positivismo criminológico italiano en la Argentina*. Ediar.
Dal Santo, L. P. (2020). Populismo penal: o que nós temos a ver com isso? *Revista Brasileira De Ciências Criminais*, *168*, 225–252
Dal Santo, L., & Sozzo, M. (2023). Special issue. Punishment in the global peripheries. *Theoretical Criminology*, *27*(4).
Dal Santo, L., & Sepúlveda Penna, C. (Eds.). (2024). *Southernising criminology: Challenges, horizons, praxis*. Abingdon.
Darke, S. (2018). *Conviviality and survival. Co-producing Brazilian prison order*. Palgrave Macmillan.
Darke, S., & Karam, M. L. (2016). Latin American prisons. In Y. Jewkes, B. Crewe, & J. Bennett (Eds.), *Handbook on prisons* (2nd ed., pp. 460–474). Routledge.
Darke, S., & Garces, C. (2017). Special issue. Informal dynamics of survival in Latin American prisons. *Prison Service Journal*, *229*.
Darke, S., Garces, C., Duno-Gottberg, L., & Antillano, A. (Eds.). (2021). *Carceral communities in Latin America: Troubling prison worlds in the 21st century*. Palgrave Macmillan.
Del Olmo, R. (1975). Limitations for the prevention of violence. The Latin American reality and its criminological theory. *Crime and Social Justice*, *3*, 21–29.
Del Olmo, R. (1981). *América Latina y su criminología*. Siglo XXI Editores.
Del Olmo, R. (1987). Criminología y derecho penal. Aspectos gnoseológicos de una relación necesaria en la América Latina actual. *Doctrina Penal*, *37*, 23–43.
Del Olmo, R. (1990). *Segunda Ruptura Criminológica*. Universidad Central de Venezuela.
Del Olmo, R. (1992). *Criminología Argentina*. Depalma.
Del Olmo, R. (1999). The development of criminology in Latin America. *Social Justice*, *26*(2), 19–45.
Dussel, E. (1977). *Filosofía de la liberación*. Edicol.
Fanon, F. (2000 [1952]). *Black skin, white masks*. Grove Press.
Faraldo-Cabana, P., & Lamela, E. (2021). How international are the top international journals of criminology and criminal justice? *European Journal on Criminal Policy and Research*, *27*, 151–174.
Ganapathy, N., & Balachandran, L. (2016). Special issue. Crime and punishment in Asia. *Journal of Contemporary Criminal Justice*, *32*(3).
Garcia, N. (2021). *Raúl Zaffaroni Criminologo* [Master's thesis in Criminology, Faculty of Legal and Social Sciences, Universidad Nacional del Litoral, Santa Fe].
Garcia, N., & Sozzo, M. (2023). For a 'marginal criminological realism': Zaffaroni and the birth of a critical perspective on the criminal question from the Global South. *Justice, Power & Resistance*, *6*(1), 50–68.
Garland, D. (2011). Criminology's pace in the academic field. In B. M. Hoyle (Ed.), *What is criminology?* (pp. 298–317). Oxford University Press.
Giamberardino, A. (2012). Os Passos de uma Criminologia Marxista: revisão bibliográfica em homenagem a Juarez Cirino dos Santos. In J. Zilio & F. Bozza (Eds.), *Estudos*

Críticos Sobre o Sistema Penal: Homenagem ao Professor Juarez Cirino dos Santos (pp. 219–240). LedZe.
Goyes, D. R. (2019). *A southern green criminology: Science against ecological discrimination*. Emerald.
Goyes, D. R. (2023). Latin American green criminology. *Justice, Power & Resistance*, 6(1), 90–107.
Goyes, D. R., & South, N. (2017). Green criminology before Green criminology: Amnesia and absences. *Critical Criminology*, 25, 165–181.
Goyes, D. R., & Sozzo, M. (2023). Latin American criminologies: Origins, trajectories and pathways. *Justice, Power & Resistance*, 6(1), 2–18.
Gramsci, A. (1977). *Quaderni dal carcere* (2nd ed.). Einaudi.
Hathazy, P., & Müller, M. (2016). Special issue. The rebirth of the prison in Latin America. *Crime, Law and Social Change*, 65(3).
Huertas García-Alejo, R. (1991). *El Delincuente y su Patología. Medicina, crimen y sociedad en el positivismo argentino*. Consejo Superior de Investigaciones Científicas.
Igbinovia, P. E. (1989). Criminology in Africa. *International Journal of Offender Therapy and Comparative Criminology*, 33(2), v–x.
Iturralde, M. (2023). The weight of empire: Crime, violence and social control - and the promise of southern criminology. In A. Aliverti, H. Carvalho, A. Chamberlen & M. Sozzo (Eds.), *Decolonizing the criminal question. Colonial legacies, contemporary problems* (pp. 53–71). Oxford University Press.
Konaté, D. (2018). *Prison architecture and punishment in colonial Senegal*. Lexington Books.
Lander, E. (Ed.). (2000). *La colonialidad del saber: eurcentrismo y ciências sociales. Perspectivas latino-americanas*. CLACSO.
Lee, M., & Laidler, K. J. (2013). Doing criminology from the periphery: Crime and punishment in Asia. *Theoretical Criminology*, 17(2), 141–157.
Lee, M., & Karen, J. (2013). Special issue. Crime and control in Asia. *Theoretical Criminology*, 17(2).
Leon, M. A. (2003). *Encierro y corrección. La configuración de un sistema de prisiones en Chile* (pp. 1800–1911). Universidad Central de Chile.
Li, E. (2018). *Punishment in contemporary China: Its evolution, development and change* (1st ed.). Taylor and Francis.
Liu, J., Hebenton, B., & Jou, S. (2013). Progress of Asian criminology: Editors' introduction. In J. Liu, B. Hebenton, & S. Jou (Eds.), *Handbook of Asian criminology* (pp. 1–7). Springer.
Macaulay, F. (2019). Prisoner capture. In R. Sieder, K. Ansolabehere, & T. Alfonso (Eds.), *Routledge handbook of law and society in Latin America* (pp. 243–258). Routledge.
Malaguti Batista, V. (2011). *Introdução crítica à Criminologia brasileira*. Revan.
Malaguti Batista, V. (2012). A Escola Crítica e a Criminologia de Juarez Cirino dos Santos. In J. Zilio & F. Bozza (Eds.), *Estudos Críticos sobre o Sistema Penal: homenagem ao Professor Cirino dos Juarez Santos* (pp. 117–128). LedZe.
Marteau, J. F. (2003). *Las palabras del orden. Proyecto republicano y cuestión criminal en Argentina (Buenos Aires, 1880–1930)*. Editores del Puerto.
Medina, J. (2011). Doing criminology in the "semi-periphery" and the "periphery". In C. J. Smith, S. X. Zhang, & R. Barberet (Eds.), *Routledge handbook of international criminology* (pp. 13–23). Routledge.
Melossi, D. (2001). The cultural embeddedness of social control: Reflections on the comparison of Italian and north-American cultures concerning punishment. *Theoretical Criminology* 5(4), 403–424.
Melossi, D., Sozzo, M., & Sparks, R. (2011). Introduction: Criminal questions: Cultural embeddedness and global mobilities. In D. Melossi, M. Sozzo, & R. Sparks (Eds.), *Travels of the criminal question* (pp. 1–14). Hart Publishing.

Moosavi, L. (2019). A friendly critique of "Asian criminology" and "Southern criminology." *British Journal of Criminology, 59*, 257–275.
Morelle, M., Le Marcis, F., & Hornberger, J. (Eds.). (2021). *Confinement, punishment and prisons in Africa*. Routledge.
Nelken, D. (2011). Theorising the embeddedness of punishment. In D. Melossi, M. Sozzo, & R. Sparks (Eds.), *Travels of the criminal question: Cultural embeddedness and diffusion* (pp. 65–92). Hart.
O'Malley, P., & Meyer, J. (2005). Missing the punitive turn? Canadian criminal justice, "balance" and penal modernism. In J. Pratt, S. Hallsworth, M. Brown, D. Brown, & W. Morrison (Eds.), *The new punitiveness: Trends, theories, perspectives* (pp. 201–2017). Willan.
Salessi, J. (1995). *Médicos, maleantes y maricas*. Beatriz Viterbo Editora.
Salvatore, R. (1992). Criminology, prison reform and the Buenos Aires working class. *Journal of Interdisciplinary History, 23*(2), 279–299.
Salvatore, R. (1996). Penitentiaries, visions of class and export economies: Brazil and Argentina compared. In R. Salvatore & C. Aguirre (Eds.), *The birth of the penitentiary in Latin America* (pp. 194–223). University of Texas Press.
Salvatore, R. (2001). Sobre el surgimiento del estado médico legal en la Argentina (1890–1940). *Estudios Sociales, XI*, 81–114.
Salvatore, R., & Aguirre, C. (1996). The birth of the penitentiary in Latin America: Toward and interpretative social history of prisons. In R. Salvatore & C. Aguirre (Eds.), *The birth of the penitentiary in Latin America* (pp. 1–43). University of Texas Press.
Salvatore, R., & Sozzo, M. (2009). Criminología moderna en América Latina y Estados Unidos (1880–1940). In L. Dammert (Ed.), *Crimen e inseguridad .Política, temas y problemas en las Americas* (pp. 19–56). FLACSO Chile/Catalonia.
Simon, J., & Sparks, R. (Eds.). (2013). *The sage handbook of punishment & society*. Sage.
Souza Cordeiro, C. S. (2020). *Doxas da crítica barattiana: a conformação de um campo criminológico crítico brasileiro* [Tesi de Doutourado em Directito, Brasília, UNICEUB].
Sozzo, M. (2006). "Tradutore Traditore." Traducción, Importación Cultural e Historia del Presente de la Criminología en América Latina. In M. Sozzo (Ed.), *Reconstruyendo las Criminologías Críticas* (pp. 353–431). Ad-Hoc.
Sozzo, M. (2007). ¿Metamorfosis de la prisión? Proyecto normalizador, populismo punitivo y 'prisión-depósito' en Argentina. *URVIO Revista Latinoamericana De Seguridad Ciudadana, 1*, 88–116.
Sozzo, M. (2009). Populismo punitivo, proyecto normalizador y 'prisión depósito en Argentina. *Revista Sistema Penal y Violencia, 1*(1), 33–65.
Sozzo, M. (2011). Los exóticos del crimen. Inmigración, delito y criminología positivista en Argentina (1887–1914). *Delito y Sociedad, 32*, 19–51.
Sozzo, M. (2015). *Locura y crimen. Nacimiento de la intersección entre dispositivo penal y dispositivo psiquiátrico*. Didot.
Sozzo, M. (2017). Los usos de Lombroso. Tres variantes en el nacimiento de la criminología positivista en Argentina. In M. Sozzo & L. Caimari (Eds.), *Historia de la Cuestión Criminal en América Latina* (pp. 27–69). Prohistoria.
Sozzo, M. (2018). Beyond the neoliberal penality thesis? Visions on the penal turn from the Global South. In K. Carrington, R. Hogg, J. Scott, & M. Sozzo (Eds.), *The Palgrave handbook of criminology and the Global South* (pp. 658–685). Palgrave Macmillan.
Sozzo, M. (2020). Criminología, mundo del derecho y modos de compromiso público: Exploraciones sobre el caso de Argentina. *Tempo Social, 32*(3), 109–146.
Sozzo, M. (2021). Public and southern criminologies: Possible encounters. In S. Playisir & T. Daems (Eds.), *Criminology and democratic politics* (pp. 59–87). Routledge.
Sozzo, M. (Ed.). (2022). *Prisons, inmates and governance in Latin America*. Palgrave Macmillan.

Sozzo, M. (2023). Reading penality from the periphery. *Theoretical Criminology*, *27*(4), 660–675.
Sozzo, M. (forthcoming). Traducción e innovación en la configuración de una perspectiva criminológica positivista en José Ingenieros (1899–1916). In J. Nuñez & M. Sozzo (Eds.), *Los viajes de las ideas sobre la cuestión criminal desde y hacia Argentina. Traducción, lucha e innovación (1880–1955)*. Max Planck Institute for the History and Theory of Law.
Sparks, R., & Loader, I. (2011). *Public criminology?* Routledge.
Sparks, R., & Loader, I. (2012). Situating criminology: On the production and consumption of knowledge about crime and justice. In M. Maguire, R. Morgan & R. Reiner (Eds.), *The Oxford handbook of criminology* (pp. 3–38). Oxford University Press.
Super, G. (2013). *Governing through crime in South Africa*. Routledge.
Travers, M. (2019). The idea of a southern criminology. *International Journal of Comparative and Applied Criminal Justice*, *43*(1), 1–12.
UNESCO. (2021). *UNESCO science report: The race against time for smarter development: Executive summary*. https://unesdoc.unesco.org/ark:/48223/pf0000377250
Unger, R. M. (2018). *Depois Do Colonialismo Mental*. Autonomia Literária.
Vasconcelos, F. T. R. (2014). *Esboço de uma sociologia política das ciências sociais contemporâneas (1968–2010): a formação do campo da segurança pública e o debate criminológico no Brasil. 2014* [Tese Doutorado em Sociologia, Faculdade de Filosofia, Letras e Ciências Humanas, USP, São Paulo].
Vasconcelos, F. T. R. (2017). As ciências sociais brasileiras e a formação do "campo da segurança pública." *Revista Brasileira de Sociologia*, *5*(9), 33–58.
Zaffaroni, E. R. (1984). *Sistemas penales y Derechos Humanos en América Latina (Primer Informe)*. Depalma.
Zaffaroni, E. R. (1988). *Criminología. Aproximación desde un margen*. Temis.
Zaffaroni, E. R. (1989). *En busca de las penas perdidas. Deslegitimación y dogmática jurídica-penal*. Ediar.
Zaffaroni, E. R. (1993). *Muertes anunciadas*. Temis.
Zaffaroni, E. R. (2022). *Colonialismo y Derechos Humanos. Apuntes para una Historia Criminal del Mundo*. Taurus.

Section 1
Penal Trajectories

Chapter 1

From *Senzalas* to Dungeons: The Constitution of the Penitentiary System in Brazil

André R. Giamberardino

Federal University of Paraná, Brazil

Abstract

The central hypothesis of the chapter is that Brazilian colonialism and slavery produced different material conditions or different governmentalities, from those at the base of the disciplinary project of the Global North, conditions that re-signified the penitentiary reform proposal. This chapter is structured into five sections: the first section introduces the hypothesis that the houses of correction were not the institutions that originated the Brazilian penitentiary system. The following section develops this idea based on an analysis of the social and economic dimensions of Brazil's colonial formation. Unlike the global North, which officially envisioned the penitentiary as the institutional foundation of a democratic society, the penitentiary in Brazil was first envisioned as a mere symbol of modernity, then as an instrument for preserving order. The third section describes how the first prisons emerged without industrialization and how the material conditions for a prison reform discourse based on discipline remained absent. The fourth section indicates the inapplicability of the original conception of discipline in a context without Protestantism, presenting the Jesuit experience as the one closest to a project of moral reform and constraint to work. Being absent the category of disciplinary power in its original form, at least regarding its economic dimension, the national penitentiary project was born from the dungeons where public and private power overlapped for the corporal punishment of the enslaved. The last section analyzes the

Punishment in Latin America: Explorations from the Margins, 19–37
Copyright © 2025 by André R. Giamberardino
Published under exclusive licence by Emerald Publishing Limited
doi:10.1108/978-1-83797-328-620241002

importation of the penal reform discourse and its adaptation in the context immediately following the abolition of slavery in 1888.

Keywords: Prison history; Brazil; punishment, Global South; slavery; colonialism

Introduction

This chapter analyzes the origin of the Brazilian penitentiary system from the political, theoretical, and empirical approach that takes the Global South as a metaphor of power relations (Carrington et al., 2016). The main works that interpreted the penitentiary invention are from the Global North and, for the most part, from the 1970s or "rediscovered" in the same decade (Foucault, 1975; Ignatieff, 1978; Melossi & Pavarini, 1977/2018; Rothman, 1971; Rusche & Kirchheimer, 1939/1999). In this chapter, these references are in dialogue with the historical process of Brazilian social formation.[1]

It is not the purpose of this chapter to review the well-known elements of works on the history of prisons. Nevertheless, some clarifications are important regarding the debate that took place during the presentation of the paper at the event "Punishment in Global Peripheries: Contemporary changes and historical continuities," at the University of Oxford (England), in June 2021.

In the literature on the macro history of prisons translated into Portuguese and influential in Brazil, works like those by Rusche and Kirchheimer (1939/1999), Foucault (1975), and Melossi and Pavarini (1977/2018) prevail, as well as a Marxist reading of the thought of Michel Foucault (Batista, 2011, p. 85), and such perspective influenced the writing of this chapter. However, this should also be problematized, considering that this is a different interpretation from the one that prevails in a broader context.

According to Koehler, for example, there was a steady decline in Marxist assumptions about the history of prisons in the second half of the 20th century. One of the protagonists of this decline was precisely the popularity of Foucault (Koehler, 2020), who absorbed and overcame several Marxian concepts with new categories, such as "civil war" and "popular illegalisms" – something that is clearer in "The Punitive Society (1972–1973)" than in "Discipline and Punish" (Harcourt, 2015; Lemos, 2020).

Even so, an important premise stemming from Marxist thought is that punitive practices precede their legal regulation and the corresponding penal theories. Beccaria's penal Enlightenment or Jeremy Bentham's utilitarianism did not invent

---

[1] An early version of this chapter was originally presented as a paper at the international conference "Punishment in Global Peripheries: Contemporary changes and historical continuities," University of Oxford (England), June 2021. I greatly appreciate the comments and contributions of Ashley Rubin and Dario Melossi, partially referred to and incorporated in this version, as well as the comments of Maximo Sozzo and Luiz Phelipe Dal Santo, the organizers of the conference.

the prison sentence. Instead, these authors theorized about punitive practices that actually emerged from the development of workhouses and houses of correction.

Rusche and Kirchheimer's (1939/1999) central hypothesis points to conditioning between the mode of production and its corresponding punitive practices, looking above all at the transition from the feudal to the capitalist economy. Reductions in the price of labor and in the reserve army of labor would reduce the value of human life (Rusche & Kirchheimer, 1939/1999, p. 35), with death sentences and corporal punishment gaining space.

Foucault, in turn, is very clear when he states that "the prison-form cannot be derived from the penal theories of Beccaria, Brissot, etc." and that "as an institution and as a practice it is derivable from the Quaker conception of religion, morality and power" (Foucault, 2015, p. 81). In the 1973 lectures, he describes a new form of power – the disciplinary power – as a new regime of truth. The "prison-form" would be a diffuse social form, rather than concentrated in the State (Harcourt, 2015, p. 244).

Likewise, in colonial formations such as the Brazilian one, punitive practices and their rationalities were materially constituted chronologically before the penal reform discourses arrived, giving new meaning to the latter. The category of discipline and the use of corporal punishment demand a critical rereading from colonization, slavery, and a predominantly rural context.

This chapter is structured in five sections as follows: the first section introduces the hypothesis that the houses of correction were not the institutions that originated the Brazilian penitentiary system. The following section develops this idea based on an analysis of the social and economic dimensions of Brazil's colonial formation. The third section describes how the first prisons emerged without industrialization and how the material conditions for a prison reform discourse based on discipline remained absent. The fourth section indicates the inapplicability of the original conception of discipline in a context without Protestantism, presenting the Jesuit experience as the one closest to a project of moral reform and constraint to work. Finally, the last section analyzes the importation of the penal reform discourse and its adaptation in the context immediately following the abolition of slavery in 1888.

The construction of a Brazilian national project and the prison reform discourse are inseparable topics. How could this project include a huge mass of those recently freed from enslavement in a context where racist and eugenic theories prevailed? The central thesis of this chapter is that the true matrices of the Brazilian penitentiary system, instead of houses of correction, were the spaces of symbiosis between public and private punitive power, represented by the dungeons of the first penitentiaries that were used to hold and flog slaves.

The Smell of Brazilwood

An important novelty appeared in Amsterdam in 1596: the *tutchhuis*, or *rasphuis* for men and *spinhuis* for women. These were one of the first houses of correction opened in Europe. The famous engraving by Melchior Fokkens depicts workers under surveillance and, higher up, a statue of justice. The well-known aim of the houses of correction was to prevent idleness and compel people to work.

Thousands of kilometers away, the Dutch competed with the Portuguese empire for space in the seas, coming to occupy part of the Brazilian Northeast between 1630 and 1654. What brings together two very distant scenarios is the smell of Brazilwood. One of the first activities performed at the Dutch *rasphuis* was precisely the work with Brazilwood extracted from the South American colony. It was "particularly suitable for the idle and lazy" (Melossi & Pavarini, 1977/2018, pp. 78–79). A historical memorandum by Jan Laurenszoon Spiegel, "Memorandum on the foundation of the tuchthuis," probably written in 1589 and mentioned by Sellin (1944, p. 53), testifies to the importance of using South American wood for disciplinary ends.

Brazil never had a correctional facility as the houses of corrections, an organized space for work constraints, even though the country's first penitentiaries were given this name. The mother institution of the Brazilian penitentiary was not the correction house, but the cellars and dungeons of 18th-century prisons, which constituted spaces overlapping public and private powers in sharing the violence imposed on slaves. This overlap became the pattern of relations established between the police, prison, and the Brazilian people before and after abolition.

The "modern and civilized" penitentiary project of the 19th century did not arrive late in Brazil: the point is that this project found rationalities and material conditions completely different and inseparable from the colonial social formation. As Salvatore and Aguirre (1996) argue, the question is not to measure how close or distant Brazil was to Europe and the USA in terms of modernity, but to understand why local elites understood, at a specific juncture, that it would be interesting to "modernize" the treatment of prisoners and the penitentiary system (p. 4), and the distinctive features of these discourses in Latin America and Brazil.

There was no delay but symbiosis; there was no rejection but a rereading, producing new forms of disciplinary practices that did not exist in experiences built under free labor. In its own way, the Brazilian colony actively participated in the same process of capital accumulation that gave rise to correctional and penitentiary institutions in Europe and the USA. However, predatory economic exploitation and the absence of a proletariat due to slavery produced different conditions for this participation, which reshaped the discourses of penal reform.

Differences are also found among the colonizers. According to John Howard, at the end of the 18th century, "the relevance of the institution [of workhouses] in Portugal and Spain is practically nil" (Melossi & Pavarini, 1977/2018, p. 118). For Sérgio Buarque de Holanda (1936/1995), "a dignified idleness has always seemed more excellent, and even more ennobling, to a good Portuguese, or a Spaniard, than the insane struggle for daily bread" (p. 38), unlike Protestant peoples. Buarque de Holanda (1936/1995), argues that the Iberian type would be *adventurous*, with "anxiety for prosperity without cost, honorific titles, positions and easy wealth" (p. 46), which would explain the predatory nature of colonization, the prohibition of the production of goods that could compete with the metropolis, and the focus on production exports, indifferent to the domestic market.

The Labor Problem and the Punitive Practices

Colonial Brazil was a huge land divided into large estates, and its economy was mostly based on export monoculture. It should not be surprising that the central problem in colonial Brazil's economy was always the need for labor. The first attempt to solve this problem was through the enslavement of indigenous people. In a short time, however, preference was given to the enslavement of Africans. The slave trade became a fundamental pillar in the organization of sugar production and the very constitution of the Brazilian people.

Therefore, it is impossible to agree with the transposition of European theoretical models to the Brazilian colonial formation, classifying it as a feudal, semi-feudal structure, or even an arm of the absolutist metropolis. What was needed to enable sugar cane cultivation in such large areas reveals not a semi-feudal organization but a mercantile, agro-industrial enterprise with a high level of capital investment. The focus on exporting also distances the slave organization from the feudal one (Furtado, 1959, p. 88). In this sense, capital accumulation was external to production.

The labor shortage was faced completely differently from Europe, not least because the initial colonial project was only trade. Settlement happened as a contingency imposed later. The enslaved worker was directly linked to production as an instrument, not a subject. Besides, the *status* of the landlords of sugar plantations was not equal to the feudal lord. While the latter "ruled people in search of their own survival," the former aimed to meet the demands of the foreign market, generating profit like a modern factory (Ribeiro, 1995, pp. 289–290).

Likewise, the fact that Portugal and its legislation – the Ordinances – were linked to an absolutist context at the time does not mean that the colony was also absolutist. Concerning the punitive practices of the Brazilian colony, if there was a feature that could not be found is exactly that of a centralized absolutism such as the monopolization of the use of force. Colonial punitive practices were fragmentary and scattered, managed much more by the personal power of the landlords of sugar plantations than directly regulated by the Portuguese Ordinances. The internal order of the plantations remained relatively free from external interference, being established by militias that repressed slave revolts and land disputes (Huggins, 1985, pp. 16–17). According to the Jesuit Jorge Benci (1705), when a slave committed a serious crime, the standard procedure was not a trial by the justice system, which was seen as something that would diminish the nobility of the landlords of sugar plantations (p. 191).

The colonial legal framework was given by the *Afonsinas* Ordinances, at the time of the arrival of Portuguese people in Brazilian lands (1500–1514); by the Manueline Ordinances (1514–1603) and finally by the Philippine Ordinances, which were in force in Brazil until its independence, followed by the publication of the Criminal Code of the Empire in 1830. The main penalties established by the Ordinances were typical of absolutism: death penalties, corporal punishment in various modalities, and exile, leaving imprisonment as an instrument of constraint to the payment of debts or custody of the convict awaiting the fulfillment of his sentence.

However, many other local regulations fragmented the regulatory system and weakened the Ordinances politically. Slaves were subjected to private violence from their masters without formal charges. Therefore, classifying historical phases according to normative changes is not an adequate method for understanding the transformations of penal practices. It is more appropriate to work with the identification of patterns and models that may even overlap at certain historical moments (Rubin, 2019a).

Portugal's central role was that of an intermediary in the trade of primary products exported by the Brazilian colony. The aim was to sell to end buyers, such as Holland and England, for greater value. Thus, Brazil supplied, first with sugar, then with gold, the capitalist expansion of pre-industrial Europe. The accumulation of capital in the colony was not reversed in developing the internal market or local industry. On the contrary, landowners bought more land, more slaves, and more luxury. The lack of investment in economic alternatives to sugar production was, in the 17th century, a determinant of the sugar company's decline in the face of global competition.

From the second half of the 16th century, *workhouses* and houses of correction appeared. Such institutions were identified as fundamental in primitive or original accumulation, that is, of separation between producer and means of production. The process of primitive accumulation was also that of transforming the means of production into capital and the direct producer into a free worker (Melossi & Pavarini, 1977/2018, p. 69). Its history is thus intertwined with the historical process of the creation of capital and the proletariat.

For this reason, prison as a punishment could not exist in pre-capitalist production systems (Melossi & Pavarini, 1977/2018, p. 57). After all, the penitentiary invention in Europe stems from the need to create the proletariat, that is, a free labor force:

> How would prison not be the quintessential punishment in a society where freedom is a good that belongs to everyone in the same way and to which everyone is linked by a "universal and constant" feeling? The loss of liberty, therefore, has the same price for everyone; better than the fine, it is the "equal" punishment. (Foucault, 1975, p. 268)

There is no way to answer this question in slavery, for the question itself must change. The Brazilian colony could not have prison as a punishment either – or an institution like the workhouses – even though it had a capitalist production system, and this was because of slavery. As part of the slave world, imprisonment contributed directly to developing the punitive practices that would emerge in the following centuries. Because of this, the post-abolition period was not one of rupture but of mere reorganization (about the experience in Louisiana, USA, see Bardes, 2020). The patterns were set up. Perhaps what existed in the Brazilian colonial formation, then, would only be the process of capital creation – from the importation of equipment and technique (Furtado, 1959, p. 83) – but without a proletariat, a demand that would only appear at the end of the 19th century.

In manufacturing, without machines, capital is invested for raw material consumption, and forced labor is characterized by low capital employment, scarce and low-quality production. At the same time, profits are secured by wage compression (Melossi & Pavarini, 1977/2018, p. 80). In industry, part of the profit goes to the payment of production and labor. However, in the Brazilian colonial economy, at least 90% of the profit remained to the landlords serving both to enable a life full of luxury and increase production (Furtado, 1959, p. 80) with a large part of payments made abroad.

A second economic activity developed in parallel to sugar was cattle farming, which favored the settlement of the Northeast of the country and helped to form a new intermediate population group. It was made up of settlers living in a subsistence economy (Furtado, 1959, p. 106). However, these poor and middle classes could not be equated with a free proletariat either.

Celso Furtado (1959) corroborates the understanding of the entire colony as a factory:

> Slave labor can be compared to the installations of a factory: the investment consists in the purchase of the slave, and its maintenance represents fixed costs. Whether the factory or the slave is working or not, the maintenance expenses will have to be spent. (pp. 85–86)

Likewise, Darcy Ribeiro described the Brazilian colonial formation as "more similar to a factory than to traditional agrarian exploitation." (Ribeiro, 1995, p. 281)

Without industrialization, the Brazilian penitentiary project was born as a factory but as a colonial factory. Moreover, the colony was also constituted as a great prison, referring not only to confinement but, above all, to the impacts of slavery on all aspects of social organization. The colonial formation has already been described, in this sense, as a huge "kidnapping institution" (Zaffaroni, 1989/1991, pp. 74–75).[2]

From the Slave Quarters to the First Jails, from the Dungeons to the Penitentiary

The most qualified scientific production on the history of prisons in Brazil comes above all from post-graduate programs in History departments. It is a literature characterized by a local and regional focus (Maia et al., 2009; Salla, 2006, pp. 107–127). It is difficult to specify when the first colonial jails appeared, without any reformist or disciplinary conception. There was, for example, a prison on *Morro do Castelo*, in the city of São Sebastião do Rio de Janeiro, in 1567 (Contrim Neto, 2006, p. 29) and *Cadeia Velha* ("Old Jail") in the first decades of the 1600s.

Most colonial prisons are linked to the 18th century, a period known as the gold and mining cycle. By that time, the population of Europeans from Portugal increased significantly. Cattle farming was stronger, and a new transport system made possible by the mining economy contributed to the integration of different regions of the country, especially in São Paulo and Rio Grande do Sul (Furtado, 1959, p. 122).

In 1737, Portugal turned the island of Fernando de Noronha into a prison. Also, in the 18th century, several "dungeon prisons" were opened, which, to this day, are referred to as "jails" and not as penitentiaries, such as the Capital Jail in

---

[2]Thinking about "confinement" as a broader analytical category than incarceration, see Harcourt, 2006. Foucault also envisioned the whole of society as a kind of total institution, stating that "the whole of society bears the penitentiary element, of which the prison is only one formulation" (Foucault, 2015, p. 94; Harcourt, 2015, p. 255).

São Paulo, the Recife Jail (1732), the Aljube Jail in Salvador, and in Rio de Janeiro the Aljube Jail, the Ilha das Cobras, the Arsenal da Marinha, and the forts of Santa Cruz and São João, and *Calabouço* (1767). The legal basis for the running of these jails came from local acts and not from the Portuguese Ordinances.

There were also picturesque punitive experiences, such as Fernando de Noronha and the *"presigangas,"* the ship jails. The first is a fascinating case: a paradisiacal prison island, without walls and with the sea as a "great jailer," in the words of José Lins do Rego in the novel *Usina*. The example of the *presigangas*, prison ships administered by the Navy in the first half of the 19th century, is also peculiar: anchored in Guanabara Bay, in the Port of Santos, in Salvador, Bahia, in Pernambuco, in Pará or the Guaíba River, in Porto Alegre, it consisted of ships that served as places of custody for political and military prisoners, condemned to forced labor, exile or corporal punishment (Trindade, 2008, pp. 166–168).

The 18th-century mining cycle did not provide material conditions for developing a disciplinary concept linked to work constraints or deprivation of freedom either. In foreign affairs, the Portuguese metropolis was weak and increasingly dependent on England. The end of the gold cycle and the decline of the mining regions brought new rural dispersion in a subsistence economy for the middle classes, while nothing weakened the slave structure (Furtado, 1959, p. 132). In this context, the set of jails was linked to the private interests of enslavers and acted as the repressive arm of local powers.

Although the economy of mining was more urban, with greater room to pursue other economic activities and develop the internal market, Portugal maintained a stance of preventing local manufacturing development (Furtado, 1959, p. 126). This attitude led to uprisings that were violently repressed and encouraged the struggle for Independence. The colonial elite feared a new revolution as the one that happened between 1791 and 1804 in Haiti. If in England in 1834, Sir George Nicholls, one of the formulators of the new *Poor Law*, said that "every poor person is a potential Jacobin" (Melossi & Pavarini, 1977/2018, p. 102), in Brazil, the fear was that every black enslaved person was a potential Haitian revolutionary (Almeida, 2019, pp. 27–28).

Therefore, preserving order through violence was a primordial concern in the early 19th century. This issue is fundamental to understanding why, a hundred years later, the mass of formerly enslaved people after abolition would continue to be seen as uneducated or not "disciplinable."

After Independence in 1822, coffee production took center stage in the Brazilian economy. But the main features remained the same: slavery, large estates, and no industrialization. In other words, without the same material basis as the Global North for the "penitentiary invention" with disciplinary content. Prison reform in Latin America failed to meet the fundamental condition of the penitentiary model, which was the demand for the development of a salaried (and urban) proletariat in a market society (Salvatore & Aguirre, 1996, p. 28).

In the first half of the 19th century, there were immense difficulties in developing local industry in the face of competition from the English textile industry and the problem of importing machinery. As Furtado (1959) concluded, industrialization was impossible in a country run by agricultural lords (p. 160).

Nevertheless, the penitentiary reform arrived, meeting these peculiar conditions and dynamics. The sense of penitentiary and its genesis can be associated not with exercising disciplinary power as a new pedagogy of subordination of the free labor force but with the peculiar relationships established between public and private authorities in the sharing of punitive practices concerning enslaved people and "free Africans."

The *dungeons* inside the prisons were peculiar spaces, rich in meaning, and can be considered the progenitors of Brazilian penitentiaries. They were places for the custody and corporal punishment on slaves, as spaces of differentiation between enslaved and non-slave prisoners (Roig, 2005, p. 42). Among its peculiarities, there was the possibility of these cellars being "rented" by the owners so that the State could be in charge of flogging their slaves or still, wait for the owner to fetch his runaway and recaptured slave.

These spaces were compared, by Melossi (2023), to the cellars of the Coliseum in Ancient Rome, because they had the same function of containing slaves to be punished. There would be a parallel between the "domestic" forms assumed by colonial punitive practices and the ancient Roman punitive practices, in which power was concentrated in the figure of the *pater familias* who held the *ius vitae necisque* – power of life and death – over women, children and slaves. It would be, therefore, different regimes, in Melossi's words: the prison as the slavery *pro tempore* of the free, on the one hand, and the prison as the permanent slavery of the unfree, on the other.

The colonial dungeons were a part of the transition to urban slavery, in which public authorities positioned themselves, in their own way, as slave masters. "*Calabouço*" (literally translated as "dungeon") was even the name of a prison in Rio de Janeiro, opened in 1767 and which remained until the first half of the 19th century exclusively to hold detained or escaped enslaved people. In 1820, the authorities charged a minimum fee of 160 reis per hundred beatings and flogged, plus 40 *reis* a day for subsistence (Holloway, 2009, pp. 255–256).

Between 1857 and 1858, enslaved people held in the Rio de Janeiro *Calabouço* jail were divided as follows: 31% as "capoeira," 25% "to be punished," and 10% as "runaway," in addition to 5.4% as "disorder," and other similar references to drunkenness, disobedience, insubordination, etc. (Holloway, 2009, p. 260). In other words, reasons for arrest and detention were not even related to the perpetration of crimes.

Salla showed how the dungeons for slaves were replicated in the São Paulo House of Correction, one of the first penitentiary buildings in the country. This penitentiary was supposed to be organized according to the logic of discipline and work, but its cellars were used for the custody of enslaved people to be punished after an escape or by order of their owners (Salla, 1999, pp. 67–68).

The dungeons also housed "free Africans," a legal status created by an 1831 Law according to which enslaved people entering Brazil would be free. Many lived with their families and worked at the São Paulo House of Correction until the late 1860s. Their movements were controlled by the government as if they were still enslaved.

In short, instead of hierarchical surveillance, examination, and normalizing sanction, the flogs prevailed both symbolically and literally.

The Category of Discipline in the Brazilian Colonial Formation

Prison reform also had an important moral or religious dimension, in addition to work. And especially in the North American experience, a strong Quaker influences. The transition from a medieval religious perspective to a Protestant one, with the change in the political meaning of charity, was decisive for developing the penitentiary systems of Philadelphia and Alburn, based on the axes of isolation, religion, and work.

Foucault argued that punishment should be investigated as a political tactic rather than as an effect of legal rules and that the effects it produces are productive/positive rather than negative/repressive ones (Foucault, 1975, pp. 30–32). Thus, the penitentiary project was never about the criminal act. It was always about the subject, producing social differentiation.

Just three decades after Damiens was taken naked to the Place de Grève in Paris, where horses dismembered him on March 2, 1757 (Foucault, 1975, pp. 9–13), the regulations for a youth detention center, also in Paris, presented a new penal rationale called disciplinary power by Foucault. The suppression of the spectacle, suffering, and pain would result from displacing the object of the punitive action from the body to the soul. According to Foucault, it is not simply a question of a quantitative reduction or mere alleviation of punishment.

It is impossible to recognize this same kind of disciplinary power in the plantations, slave quarters, and Brazilian colonial jails (similar, see Bardes, 2020, p. 23). It would also be misleading to understand colonial punitive practices as a reproduction of the pre-disciplinary punishments of the *Ancién Regime*. After all, there was no concern with the introjection of the rules by the subject, an essential element of the original concept of discipline.[3]

I would like to refer to the Jesuits, priests of the Society of Jesus, a religious order created by Inácio de Loyola in 1534. Their discourse was perhaps the closest to the concept of disciplinary power thought up in Europe. However, the context differed, as Jesuit missions lived in subsistence economies. Jesuit action was linked to a pre-capitalist ethical background and a universalist tendency, criticizing violence against the enslaved (Bosi, 1992, pp. 35–36). The Jesuit missions and reductions combined activities of catechization and exploitation of indigenous labor. It is reported that, in the region of Pará, in the 16th century, Jesuits encouraged the voluntary cooperation of indigenous labor for harvesting forest products such as cocoa, vanilla, cinnamon, and cloves, among others, without needing any coercive system (Furtado, 1959, p. 111). Prado (1942/2011) also noted that segregation measures within the Jesuit reductions came with a disciplinary regime

---

[3]In a different sense, Koerner (2006) develops the hypothesis of understanding the corporal punishment of enslaved people as an expression of disciplinary power because of the economic calculation related to the preservation of investment and the extraction of productive labor (p. 229).

"almost military, to which they were subjected, and which made them real automatons" (p. 96; also Bosi, 1992, p. 136).

The Jesuits opposed the enslavement of the indigenous people and clashed with settlers, landowners, and the Portuguese metropolis. They were ultimately attacked and expelled from Portugal and Brazilian lands in 1759.

The Italian Jesuit Jorge Benci transcribed his speeches and sermons in Bahia throughout the 16th century. In the volume published in 1705, one of the most essential documents of Brazilian history, Benci (1705) criticizes the brutality of the treatment of the enslaved and defends their catechization, despite them being "those rough people" (p. 87). According to Benci (1705, pp. 123–127), punishment has the function of "taming and disciplining" through the fear of punishment and loses effectiveness if disproportional. Furthermore, he states that the most appropriate punishment would, at first, be flogging, proportionally to the seriousness of the offenses, but no sanction would better lead to "moral reform" than prisons (Benci, 1705, pp. 183, 187).

This was probably the first time anyone argued in favor of prison sentences for moral reform in Brazil. And it is interesting to note how imprisonment and flogging went hand in hand from the beginning in the colonial slave context. According to Benci (1705, p. 188), more than any other punishment, imprisonment and floggings "break down the pride" of rebellious slaves, reinforcing obedience and subjection to the owner. The obligation to work hard would act against indolence and idleness, preventing insubordination and the wish for freedom.

The Jesuit perspective translated by Benci's texts demonstrates how even that disciplinary power outline was still far from colonial punitive practices. Moreover, it is possible to note that slavery based on racial discrimination also renders disciplinary rationality unfeasible.

Benci's whole approach is contaminated by a racist perspective through the connection between the enslavement of black people and the supposed vileness of manual labor. Benci (1705) tries to justify slavery as a sanction applied by God to the sin of Ham, who saw Noah naked and is appointed as the ascendant of the generations of "blacks who serve us" (p. 28). The author goes on to state that white people can also sin, but they need "many lessons," while blacks do not need much time to become "doctors of malice," and this because they are "more skillful for all kinds of evils" (Benci, 1705, pp. 207–209). And *that* would be the reason for the need to work.

Manual labor was then linked to slavery and to an image of vileness and infamy. Its definition as a sign of low social reputation is a peculiar trait of the history of the Brazilian Republic.

Post-Abolition: Penal Reform Between Brazilian Naturalism and Culturalism

In the USA and Europe, penal reform was shaped by optimism regarding the civilizing progress of the industrial age. Penitentiary institutions were to be laboratories for the moral reform of human beings, transformed into disciplined workers. Imperial Brazil, independent from Portugal since 1822, was no exception to this rhetoric (Salvatore & Aguirre, 1996, p. 9). Even earlier, a royal charter of July 1769 anticipated the need to build a house of correction "for the vagrant and turbulent" (de Moraes, 1923, p. 6). The aspiration to become a "civilized nation" had repercussions on the penal dimension and led to the introduction of Enlightenment principles in the first post-independence Constitution (1824), the Criminal Code of the Empire (1830) and the Code of Criminal Procedure (1832). However, "the humanitarian" concern of Brazilian jurists focused only on free men (Koerner, 2006, p. 235). Without a background like the North American Quakers' influence and the same demand for labor, which would only effectively come with the decline of slavery, what meaning would penal reform take?

In Brazil, free trade was never synonymous with free labor. The seaports opened in 1808, but "liberal" was just the name given to the new post-colonial mercantile practices. The persistence of slavery made political liberalism impossible as a cultural option or citizenship project (Bosi, 1992, pp. 198–199).

One of the first acts of Emperor Dom Pedro I concerning punitive practices was the creation of commissions to visit prisons and discuss reform measures in 1828 (Salla, 1999, p. 48; Trindade, 2008, pp. 161–162). The Committees' Reports recommended, in 1841, nocturnal segregation and common work during the day (i.e., the Alburn system), which would imply a total reorganization of the penitentiary system based on moral and religious instruction, on work, and in isolation (Salla, 1999, p. 58).

Until 1850, there was an intermediate layer of free, rural and poor producers who participated in the operation of export services (Huggins, 1985). That year, the slave trade was banned in Brazil, encouraging clandestine sales to the southern and southeastern states and generating a shortage of slaves in the Northeast. When the enslaved population began to decline, the surplus of the poor rural population became perceived as a problem and was demanded as a labor force.

Such was the context of constructing the Court House of Correction in Rio de Janeiro between 1834 and 1850. Like other of Brazil's first penitentiaries, there was a clear tension between two different paths: to be just another jail or to function effectively as a correctional facility. The first Regulation for the Court House of Correction was inspired by Alburn's system, providing for isolation and increased discipline according to the prisoner's profile. But this system never materialized. Since it was impossible to isolate the prisoners, there was a concentration of several different situations, bringing together enslaved people, those sentenced to galleys, those sentenced to simple imprisonment, and free Africans without convictions. Instead of isolation, corporal punishment of the enslaved was maintained by flogging inside the prison dungeons.

In short, the punitive practices of slavery were transposed to prison (Roig, 2005, p. 54), making the introduction of correctional work unfeasible. For example, at the Recife House of Detention, the regulation allowing the enslaved to receive a bonus for work in prison was removed from the regulation in response to complaints from the landlord of sugar mills (Maia, 1998). In this context, the meaning of prison punishment is not related to an idea of "regeneration" through work but to the violent affirmation of subordinate positions (Salla, 1999, p. 111). In 1874, an Inspection Report at the Court's House of Correction (Brasil, 2001, pp. 262–295; Koerner, 2006, pp. 211–215) recommended the adoption of the Irish progressive system developed by Walter Crofton (1862). In the progressive system, there is the possibility of transfer to less rigorous prison regimes, according to the prisoner's signs of "recovery" and according to the criteria of the prison administration. The Irish progressive system was suited to rural areas, considering that its intermediate phase would be served in an "agricultural penal colony" (Huggins, 1985, p. 66; de Moraes, 1923, p. 88). The suggestion prospered, and the progressive system was adopted by the Penal Code of 1890, the first of the Brazilian Republic.

Therefore, at that time, Brazil also had material conditions that gave a new meaning to work due to the labor shortage, but in a peculiar way. The labor supply in the mid-19th century was inelastic, consisting of 2 million enslaved people. The mortality rate was high, and the trade was illegal, with internal trafficking directed toward the coffee plantations of the South and Southeast (Furtado, 1959, p. 175). What was new was the acceleration of urbanization, with the development of railroads and farmers living more and more in the cities. As a result, the conditions were gradually established for coffee production to begin relying on wage labor and no longer on slavery (Buarque de Holanda, 1936/1995, p. 175).

In other words, the coffee farmers did not want to free the enslaved, but to replace them by shifting to free labor in the cheapest possible way (Bosi, 1992, p. 241). Workers in the subsistence sector, linked to livestock and farming, were not seen as an interesting option. The bet, as it is known, was on European immigration, founded on a belief in the innate superiority of the European worker.

Brazilian government began to establish a set of incentives for European immigration, which included payment for transportation, a guarantee of payment for the expenses of their first year of activity, and the provision of land for the cultivation of basic needs (Furtado, 1959, p. 187). However, the optimism of the elites in transforming the country into a "modern and civilized nation" presupposed the whitening of the Brazilian population.

Oliveira Vianna argued that the arrival of white Aryans would be "an imperative cause of acceleration in the march of our ethnic refinement," as the mestizos who would eventually be their descendants would tend to have increasingly white skin. The author praised the "whitening process" underway, especially in the South and São Paulo, as a "work of race refinement" (Oliveira Vianna, 1938, pp. 208–209).

Furthermore, would formerly enslaved people freed with the abolition of slavery in 1888 be automatically converted into wage workers? Two paths were possible: either the freed enslaved would start to be paid a wage, or they would abandon the old plantations and dedicate themselves to subsistence farming. Neither of these options was consummated.

One of the most perverse obstacles built by slavery was the aversion to manual labor by the newly freed. In the case of Pernambuco, Huggins found that unemployment was preferred to returning to work on the sugar plantations for a low wage (Fernandes, 1965/2008; Huggins, 1985, p. 102). After all, how to position oneself as a working class if, before that, it was necessary to understand "as a subject in the world, something that was perversely denied in the slave system" (Borges, 2019, p. 63)? Therefore, the man formed within the slave social system was "unequipped to respond to economic stimuli, the idea of accumulation is strange" (Furtado, 1959, pp. 203–204; Prado, 1942/2011, p. 303).

Meanwhile, records indicate that most arrests from the 19th to the 20th century in Brazil were for "violations of public order" (Huggins, 1985, p. 85). Poor laws aimed at criminalizing vagrancy were gaining strength since the beginning of the 19th century. The 295° article of the Criminal Code of the Empire of 1830 criminalized and defined *vagrancy* as "not having an honest and useful occupation" and "not having sufficient income," and article 296 criminalized the act of "walking around begging."

Penal control of the Afro-Brazilian population undoubtedly grew with the abolition of slavery: for example, Decree 145 of 1893 determined the "correctional prison" of beggars, vagabonds, and *capoeiras* (Flauzina, 2006, pp. 69–70; also Hertzman, 2005). Criminal justice system was organized to focus on minor offenses and misdemeanors, such as *capoeira* and vagrancy, including the formal penalty of imprisonment with work.

This period was strongly marked by the discourses of eugenics and racism (Brazilian naturalism), at first, and then by the myth of racial democracy (Brazilian culturalism). Symptomatic is the position of Caio Prado Jr, an important Marxist author, who uses terms such as "declassified" to refer to vagrants. In the author's words, "the most degraded, annoying, and harmful caste is that of the permanently unoccupied, who wander from place to place and, when the opportunity presents itself, commit crimes." And he continues:

> in the cities, vagrants are more dangerous and harmful [...]. However, the evil will be perpetuated, and only in the Republic, will the famous "capoeiras," successors of the vagrants of the colony, be eliminated from the capital. (Prado, 1942/2011, pp. 300–302)

Influenced by Oliveira Vianna, Prado (1942/2011) also stated that "the contribution of the black or Indian slave to Brazilian education is almost null," referring to "races that were still bordering on the state of barbarism" (pp. 289–293).

That was the context of reception to positivist criminology (Alvarez, 2003, p. 54). Very different from the political environment of criticism of imprisonment in which the Italian Positive School emerges, determinist theories were articulated to eugenic discourses in Brazil.

Brazilian positivists faced the theoretical dilemma of reconciling an etiological theory of criminality based on individual causes with discourses based on the analysis of racial groups. The answer was in the concept of miscegenation. Nina Rodrigues (1894) argued that there were secondary racial types with a propensity for criminal behavior according to their greater or lesser proximity to the Afro-descendant population (): the degree of melanin in the skin would be related to a criminogenic heritage that collectively characterized the dangerous classes.

Oliveira Vianna made, at the beginning of his *Evolução do povo Brasileiro* ["Brazilian people evolution"] (1938), an open praise of eugenics: "the value of an ethnic group is measured by its greater or lesser fecundity in generating superior types," considering as a superior type the "Aryan culture," which would never be assimilated by the "pure black." In short, black and indigenous people would form a passive mass on which the shaping action of the white race would act (Oliveira Vianna, 1938, pp. 172, 178).

Both in the proclamation of the Republic in 1889 and in the Revolution of 1930, when the coffee oligarchies lost power, the victorious groups were formed by military men inspired by Auguste Comte's positivism. The foundation of the Brazilian Welfare State has thus a positivist base in which "progress" is understood as possible only if accompanied by "order," as the words written on the national flag suggest. Comte really did support the idea of incorporating the proletariat into modern society. It was no coincidence that the pursuit of national unity and identity gained steam after the 1930 Revolution and Getúlio Vargas' rise to the presidency.

The book *Casa Grande e Senzala* ["The Masters and the Slaves"] by Gilberto Freyre, (1933/2003), was one of the central texts of Brazilian social thought and a decisive component in the construction of a new national identity. Among the various possible interpretations of Freyre's work, a reading that praised miscegenation fitted in very well with the new government's aims, looking for positive characteristics to describe Brazil and its people. Miscegenation came to be presented as proof of cordiality, affection, and hospitality. They would all be "pre-modern" traits of Brazilian society that would constitute not a problem but an advantage. In Freyre's (1933/2003) words, the social effects of miscegenation countered the opposition between masters and slaves (p. 33).

Similarly, Sérgio Buarque de Holanda (1936/1995) defended the absence of "racial pride" among the Portuguese, a mestizo people, which would explain the "relative inconsistency of race and color prejudices" (p. 184). This is the basis of the concept of the Brazilian as a "cordial man" and summarized, together with Freyre's work, as the myth of *racial democracy* (for the critique, see Fernandes, 1965/2008, pp. 304–327; Moura, 2019, pp. 89–138; Nascimento, 1980/2019). Though politically prevailing, the myth of racial democracy has brought together mechanisms to hide the violence inflicted on the enslaved for centuries, especially on women, and even today contributes to concealing structural racism in all layers of Brazilian society.

In this context, research into a national penitentiary project presupposes reworking the question of who is and is not part of the very nation's project. Would prisons be laboratories for "racial purification" rather than moral regeneration? The praise of miscegenation, the key to national unity from the 1930s onwards, did not explicitly oppose scientific racism. On the contrary, it concealed it, dampened it, interdicted discussion, and contributed to depoliticizing the whole penitentiary issue.

Final Considerations

The central hypothesis of this chapter is that colonialism and slavery produced different material conditions, or different moralities and governmentalities, in a Foucauldian reading (Lemos, 2020, pp. 121–122), from those at the base of the disciplinary project of the Global North, conditions that reformed and re-signified the penitentiary reform proposal.

The concepts of North and South should not have a rigidly geographical delimitation, in the sense of the critique made by Melossi (2023) to this chapter at the already mentioned seminar. In fact, there are consistent parallels between the Brazilian reality and the "South of the Northern countries." For example, the reception of criminological positivism against "African blood" in a miscegenated society occurred similarly in southern Italy, in the context of the so-called *questione meridionale*. Another parallel is the experience of combining punitive practices aimed at enslaved and free people in shaping the penitentiary system of the State of Louisiana, USA (Bardes, 2020; Bosi, 1992, p. 202, cites as examples the English and French West Indies, Cuba, and the North American cotton South).

In any case, there is an important difference from those societies in which the penitentiary was born as a disciplinary project based on the houses of correction. The distinction is about the role of the people in the construction of a national project. The goal of disciplining the proletariat, although authoritarian, presupposes "correctable" citizens who are part of the same project of a market democracy.

Post-abolition and Republican Brazil, however, was a country that was "ashamed of itself, of its biological reality" (Buarque de Holanda, 1936/1995, p. 166). The image of uncivilized multitudes replaced the idea of the correctable citizen. The dilemma was to what extent these masses would be part of a national project to modernize and unify the country after the abolition of slavery.

It is important to mention that the first revisionist work of great impact in the USA on the invention of the penitentiary, by David Rothman (1971), has not even been translated in Brazil, making it impossible to draw parallels that could also be important. In his work, Rothman defended the hypothesis that modern prisons reflected the ideal of a perfect social order to be reproduced within prison institutions as a response to the collapse of traditional forms of social control in the US post-revolutionary period (Rubin, 2019b). The new Brazilian prison system is also sometimes interpreted as a response to the supposed risk of social collapse in the post-abolition period. But there is no point in claiming that there was a search for a perfect order to be reproduced inside Brazilian prisons. Rothman's interpretation has been criticized for focusing excessively on the Jacksonian era, ignoring the social dynamics that preceded it. Similarly, it is impossible to understand Brazil's penitentiary invention by looking only at the period following the abolition of slavery.

In short, the productive function of social differentiation in Brazilian society has obeyed peculiar dynamics and conditions. Unlike the global North, which officially envisioned the penitentiary as the institutional foundation of a democratic society, the penitentiary was seen in Brazil first as a mere symbol of modernity, then as an instrument for preserving order (Salvatore & Aguirre, 1996, p. 24). As a mere symbol, it tolerates the preservation of private punitive power over the enslaved and its sharing with the public authorities. Subsequently, this supposedly democratic basis for the penitentiary project continued to lack political will for the social and political inclusion of everyone in the new Republic. The rhetorical commitment to "self-government" has always only meant controlling and preserving order through violence. In Comtian positivist thinking and as the Brazilian flag states, progress presupposes authoritarian order.

Brazil's colonial formation was also constituted as a prison and factory, but throughout the whole territory, not limited to houses of correction. Absent the category of disciplinary power in its original form, at least regarding its economic dimension, the national penitentiary project was born from the dungeons where public and private power overlapped for the corporal punishment of the enslaved.

Finally, there is the issue of the impact of centuries of slavery on the cultural formation of Brazilian elites. The legacy of the patriarchal clan as an economic, social, administrative, and religious unit of the colonial formation is the weakening of the idea of public authority (Prado, 1942/2011, p. 305). At the same time, the elites cultivate an aristocratic self-image that spreads throughout the population. Buarque de Holanda (1936/1995) observed simple carpenter officers dressing like nobles, "using" the descendants of formerly enslaved people to carry their tools, trying to differentiate themselves from the humbler people (pp. 87, 113).

The "master and slave" mentality, therefore, proved resistant to urbanization and industrialization, invading cities throughout the 20th century. The same elites are today alien to the idea of the common good, "suffering from inequality" (Ribeiro, 1995, pp. 216–217). They still occupy decisive positions in politics and the criminal justice system, above all by prosecuting and sentencing people to prison.

References

Aguirre, C. (2009). Cárcere e sociedade na América Latina, 1800–1940. In C. Maia, F. Sá Neto, & M. Bretas (Eds.), *História das Prisões no Brasil* (pp. 35–77), Rocco.
Almeida, S. (2019). *Racismo estrutural*. Pólen.
Alvarez, M. C. (2003). *Bacharéis, Criminologistas e Juristas: saber jurídico e nova escola penal no Brasil*. Método.
Bardes, J. (2020). *Mass incarceration in the age of slavery and emancipation: Fugitive slaves, poor whites and prison development in Louisiana, 1805–1877* [Ph.D. thesis, Tulane University].
Batista, V. M. (2011). *Introdução crítica à criminologia brasileira*. Editora Revan.
Benci, J. (1705). *Economia christãa dos senhores no governo dos escravos*. Officina de Antonio de Roffi na Praça de Ceri.
Borges, J. (2019). *Encarceramento em massa*. Pólen.
Bosi, A. (1992). *Dialética da colonização*. Companhia das Letras.
Brasil. (2001). Relatorio da Commissão Inspectora da Casa de Correcção da Corte/1874. *Revista Brasileira de Ciências Criminais*, n. 35 (pp. 262–295). Revista dos Tribunais.
Buarque de Holanda, S. (1995 [1936]). *Raízes do Brasil* (26th ed). Companhia das Letras.
Carrington, K., Hogg, R., & Sozzo, M. (2016). Southern criminology. *The British Journal of Criminology, 56*(1), 1–20.
Contrim Neto, A. B. (2006). As primeiras prisões no Rio de Janeiro: A Cadeia Velha e o Aljube. *Revista da Academia Brasileira de Letras Jurídicas*, n. 29 (pp. 29–33). Rio de Janeiro.
Crofton, W. (1862). *A brief description of the Irish Convict System*. Emily Faithfull.
Fernandes, F. (2008 [1965]). *A integração do negro na sociedade de classes* (5th ed.). Globo.
Flauzina, A. L. P. (2006). *Corpo negro caído no chão: o sistema penal e o projeto genocida do Estado brasileiro*. Master in Law, Universidade de Brasília.
Foucault, M. (1975). *Surveiller et punir: Naissance de la prison*. Gallimard.

Foucault, M. (2015). *A sociedade punitiva: Curso no Collège de France (1972–1973)*. Martins Fontes.
Freyre, G. (2003 [1933]). *Casa Grande e Senzala: formação da família brasileira sob o regime da economia patriarcal* (48th ed.). Global.
Furtado, C. (1959). *Formação econômica do Brasil*. Companhia das Letras.
Harcourt, B. (2006). From the asylum to the prison: Rethinking the incarceration revolution. *Texas Law Review*, *84*(7), 1751–1786.
Harcourt, B. (2015). Situação do Curso. In M. Foucault, *A Sociedade Punitiva: Curso no Collège de France, 1972–1973* (pp. 241–281). Martins Fontes.
Hertzman, M. (2005). *Workers into vagrants: Policing Rio de Janeiro before (and after) Music was the Point, 1890–1940* [Ph.D. thesis, University of Wisconsin].
Holloway, T. (2009). O Calabouço e o Aljube do Rio de Janeiro no século XIX. In C. Maia, F. Sá Neto, & M. Bretas (Eds.), *História das Prisões no Brasil* (pp. 253–281). Rocco.
Huggins, M. (1985). *From slavery to vagrancy in Brazil*. Rudgers University Press.
Ignatieff, M. (1978). *A just measure of pain. The penitentiary in Industrial Revolution 1750–1850*. McMillan.
Koehler, J. (2020). Don't talk to me about Marx any more!. *Punishment and Society*, *22*(5), 731–735.
Koerner, A. (2006). Punição, disciplina e pensamento penal no Brasil do século XIX. *Lua Nova*, v. 68, São Paulo (pp. 205–242).
Lemos, C. (2020). *Criminologia Foucaultiana*. Casa do Direito.
Maia, C. (1998). Quando a liberdade não é um bem que pertence a todos: as condições de vida dos escravos na Casa de Detenção da cidade do Recife. *Clio – Revista de Pesquisa Histórica* (pp. 19–27), Recife, 1/17.
Maia, C., Sá Neto, F., & Bretas, M. (Eds.). (2009). *História das Prisões no Brasil*. Rocco.
Melossi, D. (2023). Servitude for a time: From the permanent slavery of the unfree to the slavery pro tempore of the free. *Punishment and Society*, *25*(5), 1207–1232.
Melossi, D., & Pavarini, M. (2018 [1977]). *Carcere e fabbrica* (4th ed.). Il Mulino.
de Moraes, E. (1923). *Prisões e instituições penitenciárias no Brazil*. Sociedade Anonyma.
Moura, C. (2019). *Sociologia do Negro Brasileiro*. Perspectiva.
Nascimento, A. (2019 [1980]). *O Quilombismo: documentos de uma militância pan-africanista*. Perspectiva.
Oliveira Vianna. (1938). *Evolução do povo brasileiro* (3rd ed.). Nacional.
Pedroso, R. C. (2003). *Os signos da opressão. História e violência nas prisões brasileiras*. Imprensa Oficial do Estado.
Prado, C., Jr. (2011 [1942]). *Formação do Brasil Contemporâneo*. Companhia das Letras.
Ribeiro, D. (1995). *O povo brasileiro*. Companhia das Letras.
Rodrigues, N. (1894). *As raças humanas e a responsabilidade penal no Brasil*. Editora Guanabara.
Roig, R. D. E. (2005). *Direito e prática histórica da execução penal no Brasil*. Revan.
Rothman, D. (1971). *The discovery of asylum. Social order and disorder in the New Republic*. Little Brown and Co.
Rubin, A. (2019a). History of the prison. In M. Deflem (Ed.), *The handbook of social control* (pp. 279–292). John Wiley & Sons Ltd.
Rubin, A. (2019b). Beyond Rothman: Revisiting *The Discovery of Asylum*. *Annual Review of Law and Social Science*, *15*, 137–154.
Rusche, G., & Kirchheimer, O. (1999 [1939]). *Punição e estrutura social [Punishment and social structure]*. Freitas Bastos.
Salla, F. (1999). *As prisões em São Paulo 1822–1940*. Fapesp.
Salla, F. (2006). A pesquisa sobre as prisões: um balanço preliminar. In A. Koerner (Ed.), *História da Justiça Penal no Brasil* (pp. 107–127). Ibccrim.

Salvatore, R., Aguirre, C., & Joseph, G. (Eds.) (2001). *Crime and punishment in Latin America*. Duke University Press.
Salvatore, R., & Aguirre, C. (Eds.). (1996). *The birth of penitentiary in Latin America. Essays on criminology, prison reform and social Control 1830–1940* (pp. 1–43). University of Texas Press.
Sellin, T. (1944). *Pioneering in penology*. University of Pennsylvania Press.
Trindade C. (2008). A reforma prisional na Bahia oitocentista. *Revista de História, 158*, 157–198.
Zaffaroni, E. R. (1991 [1989]). *Em busca das penas perdidas [En busca de las penas perdidas]*. Revan.

Chapter 2

Punitive Turn or Punitive Imperialism? Analyzing the Transformation in the Ecuadorian Penal Realm

Martha Vargas Aguirre

University of Ottawa, Canada

Abstract

Criminological research, particularly in the Anglo-Saxon academic realm, has extensively examined the sharp increase in incarceration rates since the mid-1970s. Referred to as the "sociologies of the punitive turn" (Carrier, 2010), these studies argue that this surge reflects a sudden and harsh transformation in the logic governing penal practices and discourse. Some findings even suggest that this punitive shift has a global reach, impacting regions like Latin America. This broader narrative prompts an inquiry into whether a similar punitive turn occurred in Ecuador, a South American nation. Examination of prison demographics and legal frameworks in this country reveals a notable increase in incarceration rates during the 1990s, closely linked to drug trafficking control policies led by the United States. Consequently, I suggest that while the influence of neoliberal rationality, characteristic of the punitive turn, is evident, it's more aptly described as a manifestation of punitive imperialism. Thus, it is imperative to analyze shifts in punishment trends within the framework of imperial dynamics, particularly considering the economic dependency of peripheral countries.

Keywords: Ecuador; drugs; Latin America; punishment; policy; neoliberalism

Introduction

The 1980s marked the peak of the emergence of neoliberalism, understood as a socio-economic model that upholds the notion of letting markets and individuals function with minimal intervention. It advocates for the primacy of competition and individualism within markets while harboring strong reservations toward the equitable distribution of resources and fostering collective solidarity (Peck et al., 2018). In this context, significant economic and political restructurings unfolded, sparking a multitude of scholarly investigations into their effects. These inquiries have consistently levied robust criticisms against the rationality underpinning the neoliberal model. They assert that its deployment has fundamentally reshaped the landscape of employment, leading to heightened rates of unemployment, and exacerbating social and economic marginalization among vulnerable social groups (Kiely, 2007).

Furthermore, the advent of neoliberalism coincided with a notable phenomenon: a significant surge in incarceration rates (Brown, 2013). Criminological research (mainly in the Anglo-Saxon academic scene) has studied the exponential increase in incarceration rates that started in the mid-1970s. Many of these studies, called "sociologies of the punitive turn" (Carrier, 2010) claim that this phenomenon, not linked to an increase in crime rates, responds to a sudden and draconian metamorphosis in the logic underlying the practices and discourses of the penal realm. This sudden and dramatic change has been denominated "punitive turn," and it is linked to the implementation and development of neoliberalism (Bell, 2011; Giorgi, 2016; Hallsworth, 2002; Pakes, 2006; Wacquant, 2009).

The political, economic, and social restructuring brought about by this political-economic system resulted in the exacerbation of the coercive penal power of the State, which started to manage social issues through the criminal system. In this sense, prisons became poverty (which notoriously increased due to neoliberalism) management institutions (Bell, 2011; Miller, 2014; Wacquant, 1999, 2001, 2003, 2009). In this vein, these research endeavors develop their analyses focusing on the United States and the United Kingdom (Carrier, 2010). However, their conclusions estimate that this punitive turn has a global reach encompassing Latin America (Müller, 2012; Wacquant, 2003, 2008).

For more than three decades, Latin American countries experimented with neoliberal models of government, resulting in a structural adjustment of economic and social policies (Danani, 2008) that have seemingly been extended to the limits of criminal policy (e.g., Iturralde, 2010; Wacquant, 2008). In this context, the prison population in Latin America started to increase significantly, a trend linked to the increasing severity of penal policy (Hathazy & Müller, 2016). Consequently, a question arises: are the specificities of the Latin American context indicative of a discernible punitive turn within this region? This chapter aims to answer this question by focusing on one country, Ecuador.

The examination of the "punitive turn" trend within academic discourse has faced substantial criticism, largely stemming from its inclination toward explanations that are both overgeneralizing and reductionist in nature. Critics argue that these broad assertions neglect the intricate and diverse dynamics involved in the development of criminal policies. Furthermore, the inherent contextual constraints of the punitive turn framework impede its capacity to grasp the intricacies and complexities inherent in the evolution of penal systems (e.g., Carrier, 2010; Lacey, 2010; Mayer, 2010; Nelken, 2010; O'Malley, 2014; Piven, 2010). Similar critiques are also present in analyses focusing on the Global South. In this context, Sozzo's (2018) analysis of the South American context serves as a prime example. His work underscores the importance of studying the specific characteristics of the region, challenging the prevailing "neo-liberal penality thesis," and advocating for a nuanced, context-specific approach.

Following this perspective, I posit that particularities of the Ecuadorian context offer valuable insights into the complexities of carceral population growth. While the country did experience a surge in incarceration rates starting in the 1990s (Pontón Cevallos & Torres, 2007), coinciding with the peak of economic neoliberal restructuring (Bonilla, 1991), a closer examination reveals additional contributing factors.

Analysis of prison demographics and shifts in the legal framework indicate that other events also influenced these changes. Specifically, the increase in Ecuador's prison population is closely tied to drug trafficking control policies led and designed by the United States. This includes the implementation of commercial agreements such as the Andean Trade Preference Act (ATPA), which was in effect between 1991 and 2001 and subsequently replaced by the Andean Trade Promotion and Drug Eradication (ATPDE), operative from 2002 to 2013.

These agreements were unilateral preferential treaties that the US government implemented throughout the 1990s and 2000s with four member countries of the Andean Community of Nations (Peru, Colombia, Bolivia, and Ecuador). Their purpose was to grant preferential access to a significant number of Andean products while simultaneously enforcing anti-drug trafficking policies in the beneficiary states (Ramírez-Loayza et al., 2023). Within this framework, this chapter explores how anti-drug trafficking policies, promoted by the United States, and implemented in Ecuador since the 1990s, impacted crime regulation in this Andean country during the last 14 years of its neoliberal period (1992–2006).

Therefore, I argue that the changes in Ecuador's criminalization processes during this period are linked to a governance strategy already outlined within the framework of US policy. This implementation was facilitated due to Ecuador's economic and commercial dependence on the United States. Accordingly, examining the specifics of this context suggests that while the neoliberal model defining the so-called punitive turn did impact the shift in punishment trends in Ecuador, this transformation is more accurately characterized as a form of *punitive imperialism*.

Inspired by the concept of penal imperialism, developed by Baker (n.d.) to explain the new legal order that criminalizes human mobility, I posit that the shifts in the punitive realm cannot be analyzed without considering the imperial dynamics between Latin America and the United States. It is precisely within this framework that I analyze the case of Ecuador, focusing on the moment in which the United States began to have more interference in the penal field in this country.

Therefore, to understand these dynamics, this chapter describes and studies how the ATPDA and the ATPDE were directly related to the increased criminal repression in this periphery country, and its subsequent high rates of imprisonment. In this sense, this chapter also aims to propose a theoretical view where the transformations in the criminalization processes should be studied in close consideration of the imperialist dynamics that define peripheral countries like Ecuador.

The opening section of this chapter sheds light on the concept of the punitive turn, providing insight into how this perspective helps explain the rise in incarceration rates. Moving on, the second part delves into the complex dynamics of punitive measures in Ecuador. Here, I expose how a mix of neoliberal economic policies and the influence of the United States anti-drug efforts have shaped Ecuador's approach to dealing with crime. Lastly, the third section closely examines the detailed requirements and procedures Ecuador followed to combat drug trafficking. Through this analysis, I explain how these demands have led to significant changes in Ecuador's prison population, illustrating the impact of punitive imperialism on the country's justice system.

Punitive Turn: An Encompassing Logic

The research conducted within the framework of the punitive turn explores the effects of neoliberalism on political, economic, and social structures, which have given rise to a new mode of governance reshaping contemporary societal institutions, including those involved in crime control. Consequently, the significant societal transformations in Western societies, marked by a notable reduction in state intervention, have generated a generalized climate of anxiety-threatening social order (Welch, 2003). As a result, these societies are experiencing the emergence of a new governmental rationality that prioritizes repression as a means of asserting political authority and mitigating potential social unrest (Pitts, 2012). This transformation heightened the coercive authority of the State and prompted the use of the criminal justice system to address social concerns. Consequently, there has been an unprecedented surge in the punitive nature of criminal policies, indicative of a broader societal trend toward more punitive approaches to crime and social control.

Carrier (2010) states that these studies identify three main symptoms of this contemporary dynamic of punishment. The first is related to the continuous and expansive increase in the prison population. The second one is linked to the development of a post-disciplinary penalty; the criminal justice system is not conceived as a disciplinary normalization device anymore (Foucault, 2015), but as a mechanism to neutralize a dangerous class of undesirables (Feeley & Simon, 1992). Finally, the third symptomatic manifestation emphasizes the importance of crime control within the political sphere. In this context, there is a prevalence of practices and discourses that are heavily mediated, characterized by their simplistic presentation, and infused with emotional appeal.

Certain analyses posit that this punitive trend extends beyond core countries alone, encompassing peripheral countries, including those in Latin America (Arriagada Gajewski, 2012; Iturralde, 2010; Müller, 2012; Núñez Rebolledo, 2019; Wacquant, 2003). The adoption of neoliberalism and its free-market economic policies throughout the 1980s and the 1990s in this region precipitated premature deindustrialization, fostered labor market segmentation, and aggravated social inequalities (Danani, 2008). In the face of growing social and economic precarity, Latin America witnessed unprecedented growth in its imprisonment rates.[1]

In this context, during the 1990s, Ecuador also witnessed a significant increase in incarceration rates (Pontón Cevallos & Torres, 2007), which coincided with the government's adoption of neoliberal economic policies. While the spread of neoliberal economic policies in Latin America during the 1980s and 1990s reflects trends seen in core countries, such as heightened inequality, poverty, and incarceration rates, as highlighted by sociologists studying the punitive turn, it remains to be explored whether these phenomena truly align with the logic of preventing social unrest and managing undesirable populations, as proposed by these scholars. This chapter will delve further into these inquiries in the subsequent sections.

It is essential to mention that the data from 2008 onward shows a decline in the prison population, coinciding with the shift to a leftist government in Ecuador. This political transition mirrors the broader trend seen across Latin America that started in the late 1990s, known as the "Pink Tide wave," characterized by the rise of left-leaning governments critical of neoliberalism. Beginning with the election of President Chavez in Venezuela, this movement later extended to countries like Brazil, Bolivia, and Argentina (Ellner & de Sousa Santos, 2020). Ecuador experienced a similar political shift in 2007 with the election of ex-president Rafael Correa (Sánchez & Pachano, 2020).

During the tenure of these leftist governments, there was a noticeable decrease in the prison population of two countries signatories of the ATPDA and the ATPDEA agreements, Bolivia and Ecuador. To some extent, this decline in prison population during the administrations of leftist governments may be attributed to their disengagement from the United States' war on drugs[2] (Aguirre Salas et al., 2020; Edwards & Youngers, 2010; Giacoman, 2011; Hesselroth, 2015; Polga-Hecimovich, 2020). However, it is important to acknowledge that this aspect falls outside the scope of this chapter, which primarily focuses on the neoliberal period as the foundational framework for the so-called punitive turn.[3]

---

[1] Incarceration rates in Latin America underwent a dramatic shift starting in the 1990s, surpassing 150 inmates per 100,000 people (Sozzo, 2022). By 2020, overcrowding in the region averaged 64%, with countries like Guatemala reaching an alarming 233% (Alvarado et al., 2020). By 2023, it is estimated that the prison population in this region has surged by 70% (Población carcelaria, 2023). Despite occasional decreases, these numbers have continued to rise unchecked throughout the first two decades of the 2000s (World Prison Brief, n.d.).
[2] The chart also shows an increase starting in 2010, which coincides with the leftist government of Correa, who was in power until 2017. For an analysis of this trend, see Aguirre Salas et al. (2020).
[3] To explore the rise in punitiveness within penal policies during the left-wing administrations of Argentina, Brazil, and Uruguay, refer to Sozzo's (2018) work.

The Particularities of Punitive Repression in Ecuador

Crime control and punishment are defined by the specificities of the context where they are developed (Aas, 2010; Loader & Sparks, 2004). In this regard, it is crucial to recognize the importance of cultural values, historical contexts, and societal norms in shaping perspectives on crime, punishment, and justice (Melossi, 2004). These elements exert significant influence on the strategies employed by societies to address criminal conduct and maintain social order. Therefore, comprehending crime control mechanisms and punitive measures requires a comprehensive examination of the broader socio-cultural milieu in which they operate.

To understand the transformation in the field of repression that occurred in Latin America, particularly in Ecuador, following neoliberal restructuring, analyses must pay attention to the specificities of the processes that facilitated these changes (Sozzo, 2018). It is essential to consider that the dynamics of neoliberalism implementation and its subsequent consequences in this region do not conform to the same patterns observed in core countries.

On one hand, neoliberal logic defined Ecuadorian politics from the 1980s[4] onwards. However, this Andean country did not experience the same structural process of economic, political, and social transformation as core countries. Although a similar trend in terms of rising unemployment can be identified between core countries and this country of the periphery (Uquillas, 2007) we cannot speak of massive expulsion of the working population and subsequently of a punitive transformation necessary to manage the mass of "new poor" (Wacquant, 2009) through the criminal system, as claimed by theorizations of the punitive turn.

Despite the escalation of poverty and inequality stemming from neoliberal restructuring, Ecuador's economy has long grappled with inherent disparities and a prevalence of informal employment (Costales-Montenegro & Rondón, 2014). Unlike the United States, where neoliberalism catalyzed the erosion of welfare systems, Ecuador did not witness a similar dissolution. Much like many Latin American counterparts, Ecuador lacked a welfare model in the strictest sense (Delgado & Porto, 2021). This country relied on limited social welfare initiatives targeting vulnerable demographics (Rosero, 2018). These efforts often encountered limitations in efficacy and scope due to multifaceted economic, political, and social constraints. Challenges including economic volatility, political instability, and institutional frailty impeded Ecuador's ability to establish comprehensive social welfare provisions (Chávez Zavala, 2016; Vos, 2000; Yasunaga Kumano, 2020).

Furthermore, like the rest of Latin America, Ecuador embraced neoliberalism within a context of economic and political dependence on the United States (Russell, 2006). The historical relationship between this region and the North American power has been marked by imperialist dynamics. Thus, neoliberalism enters the region sustained by an imperialist logic that shapes the relations

---

[4]Neoliberalism was implemented in Ecuador in the presidency of León Febres Cordero who was in power from 1984 until 1988.

between this country and the Latin American periphery (Harvey, 2005). Consequently, comprehending the transformation in Ecuador's punitive landscape necessitates an examination of the imperialist control mechanisms that define the relationships between core nations and the periphery (Carrington et al., 2016, 2018; Sozzo, 2023). Therefore, as we confront distinct structural transformations but observe parallel outcomes, such as increased incarceration rates and heightened repressive inclinations, it becomes imperative to scrutinize the specificities of the context in which these shifts occurred.

First, if we analyze the demographic profile of incarceration starting in the 1990s, the decade in which the rate of incarceration began to grow exponentially in Ecuador, we can see that the most predominant crimes are drug-related (Gallardo & Núñez Vega, 2006; Núñez Vega, 2005). In contrast, in previous decades crimes against property were those with the highest incidence (Vega Uquillas et al., 1987). Thus, observing this trend, the change in punitive trends in Ecuador should be studied within the frame of the anti-drug policy implemented at this time in the country. This policy is linked to the war on drugs enacted by the United States. Hence, the surge in incarcerations aligned with Ecuador's participation in the US drug war policy.

Until 1990, Ecuador kept its distance from this policy against drug trafficking, which is why this country did not ratify the "Cartagena Declaration."[5] Ecuador did not feel concerned by the United States interests, as the country was not one of the main producers of these substances. However, in 1992, after participating in the "San Antonio Texas Anti-Drug Summit," President Rodrigo Borja (in power from 1988 to 1992) adopted a radical change in Ecuador's position and decided that the country's participation in the fight against drugs was essential (Robayo & Leiva Ponce, 2005). Borja joined this "war" arguing that narcotraffic, as an international crime, should be fought by Ecuador even if the country was not a direct part of the problem.[6]

At this stage, Ecuador and the United States considered that this Andean country should form part of this fight to prevent it from becoming an economy dependent on drugs. Consequently, in 1991, Ecuador signed the Andean Trade Preference Act (ATPA) with the United States for the first time. The primary objective was "to provide the Andean countries with legal economic alternatives to the cultivation and production of illicit narcotics" (House Report No. 110-529, 2008).

---

[5]The "Cartagena Declaration" was signed in 1990 by Bolivia, Peru, and Colombia with the United States to develop multilateral strategies to combat drug trafficking.
[6]In his speech the former Ecuadorian president, Borja proclaimed: drugs are not part of our exports nor are they part of our economy, but naturally that does not excuse us from our joint responsibility against this modern madness of drug trafficking and consumption, close to which there is enormous economic power, it is a plague that does not border any frontier and therefore must receive a concerted bilateral and multilateral response for that fight to succeed (Robayo & Leiva Ponce, 2005, p. 104).

Within the framework of this agreement, certain products exported to the United States from the Andean countries of Bolivia, Colombia, Ecuador, and Peru would receive a duty-free exemption. In other words, they would enter the US economy without being affected by tariffs. The ATPA agreement came to an end in December 2011 but was subsequently renewed through the Andean Trade Promotion and Drug Eradication Agreement (ATPDEA), which was in force until July 2013.

In the case of Ecuador, one of the main destinations of most of its exports is the United States, so the signing of a trade agreement of this type was considered an important strategic move for this country's economy (Rubio Ríos, 2008). Under the ATPA and ATPDEA, 6,900 Andean products were part of this exemption (Barreiro, 2002). Thus, this treaty meant that the Andean countries would be able to enter the US market more easily.

These agreements sought to improve Ecuador's economy. Although there were indeed certain benefits for Ecuador's exports, the tariff preferences did not bring the expected results. Throughout these agreements, the United States had control over the entry of products into its market and Ecuador did not achieve the expected economic diversification (Jácome, 2004); it did not cease to be an economy dependent on primary products exports, primarily oil[7] (Benítez & Larrea, 2003). Consequently, the ATPA and ATPDEA did not allow this country to diversify its import structure or obtain greater penetration in the US market (Jácome, 2004). Likewise, there was no significant impact on the reduction of social inequality and poverty in this country (Vos & Leon, 2003). Therefore, the dynamics of this agreement only reaffirmed Ecuador as a peripheral country dependent on the central economy of the United States.

This form of bilateral agreement, along with Free Trade Agreements, is typically advocated with the aim of enhancing the economic growth of peripheral nations by optimizing resource allocation and increasing their competitiveness in the global market (Bell Lara & Dello Buono, 2020). However, as mentioned above, the results of these agreements were not as promising as they were intended to be. Trade agreements with Ecuador, as well as with the rest of Latin America, have allowed the United States to penetrate these markets more easily. From a dominant position, the United States imposes conditions whose non-compliance can culminate in the unilateral suspension of the agreements (Huerta González, 2007).

Trade agreements such as the ATPA and the ATPDEA also allow a more flexible entry of products and investments into peripheral countries. Therefore, the United States can control strategic sectors and promote policies that support the interests of transnational companies (Bell Lara & Dello Buono, 2020). Hence, countries like Ecuador are unable to superimpose their national interests and erode the chains of economic dependence. In this context, countries seeking to benefit from the exemptions established in the APTA and APTDE were to

---

[7]For example, according to data from the Statistics of the Central Bank of Ecuador (Banco Central de Ecuador, n.d.), of the over 800 products duty-free products that could enter the United States, exports were only concentrated in four primary products.

comply with certain conditions that would make them eligible candidates. These conditions were not only related to the characteristics of the imported products but also extended to the field of domestic criminal legislation. If the exporting country failed to comply with the requirements imposed, the agreements could be unilaterally suspended (Gloeckner, 2023).

Numerous Latin American nations, seeking avenues for economic and social advancement, have engaged in bilateral agreements with the United States (Huerta González, 2007). As a result, nations like Ecuador have found themselves trapped in a cycle of dependency, ostensibly promoting economic development but perpetuating imperialist dynamics (Harvey, 2005) and upholding the legacy of colonialism. This sustains enduring manifestations of oppression, exploitation, and inequality in Latin American societies, as well as other global regions, up to the present day (Kohli, 2019).

In this respect, throughout the duration of the ATPA and ATPDEA agreements, they functioned as mechanisms for the expansion of economic imperialism. This dynamic characterizes the relationship between core countries, which possess significant capabilities for innovation and technological advancement, leading to the manufacturing of goods, and those in the periphery, whose economies rely on exporting raw materials to the economic systems of the center (Jorgenson & Kick, 2003).

Ecuador's economic dependence on the United States and the dynamics of economic imperialism that sustain it have been a long-standing constant in this country, and the Andean preference agreements are just one more expression of it. It has been argued that imperialism is not only limited to the economic aspect, but it can also extend to other areas and thus take various forms (Harvey, 2005). These dynamics can initially be framed by the economic sphere and quickly reach other realms such as politics, communication, military (Galtung, 1971), culture (Rothkopf, 1997), and migration regulation (Baker, n.d.; Walia, 2014) resulting in various forms of imperialism that act in an intertwined manner.

In this framework, the Andean preference treaties are expressions of economic imperialism in Andean countries such as Ecuador, and they foster economic dependence on the United States. However, the underlying premise of these agreements, centered on combating drug trafficking, also introduces imperialist dynamics that permeate the country's criminal justice system. In essence, these tariff preference treaties facilitate the extension of punitive imperialism.

In this vein and drawing from Baker (n.d.) concept of penal imperialism, which describes the power dynamics that define border politics, I posit that Ecuador's participation in the war on drugs policy is the outcome of the same logic. Therefore, the ATPA and APTDEA agreements were mechanisms through which a core country like the United States. extended its rule outside its nation-state boundaries.

Baker (n.d.) claims that penal imperialism is an expression of penal power that is deep-seated in colonizing dynamics, relies on military power, and operates in a transnational space. In this vein, penal imperialism seeks to regulate and control borders and people who cross them through logics and practices initially conceived for the criminal justice system. Following this line of thought, I estimate that Bakers (n.d.) description not only illustrates the reality of border regimes but can also be identified in the dynamics that define criminal policy transfer between core countries like the United States and periphery nations like the Andean countries. However, as we are not analyzing border crossing regulation, we estimate that in this context the word "punitive" will describe better the dependency and domination relation guiding the ATPDA and ATPDE agreements, as well as the transformations in the criminal justice system that took place in Ecuador during the 1980s and 1990s.

The word "punitive" comes from the Latin word "punier," which means "to inflict a penalty on" (Simpson, 2000). This concept does not only refer to forms of direct punishment related to the criminal realm, but it also describes troublesome consequences related to a certain action or omission. Hence, these consequences are not necessarily a punishment dictated by a criminal sentence, they could also be economic, social, and political outcomes. However, they will be unpleasant results that seek to reprimand or repress the entity that receives them (Soca, 2018). Therefore, in the case of the relationship between Ecuador and the United States, the troublesome consequences were not only limited to the penal realm (through drug-enforcement criminal policy), but they also extended to the potential suspension or cancelation of these economic agreements if Ecuador did not comply with the US government requirements. Hence, as the consequences are not limited to criminal punishment, but extend to the economic spheres, we consider that punitive imperialism catches the domination dynamics in place.

Punitive Imperialism: Conditions Related to Drug-Enforcement

Within the framework of ATPA and ATPDE agreements, members had to have certain eligibility criteria, one of which was to "meet the narcotics cooperation certification criteria" (Rosen, 2021, p. 13). In this context, The Foreign Assistance Act of 1961 requires the President to annually submit to Congress a list of nations involved in illicit drug production and trafficking, with Ecuador among them. Certification is granted to countries that have "'cooperated fully' with US narcotics reduction goals or has taken 'adequate steps on its own' to achieve full compliance" (Narcotics Certification of Drug Producing and Trafficking Nations: Questions and Answers, 2000, p. 1).

The precise requirements and procedures for Ecuador's compliance were detailed in confidential annual bilateral agreements (Edwards & Youngers, 2010). However, the Ecuadorian press disclosed reportedly conditions, which included a mandate for a 10% annual increase in drug seizures, a 15% rise in confiscations of arms and chemical weapons, and a 12% surge in the number of legal proceedings related to drug trafficking (FFAA y Policía, 2003). Although this information was exposed in 2003, it is plausible to infer that the requirements set forth during the existence of these trade agreements remained consistent throughout their duration.

It is noteworthy that Ecuador's involvement in the American war on drugs stretches back several years, marked by the initial bilateral agreement signed between Ecuador and the United States in 1985, during the presidency of Febres Cordero (Bonilla, 1991). Consequently, by the time the ATPA came into effect,

Ecuador had already been actively engaged in this campaign, although its efforts were further intensified during the 1990s. In this content, in September 1990, during Borja's presidency, the "Ley de Substancias Estupefacientes y Psicotropicas" (Law on Narcotic and Psychotropic Substances), better known as Law 108, was enacted. This legislation, along with subsequent reforms, served as a significant punitive measure against drug trafficking and aligned with the expectations of the United States. At the time, it was considered one of the most stringent laws against drug trafficking in Latin America (Paladines, 2016).

The influence of the United States played a crucial role in the passage of Law 108. This influence had steadily grown since 1985, marked by continuous collaboration in drug control initiatives. Over time, it intensified, placing mounting pressure on Ecuador. The country found itself caught between the expectations of the United States and the escalating global focus on combating drug trafficking (Edwards, 2003). This dynamic underscores Ecuador's dependency on the United States and sheds light on the mechanisms of punitive imperialism at play.

Before the enactment of Law 108, Ecuador's anti-drug legislation also approached drug-related issues as public health concerns, rather than solely treating them as criminal matters. For instance, the 1970 "Ley de Control y Fiscalización del Tráfico de Estupefacientes" (Control and Enforcement Law on Drug Trafficking) contained a specific section dedicated to individuals struggling with substance abuse, mandating that they receive medical attention and, if necessary, participate in rehabilitation programs.[8] However, after this period, Ecuadorian legislation shifted toward a more stringent approach,[9] aligning with the prohibitionist tendencies of international drug agreements at the time. Although harsher penalties were introduced, they were applied only in exceptional circumstances, and the health-centered approach remained (Edwards & Youngers, 2010).

The implementation of Law 108 represented a significant shift in Ecuador's approach to drug-related matters. It completely removed the section addressing drug issues as a public health concern and abolished distinctions based on the scale of involvement in drug activities. Both drug consumers and small-scale and large-scale traffickers were treated similarly under the law. Additionally, defendants' rights were curtailed, requiring them to prove their innocence, while special procedures were introduced. Prescription periods were extended, and penalties were substantially increased. These changes, as noted by Núñez Vega (2005), led to the creation of what can be considered a penal subsystem within Ecuador's legal framework.

Through Law 108, Ecuador adopted a widespread practice in the American criminal system, mandatory minimum penalties. In this context, all drug offenses were punished with a minimum sentence of 10 years of imprisonment.

---

[8]This was stated in Title II, articles 22–28 of this law, which was published in the Official Registry No. 105 of November 1970.
[9]The legislation from 1970 was replaced in 1987 by the Ley de Control y Fiscalización del Tráfico de Estupefacientes y Sustancias Psicotrópicas (Control and Enforcement Law on the Traffic of Narcotic Drugs and Psychotropic Substances), published in the Official Registry No. 612 of January 1987.

Consequently, all offenders, regardless of the seriousness of the crime, were judged in the same way, including drug users and micro-traffickers (Edwards, 2010). Drug use was one of the most serious offenses in the Penal Code. A user could receive 10 years in prison, an unreasonable penalty in a country where homicide was punishable by 16 years (Ecuadorian Penal Code, 1971).

Similarly, this legislation exacerbated the lack of independence of the judiciary in Ecuador (Estrella et al., 2011). In this regard, to further their interests, American neoliberal policies have advocated and financed judicial reforms throughout Latin America (Gloeckner, 2023). In the case of Ecuador, the recommendations made by the United States in the elaboration and application of Law 108 determined the need for a review of all judicial decisions by the Supreme Court to avoid corruption. Therefore, to avoid reviews for corruption, which took place in the case of judgments of acquittal, most trials related to drug offenses ended up in guilty verdicts (Vásconez, 2006).

As previously mentioned, at the time that ATPA and the ATPDE were signed, Ecuador was mainly a transit country, so drug trade within the country was mainly a small-scale informal activity (UNODC, 2015). Therefore, in the absence of intense drug-related criminality, the pressure to comply with US conditions meant that much of Ecuador's drug enforcement efforts were concentrated on criminalizing minority dealers from the most vulnerable social groups. In this sense, a hunt for micro drug dealers took place, which Núñez Vega (2005) accurately named "cacería de brujos" (witch hunt) as the term "brujo" (witch) is the colloquial term used in Ecuador to refer to a small-scale drug dealer.

The war on drugs policies adopted by Ecuador in the frame of punitive imperialism profoundly transformed the configuration of Ecuador's prison population. By observing the data related to the Ecuadorian prison population we may state that the number of people detained for drug-related offenses increased in an unprecedented way since the 1990s. Thus, in the mid-19th century, the most significant crimes for which people were incarcerated in Ecuador were murders with a percentage of 19%, followed by robbery (16.5%) and assault and battery (14%). Toward the end of the 19th century, President García Moreno focused punitive efforts mainly on crimes against morality, such as drunkenness or concubinage (Castro Proaño, 1987). During the 20th century and until the mid-1980s, the most important crimes were related to property. It was after this period that Ecuador began to experience a progressive growth in the criminalization of drug-related crimes (Edwards & Youngers, 2010).

Between 1972 and 1985, the number of individuals incarcerated for drug-related offenses began to gradually rise. However, throughout the 1990s, particularly after the implementation of Law 108, this category of crime became increasingly prevalent within Ecuadorian prisons (Edwards, 2003; Núñez Vega, 2005; Paladines, 2016). In 1996, Ecuador witnessed a peak in the number of individuals detained for drug offenses, leading to significant prison overcrowding (Edwards & Youngers, 2010).

The situation began to improve slightly in 1997 when certain legal benefits were extended to incarcerated individuals. These efforts to address prison overcrowding were the result of reforms to the Code of Execution of Sentences and Social Rehabilitation and the issuance of a new Constitution in 1998. Some of these reforms included the introduction of the "dos por uno" (two for one) policy, which doubled the number of days that could be deducted from a sentence for good behavior. In other words, prisoners could earn an additional day of reduction for each day of good behavior. Additionally, individuals held in pretrial detention for more than 1 year were released. Likewise, drug use was decriminalized in 1998 (Mora Enríquez, 2003). However, this measure did not entirely resolve the issue, as many users continued to face charges of drug trafficking. The complexity of this situation was compounded by the logistical hurdles in proving that defendants were mere drug users.[10]

It is important to note that the composition of Ecuador's prison population underwent significant changes beyond the shift in the dominant crime types within the criminal justice system. There was also a noticeable rise in the criminalization of women, particularly in the context of drug-related offenses. Before the 1980s, the majority (82%) of crimes leading to female incarceration were offenses against individuals (Vegas Uquillas et al., 1987). However, with the onset of economic crises in Latin America during the 1980s, drug-related crimes began to surge, accounting for 38.24% of female incarcerations during that decade. This trend escalated further in 1996, with rates soaring to 73.6%, and peaked at 77% by 2005. These increases coincided with the period during which the ATPA and the ATPDEA were in force (Edwards, 2010).

The rise in the incarceration of women for drug-related offenses has been attributed to the phenomenon of female poverty by some scholars. For instance, Davis (2011) argues that neoliberal policies promoting labor flexibility have exacerbated economic hardships for women. In Latin America, a significant portion of informal work is undertaken by women (Ramirez Vigoya, 2015), particularly those from the most vulnerable social strata who struggle to find formal employment opportunities. The Economic Commission for Latin America and the Caribbean (ECLAC) highlights the challenges faced by these women in accessing the formal labor market, leaving informal work as their primary option, a situation exacerbated by the adoption of neoliberal models in the region (Angarita, 2008).

In societies where women's access to stable employment is precarious, the rise in unemployment rates during neoliberalism disproportionately affects impoverished women (Cobo & Posada, 2006). This phenomenon, known as the "feminization of poverty," has led to an increase in women's involvement in the micro-trafficking of drugs in Ecuador (Edwards, 2010), reshaping the landscape

---

[10]Following the decriminalization of drug use, the identification of an individual as an addict was initially determined through a psychosomatic examination conducted by a physician. However, the final decision regarding the individual's status was left to the discretion of the judge. This approach raised concerns as the evaluation relied on the defendant's ability to prove a long history of substance abuse. It wasn't until 2013 that a more objective method for determining drug consumption was established. This involved the implementation of a table specifying the quantity of drugs, categorized by type, that an individual could possess to be classified as a consumer.

of what constitutes female criminality. Traditional criminological research has often associated women with certain types of crimes such as infanticide or matricide (Frigon, 2003). However, recent decades have seen a shift in contexts where poverty drives women to engage in drug-related offenses.

This transformation has resulted in heightened criminalization of women, particularly in environments where small-scale drug trafficking is targeted by law enforcement. Consequently, the punitive measures characteristic of criminal policies during the ATPA and ATPDEA agreements have disproportionately affected vulnerable Ecuadorian women. Incarcerating them has only served to exacerbate and perpetuate the cycle of violence and poverty in which these marginalized women find themselves (Gustafson, 2013).

The enactment of Law 108 in Ecuador marked a significant shift in the nation's approach to drug-related offenses, reflecting broader trends influenced by global pressures, notably from the United States. While intended to combat drug trafficking, this legislation had far-reaching consequences for Ecuador's legal system and its incarcerated population. The substantial increase in incarceration rates, especially among vulnerable demographics like women and economically disadvantaged individuals, highlights the intricate interplay between economic conditions, political structures, and the implementation of punitive measures. Furthermore, Ecuador's engagement in anti-drug agreements with the United States emphasizes the intricate network of international relations influencing domestic strategies in combating drug-related crimes, which are deeply entrenched in dynamics that continue to perpetuate imperialism and colonialism.

Conclusion

During the 1980s and 1990s, Ecuador witnessed a surge in incarceration rates and a notable shift in the composition of its prison population. Núñez Vega (2005) contends that this transformation is intricately linked to the broader historical trajectory of the nation. Building upon this assertion, in this chapter, I argue that examining the historical evolution of Ecuador provides valuable insights into the patterns of criminalization within the country. However, it is imperative to acknowledge that historical processes are fundamentally shaped by power dynamics, and all instances of criminalization serve as manifestations of these dynamics.

When examining how the war on drugs shaped Ecuadorian criminal policy, it's essential to note that, at its inception, Ecuador wasn't significantly impacted by large-scale drug trafficking. Nevertheless, it adopted stringent measures, mirroring US directives to combat the issue, despite its incongruence with the local context. This adoption of a "made in U.S.A." punitive approach was largely driven by economic pressures stemming from the conditions outlined in the ATPDA and ATPDE agreements.

The imperialist dynamics that define the economic relationship between the United States and Ecuador, influenced its punitive trends. Consequently, Ecuador found itself subject to the transfer of the US war on drugs policy, reflecting a form of punitive imperialism. This transfer extended beyond economic dependency to encompass criminal policy, wherein the United States effectively extended its influence over Ecuadorian society. In essence, the transformation in Ecuador's criminalization processes can be viewed as the replication of a governance model already established within the framework of US policy, facilitated by Ecuador's economic and commercial dependence on the former.

References

Aas, K. F. (2010). Global criminology. In E. McLaughlin & T. Newburn (Eds.), *The SAGE handbook of criminological theory* (pp. 427–443). Sage.

Aguirre Salas, A., Léon, T., & Ribadeneira, N. (2020). Sistema penitenciario y población penalizada durante la Revolución Ciudadana (2007–2017). *URVIO Revista Latinoamericana de Estudios de Seguridad, 27*, 94–110. https://doi.org/10.17141/urvio.27.2020.4303

Alvarado, N., Villa-Mar, K., Jarquín, M. J., Cedillo, B., & Forero, D. (2020). *Las cárceles de América Latina y el Caribe ante la crisis sanitaria del COVID-19*. IDB Publications. https://doi.org/10.18235/0002607

Angarita, A. T. (2008). *Drogas, cárcel y género en Ecuador: La experiencia de mujeres" mulas"*. Flacso-Sede Ecuador.

Arenas, L. C., & Gómez, G. I. (2000). En busca de justicia en los tiempos de las reformas judiciales: estudios de caso en Colombia, Perú y Venezuela. *Revista El Otro Derecho*.

Arriagada Gajewski, I. (2012). De cárceles y concesiones: Privatización carcelaria y penalidad neoliberal. *Revista de Derecho (Valdivia), 25*(2), 9–31. https://doi.org/10.4067/S0718-09502012000200001

Banco Central del Ecuador. (n.d.). *Comercio exterior*. Retrieved July 24, 2024, from https://www.bce.fin.ec/comercio-exterior

Baker, V. (n.d.). *Penal imperialism: The rise and return of transnational penal orders*. https://www.law.uci.edu/centers/glas/activities/transnational-ordering-criminal-justice/abstract-barker.html

Bell, E. (2011). *Criminal justice and neoliberalism*. Springer.

Bell Lara, J., & Dello Buono, R. A. (2020). Imperialismo y neoliberalismo. *Revista Estudios del Desarrollo Social: Cuba y América Latina, 8*(1). http://scielo.sld.cu/scielo.php?script=sci_abstract&pid=S2308-01322020000100017&lng=es&nrm=iso&tlng=es

Benítez, F. F., & Larrea, C. (2003). *Impactos ambientales de las políticas de liberalización externa y los flujos de capital*. El caso de Ecuador.

Bonilla, A. (1991). Ecuador: Actor internacional en la guerra de las drogas. In B. Bagley, A. Bonilla, & A. Páez (Eds.), *La economía política del narcotráfico: El caso ecuatoriano* (pp. 9–45). https://biblio.flacsoandes.edu.ec/libros/digital/45018.pdf

Brown, D. (2013). Prison rates, social democracy, neoliberalism and justice reinvestment. In K. Carrington, M. Ball, E. O'Brien, & J. M. Tauri (Eds.), *Crime, justice and social democracy: International perspectives* (pp. 70–85). Palgrave Macmillan UK. https://doi.org/10.1057/9781137008695_5

Carrier, N. (2010). Sociologies anglo-saxonnes du virage punitif. *Champ pénal/penal field (Vol. VII)*. https://doi.org/10.4000/champpenal.7818

Carrington, K., Hogg, R., Scott, J., Sozzo, M., & Walters, R. (2018). *Southern criminology*. Routledge. https://doi.org/10.4324/9781315194585

Carrington, K., Hogg, R., & Sozzo, M. (2016). Southern criminology. *The British Journal of Criminology, 56*(1), 1–20. https://doi.org/10.1093/bjc/azv083

Castro Proaño, R. C. (1987). La criminalidad en el Ecuador entre 1841 y 1850. In *Archivos de Criminología, Neuro-psiquiatría y Disciplinas Conexas*, Número 28, 3ª época, Vol. XXVI (pp. 81–98). Quito, Facultad de jurisprudencia, Ciencias Políticas y Sociales de la Universidad Central del Ecuador.

Chávez Zavala, P. (2016). Regímenes de Bienestar y gobiernos "progresistas" en América Latina: Los casos de Venezuela, Ecuador y Bolivia. *Iberoamericana, 87*, 112.

Cobo, R., & Posada, L. (2006). *La feminización de la pobreza. Mujeres en Red. Madrid, s/f, 2. L'homicide conjugal au féminin: d'hier à aujourd'hui.* Éditions du Remue-Ménage.

Costales-Montenegro, R., & Rondón, I. G. (2014). Las políticas neoliberales en América Latina y su impacto en el sector de la salud: caso Ecuador. *Observatorio de la Economía Latinoamericana* (197).

Danani, C. C. (2008). América Latina luego del mito del progreso neoliberal: las políticas sociales y el problema de la desigualdad. *Ciências Sociais Unisinos, 44*(1), 39–48.

Davis, A. Y. (2011). *Are prisons obsolete?* Seven Stories Press.

Delgado, M. G., & Porto, L. V. (2021). The welfare state: General characteristics, obstacles and challenges in Latin America (Spanish text). *E-Revista Internacional de La Proteccion Social, 6*(1), 107–140.

Edwards, S. G. (2003). *Políticas y Prisiones para el Control de Drogas Ilícitas: El Costo Humano.* WOLA. https://www.wola.org/sites/default/files/downloadable/Drug%20Policy/past/ddhr_ecuador_memo4_esp.pdf

Edwards, S. G. (2010). *La legislación de drogas de Ecuador y su impacto sobre la población penal en el país.* WOLA. https://www.wola.org/sites/default/files/downloadable/Drug%20Policy/2011/Spanish/sistemas%20sobrecargados-resumen%20ecuador-web.pdf

Edwards, S. G., & Youngers, C. A. (2010). Drug law reform in Ecuador: Building momentum for a more effective, balanced and realistic approach. *Policy.* https://www.wola.org/sites/default/files/downloadable/Drug%20Policy/2011/Spanish/joint%20pubs/ecuador%20memo.pdf

Ellner, S., & de Sousa Santos, B. (2020). *Latin America's pink tide: Breakthroughs and shortcomings.* Rowman & Littlefield.

Estrella, C., Pontón, D., Pontón, J., & Núñez, J. (2011). Análisis de la ley de drogas desde una perspectiva socio-política. Diagnóstico de la ley de sustancias estupefacientes y psicotrópicas. p. 76, cuadro 12, Quito.

Feeley, M. M., & Simon, J. (1992). The new penology: Notes on the emerging strategy of corrections and its implications. *Criminology, 30*(4), 449–474.

FFAA y Policía. (2003, October 12). *El Comercio,* A7.

Foucault, M. (2015). *The punitive society: Lectures at the Collège de France 1972–1973.* Palgrave Macmillan.

Frigon, S. (2003). *L'homicide conjugal au féminin: d'hier à aujourd'hui.* Éditions du Remue-Ménage.

Gallardo, C., & Núñez Vega, J. (2006). *Una Lectura cuantitativa del sistema de carceles en Ecuador.pdf.* FLACSO Sede Ecuador. https://adsdatabase.ohchr.org/IssueLibrary/CLAUDIO%20GALLARDO%20Y%20JORGE%20NUNEZ%20VEGA_Una%20Lectura%20cuantitativa%20del%20sistema%20de%20carceles%20en%20Ecuador.pdf

Galtung, J. (1971). A structural theory of imperialism. *Journal of Peace Research, 8*(2), 81–117.

Giacoman, D. (2011). Drug policy and the prison situation in Bolivia. In P. Metaal & C. Youngers (Eds.), *Systems overload. Drug laws and prisons in Latin America* (pp. 21–29). Transnational Institute/WOLA. https://www.wola.org/sites/default/files/downloadable/Drug%20Policy/2011/WOLATNI-Systems_Overload-bolivia-def.pdf

Giorgi, A. D. (2016). *Re-thinking the political economy of punishment: Perspectives on postfordism and penal politics.* Routledge. https://doi.org/10.4324/9781315244273

Gloeckner, R. J. (2023). Las reformas de los sistemas de justicia criminal latinoamericanos: ¿Modelos acusatorios, racionalidad neoliberal? Reforming Latin American criminal justice systems: Accusatory models, neoliberal rationale? *Cadernos de Dereito Actual, 20,* Article 20.

Gustafson, K. (2013). Degradation ceremonies and the criminalization of low-income women. *UC Irvine Law Review, 3,* 297.

Hallsworth, S. (2002). The case for a postmodern penality. *Theoretical Criminology, 6*(2), 145–163. https://doi.org/10.1177/136248060200600202

Harvey, D. (2005). From globalization to the new imperialism. *Critical Globalization Studies, 91*, 100.

Hathazy, P., & Müller, M.-M. (2016). The rebirth of the prison in Latin America: Determinants, regimes and social effects. *Crime, Law and Social Change, 65*(3), 113–135. https://doi.org/10.1007/s10611-015-9580-8

Hesselroth, A. (2015). The decolonization of Bolivia's antinarcotics policy. *Bolivian Studies Journal, 21*, 59–99. https://doi.org/10.5195/bsj.2015.134

House Report No. 110-529. (2008). https://www.govinfo.gov/content/pkg/CRPT-110hrpt529/html/CRPT-110hrpt529.htm

Huerta González, A. (2007). Los tratados de libre comercio impulsados por Estados Unidos en América Latina y la profundización del subdesarrollo. *Contaduría y administración* (221), 09–37.

Iturralde, M. (2010). Democracies without citizenship: Crime and punishment in Latin America. *New Criminal Law Review, 13*(2), 309–332. https://doi.org/10.1525/nclr.2010.13.2.309

Jácome, H. (2004). A las puertas del abismo. Las implicaciones del TLC para Ecuador. *Íconos: Revista de Ciencias Sociales*, (20), 6–13.

Jorgenson, A. K., & Kick, E. L. (2003). Introduction: Globalization and the environment. *Journal of World-Systems Research, 9*(2), 195–203.

Kiely, R. (2007). Poverty reduction through liberalisation? Neoliberalism and the myth of global convergence. *Review of International Studies, 33*(3), 415–434.

Kohli, A. (2019). *Imperialism and the developing world: How Britain and the United States shaped the global periphery*. Oxford University Press.

Lacey, N. (2010). Differentiating among penal states. *The British Journal of Sociology, 61*(4), 778–794. https://doi.org/10.1111/j.1468-4446.2010.01341.x

Loader, I., & Sparks, R. (2004). For an historical sociology of crime policy in England and Wales since 1968. *Critical Review of International Social and Political Philosophy, 7*(2), 5–32.

Mayer, M. (2010). Punishing the Poor—a debate: Some questions on Wacquant's theorizing the neoliberal state. *Theoretical Criminology, 14*(1), 93–103. https://doi.org/10.1177/1362480609352890

Melossi, D. (2004). The cultural embeddedness of social control: Reflections on a comparison of Italian and North American cultures concerning punishment. In *Criminal justice and political cultures*. Willan.

Miller, R. J. (2014). Devolving the carceral state: Race, prisoner reentry, and the micropolitics of urban poverty management. *Punishment & Society, 16*(3), 305–335. https://doi.org/10.1177/1462474514527487

Mora Enríquez, D. (2003). *aplicacion del regimen progresivo: Ubicacion poblacional carcelaria y clasificacion de los centros de rehabilitacion social y de los internos o presos de acuerdo a las nuevas normas del codigo de ejecucion de penas y rehabilitacion social y su reglamento y en la constitucion politica del ecuador*. Instituto de Altos Estudios Nacionales.

Müller, M.-M. (2012). The rise of the penal state in Latin America. *Contemporary Justice Review, 15*(1), 57–76. https://doi.org/10.1080/10282580.2011.590282

Narcotics Certification of Drug Producing and Trafficking Nations: Questions and Answers. (2000). CRS Report of Congress. https://www.everycrsreport.com/files/20000327_98-159_944ec433b395f62a5b38a1d6492f2209fab35f67.pdf

Nelken, D. (2010). Denouncing the penal state. *Criminology & Criminal Justice, 10*(4), 331–340. https://doi.org/10.1177/1748895810382382

Núñez Rebolledo, L. (2019). The punitive turn, neoliberalism, feminism and gender violence. *Política y Cultura, 51*, 55–81. https://doi.org/10.24275/RVNN3774

Núñez Vega, J. (2005). *Cacería de brujos: Drogas ilegales y sistema de cárceles en Ecuador* [Master thesis, FLACSO Sede Ecuador]. http://repositorio.flacsoandes.edu.ec/handle/10469/956

O'Malley, P. (2014). Prisons, neoliberalism and neoliberal states: Reading Loïc Wacquant and prisons of poverty. *Thesis Eleven, 122*(1), 89–96. https://doi.org/10.1177/0725513614530068

Pakes, F. (2006). The ebb and flow of criminal justice in the Netherlands. *International Journal of the Sociology of Law, 34*(3), 141–156. https://doi.org/10.1016/j.ijsl.2006.08.001

Paladines, J. (2016). *Cárcel y drogas en Ecuador: el castigo de los más débiles*. Pensamiento Penal.

Pitts, J. (2012). The third time as farce: Whatever happened to the penal state?. In P. Squires & J. Lea (Eds.), *Criminalisation and advanced marginality* (pp. 61–84). Policy Press. https://bristoluniversitypressdigital.com/edcollchap/book/9781447300021/ch004.xml

Peck, J., Brenner, N., & Theodore, N. (2018). Actually existing neoliberalism. In D. Cahill, M. Cooper, M. Konings, & D. Primrose (Eds.), *The SAGE handbook of neoliberalism* (pp. 3–15). SAGE Publications Ltd. https://doi.org/10.4135/9781526416001

Piven, F. F. (2010). A response to Wacquant. *Theoretical Criminology, 14*(1), 111–116. https://doi.org/10.1177/1362480609353340

Población carcelaria. (2023, November 23). *DW*. https://www.dw.com/es/la-poblaci%C3%B3n-carcelaria-en-am%C3%A9rica-latina-se-dispar%C3%B3-un-70-en-20-a%C3%B1os/a-67538285

Polga-Hecimovich, J. (2020). Reshaping the state: The unitary executive presidency of Rafael Correa. In F. Sánchez & S. Pachano (Eds.), *Assessing the left turn in Ecuador* (pp. 15–39). Springer International Publishing. https://doi.org/10.1007/978-3-030-27625-6_2

Pontón Cevallos, J., & Torres, A. (2007). *Cárceles del Ecuador: Los efectos de la criminalización por drogas*. http://repositorio.flacsoandes.edu.ec/handle/10469/1399

Ramírez-Loayza., D. K., Castillo-Aguirre., M. M., & Zamora-Campoverde., M. A. (2023). Evolución de los Arreglos Comerciales Preferenciales Otorgados por Estados Unidos a Ecuador. *Economía y Negocios, 14*(1), 115–134. https://doi.org/10.29019/eyn.v14i1.1072

Ramirez Vigoya, A. (2015). Caracterización Del Mercado Laboral Femenino En Colombia Frente Al Neoliberalismo: Una Mirada Al Sector Rural.

Robayo, L., & Leiva Ponce, J. (2005). Relaciones Ecuador-Estados Unidos Presidencia de Rodrigo Borja. In *Las relaciones Ecuador-Estados Unidos en 25 años de democracia (1979–2004)* (pp. 89–112). Editorial Abya Yala.

Rosen, L. W. (2021). *The U.S. "Majors List" of illicit drug-producing and drug-transit countries*. https://crsreports.congress.gov/product/pdf/R/R46695/2

Rosero, D. A. (2018). Estado de bienestar en ecuador: Pensiones. *Boletín Academia Nacional de Historia, 96*(199), Article 199.

Rothkopf, D. (1997). In praise of cultural imperialism? *Foreign Policy, 107*, 38–53.

Rubio Ríos, M. L. (2008). *El impacto de las ATPDEA en la agenda comercial de política exterior del Ecuador* [Master thesis, FLACSO sede Ecuador]. http://repositorio.flacsoandes.edu.ec/handle/10469/483

Russell, R. (2006). América Latina para Estados Unidos: ¿especial, desdeñable, codiciada o perdida. *Nueva sociedad, 206*, 48–62.

Sánchez, F., & Pachano, S. (Eds.). (2020). *Assessing the left turn in Ecuador*. Springer International Publishing. https://doi.org/10.1007/978-3-030-27625-6

Simon, J. (1997). Governing through crime. In L. M. Friedman, & G. Fisher (Eds.), *The crime conundrum: Essays on criminal justice* (pp. 171–189). Westview Press.

Simpson. (2000). *Cassell's Latin-English, English-Latin dictionary* (5th ed.). Continuum.

Soca, R. (2018). *El origen de las palabras: diccionario etimológico ilustrado*. Rey Naranjo.

Sozzo, M. (2018). Beyond the 'Neo-liberal Penality Thesis'? Punitive turn and political change in South America. In K. Carrington, R. Hogg, J. Scott, & M. Sozzo (Eds.), *The Palgrave handbook of criminology and the Global South* (pp. 659–685). Springer International Publishing. https://doi.org/10.1007/978-3-319-65021-0_32

Sozzo, M. (2022). Introduction: Inmate governance in Latin America. Context, trends and conditions. In M. Sozzo (Ed.), *Prisons, inmates and governance in Latin America* (pp. 1–32). Springer International Publishing. https://doi.org/10.1007/978-3-030-98602-5_1

Sozzo, M. (2023). Reading penalty from the periphery. *Theoretical Criminology, 27*(4), 660–675. https://doi.org/10.1177/13624806231199749

UNODC (United Nations Office on Drugs and Crime). (2015). *Informe de monitoreo de territorios afectados por cultivos ilícitos*. https://bit.ly/39hPdcl

Uquillas, C. A. (2007). *El fracaso del neoliberaliso en el Ecuador y alternativas frente a la crisis*. https://www.eumed.net/libros-gratis/2007c/313/313.pdf

Vega Uquillas, V., Gonzalez Miño, M., & Rivadeneira, S. (1987). Tendencias de la criminalidad en el Ecuador. In *Archivos de Criminología, Neuro-psiquiatría y Disciplinas Conexas* (pp. 99–109).

Vos, R. (2000). *Ecuador 1999: Crisis económica y protección social*. Editorial Abya Yala.

Vos, R., & Leon, M. (2003). *Dolarización, dinámica de exportaciones y equidad: ¿cómo compatibilizarlas en el caso de Ecuador?* (Vol. 5). Unidad de Información y Análisis--SIISE--de la Secretaría Técnica del Frente Social.

Wacquant, L. (1999). *Les prisons de la misère*. Raisons d'agir.

Wacquant, L. (2001). The penalisation of poverty and the rise of neo-liberalism. *European Journal on Criminal Policy and Research, 9*(4), 401–412. https://doi.org/10.1023/A:1013147404519

Wacquant, L. (2003). Toward a dictatorship over the poor?: Notes on the penalization of poverty in Brazil. *Punishment & Society, 5*(2), 197–205. https://doi.org/10.1177/146247450352004

Wacquant, L. (2008). The militarization of urban marginality: Lessons from the Brazilian metropolis. *International Political Sociology, 2*(1), 56–74. https://doi.org/10.1111/j.1749-5687.2008.00037.x

Wacquant, L. (2009). *Punishing the poor: The neoliberal government of social insecurity*. Duke University Press.

Walia, H. (2014). *Undoing border imperialism*. AK Press.

Welch, M. (2003). Force and fraud: A radically coherent criticism of corrections as industry. *Contemporary Justice Review: CJR, 6*(3), 227–240.

World Prison Brief. (n.d.). *Highest to lowest-prison population total*. Institute for Crime & Justice Policy Research, Birkbeck University of London. Retrieved April 4, 2024, from https://www.prisonstudies.org/map/south-america

Yasunaga Kumano, M. (2020). La desigualdad y la inestabilidad política en América Latina: Las protestas en Ecuador, Chile y Colombia. *bie3: Boletín IEEE, 18*, 366–382.

Chapter 3

Criminal Justice Reform, Americanization, and Conviction without Trial in Argentina

Máximo Sozzo

National University of Litoral, Argentina

Abstract

This chapter addresses the hypothesis that the criminal justice reforms toward an accusatory/adversarial model produced in Latin America from the 1980s onwards have meant a mutation in its way of functioning that can be read as an "Americanization." Specifically, this general question is addressed by analyzing the introduction, in these reform processes, of mechanisms of conviction without trial – in their majority inspired by the "plea bargaining" of the Anglo-American tradition – that have a significant impact on the way in which the power to punish is exercised in most of the countries of the region today. This discussion is elaborated from a case study on the Province of Santa Fe (Argentina). It is argued that in the "law in books" the introduction of this type of mechanism has frequently implied a "weak Americanization," since it was a "legal translation" (Langer, 2006) that not only generated "adoptions" but also "innovations" with respect to the parameters of the Anglo-American tradition. But it also shows how this can be combined with a "strong Americanization" in the "law in action," differentiating the dimension of the dynamics from the dimension of the effects, based on two key observations: the weakness and infrequency of judicial control of the agreements reached by the parties and the enormous preponderance of convictions without trial. In this way, it is intended to make the idea of "Americanization" of criminal justice more complex, differentiating levels (in books/in action) and dimensions (dynamics/results).

Keywords: Americanization; criminal justice; plea bargaining; law in books; law in action; legal reform

Criminal Justice Reform: Programs and Influences

Over the last 35 years, a series of criminal justice reforms have taken place in Latin America. These reforms have sought to drastically change the dynamics of the criminal justice functioning. They have been commonly defined, both by their promoters and their observers, as the passage from an "inquisitorial model" to an "accusatorial/adversarial model."[1]

In general, these changes have been persistently encouraged by claiming three objectives: (a) to generate a greater capacity to respect and protect the guarantees and rights of the accused, but also of the victims – the latter presented as a novelty compared to its complete lack of consideration in the past; (b) to increase the speed of its operation, producing greater effectiveness and efficiency, in terms of more cases resolved in less time and with less expense; (c) to increase the transparency of these state institutions, in relation to the orality and openness of their procedures and the possibility, therefore, for citizens to directly witness them and the results they reach.

A "program" (Garland, 2018, pp. 121–125) was structured around each of these objectives, understood as a complex discursive amalgam that defined not only "why" and "what for" criminal justice reform, but also the "what" and "how" of it. Each of these programs contained a promise to achieve an ideal for the new criminal justice, in relation to its specific objective: a "rights-based" justice, a "managerial" justice, and a "democratic" justice. These different objectives and ideals, in turn, have been translated in the framework of each program into a whole series of proposals for particular measures for their realization – the "what" and the "how" – in the reformed criminal justice system.

In the processes of change in the criminal justice system that have taken place throughout this period in different jurisdictions, these three programs – with their objectives, ideals and measures – have coexisted within the framework of combinations whose balances have varied to a certain extent. These variations have had to do with the different orientations of the various actors who have been fighting in the academic, political and judicial fields in favor of these processes of change. In all their diversity, these actors have proposed their own balance of these programs. But this has not prevented certain recurrent combinations from becoming dominant in specific times and spaces.

If we take the case of Argentina, it is possible to state with reasonable certainty that at the time of its emergence, during the 1980s and early 1990s, the reformist

---

[1] Among the many recent examples of this way of presenting criminal justice reform processes in Latin America, from a partisan viewpoint, starting with an international organization that has played an important role in its promotion and monitoring – the Justice Studies Center of the Americas (Ciocchini, 2017, pp. 324–326; Gutiérrez, 2014a, p. 81; Hathazy, 2020, pp. 34–36; Langer, 2007, pp. 655–656; Palacios, 2011, pp. 63–65;), see Fuchs et al. (2018). For an in-depth exploration of the meanings of these two categories, "inquisitorial model" and "accusatorial model" and their roles and limitations in the academic debate about the functioning of criminal justice in comparative terms, see Langer (2014).

discourses deployed, with particular intensity, the program of "rights-based justice" in a context marked by the legacy of authoritarianism and the transition to democracy. This did not prevent, in that specific time and space, the presence of those two other programs of change in the discourses of reformist actors. However, they were to some extent subordinated to the "rights-based justice" (Anitua, 2017, p. 147; Ciocchini, 2018, pp. 22, 27; Gutiérrez, 2014a, pp. 79–80, 2014b, p. 75, 2016, p. 163; Hathazy, 2020, pp. 28–29; Langer, 2007, pp. 637–641; Mira, 2020a; pp. 42, 49–51; Sozzo, 2011a, pp. 6–25, 2013, pp. 204–208). Now, in this national context, this balance seems to have been modified over time, significantly growing the strength of the "managerial justice" program. This change in direction seems to be linked to two main elements. On the one hand, to the gradual installation of the "insecurity crisis" which has brought street crime to the center of the public and political agenda. On the other hand, to the strong affinity of this program with the neoliberal ethos that played a fundamental role in the economic and social policies during the governmental administrations of Presidents Menem (1989–1999) and De la Rua (1999–2001) (Ciocchini, 2018, pp. 24, 27; Ganón, 2007, pp. 445–451; Gutiérrez, 2014a, p. 81, 2014b, pp. 76–80, 2016, pp. 159–160; Langer, 2007, pp. 632–633; Sozzo, 2011a, pp. 24–26, 2016, pp. 306–311, 2018, pp. 665–666). There is important evidence of this change in social research on criminal justice reform in the Province of Buenos Aires – the most extensively studied case so far in the country (Bessone et al., 2020; Ciocchini, 2012, 2013, 2017, 2018; Ganón, 2007; Gutierrez, 2017; Kostenwein, 2012, 2016, 2017, 2020a, 2020b; Museri, 2019).[2] But symptoms in the same direction have also been observed recently in the cases of the City of Buenos Aires and the Province of Santa Fe (Sicardi, 2019, 2020; Sozzo et al., 2015a, 2015b, 2016; Sozzo et al., 2019; Taboga, 2021).[3]

The existence of specific combinations of these reform programs that become dominant in a given time and space does not cancel out the existence of constant struggles over the direction and content of change. Actors who consider themselves and are considered reformists may have antagonistic visions around certain key decisions and measures and push to orient them in different directions (Langer, 2007, p. 656). In addition, reformist actors face resistance from actors in the political, academic and judicial fields who oppose the reform processes – or certain measures included in them – with different intensities and modalities

---

[2] Criminal justice competencies in Argentina are divided between the federal sphere – in relation to federal crimes – and 23 provinces – in relation to common crimes. In addition, the city of Buenos Aires has had a special status since 1994 and has been slowly building its own criminal justice system. Traditionally – and even today, in part – the institutions of the administration of criminal justice with respect to common crimes – not federal offenses – committed in the city of Buenos Aires – as a federal district – were subject to the "national" criminal justice – depending on the Judicial Branch of the Nation.

[3] To what extent this is true in other Argentine jurisdictions is something that remains unexplored from a social research point of view and constitutes an important question to be investigated in the future.

(Langer, 2007, pp. 656–657). This gives rise to a series of transactions and compromises around what is possible. Sometimes there has even been the adoption, over time, of decisions and measures that are labeled as "counter-reformist" by some observers and players (Gutiérrez, 2014a, p. 84). This also constitutes a source of variation across time and space.

In this sense, the general and simple description of a shift from an "inquisitorial model" to an "accusatorial/adversarial model" of criminal justice can be misleading, emphasizing a uniformity that makes us lose sight of the significant degree of diversity that persists in criminal justice reform processes in Latin America. Even this important degree of variation can exist within the same national context, as is clearly the case in Argentina, where diverse reform processes have coexisted, with specific characteristics and temporalities in its jurisdictions.[4]

Criminal justice reform processes in Latin America were born in the 1980s from the configuration of a network of "reformers" and "activists," composed of criminal law and criminal procedure jurists, criminal justice operators, actors from the world of politics and non-governmental and international organizations, which began to weave in the Argentine context and later acquired regional dimensions (Binder, 2016, pp. 71–72; González Guarda, 2015, pp. 87–91, 2016, pp. 158–161; Hathazy, 2020, pp. 27–31; Langer, 2007, pp. 642–646, 651; Mira, 2020a, pp. 42–43). In this network, ideas around criminal justice reform were initially constructed taking into consideration the debates and experiences around European criminal justice systems, with the German context being particularly prominent. In turn, these ideas implied a sort of updating of the criminal procedural law school of the National University of Córdoba and its experiences in reforming provincial criminal procedural codes in Argentina since the late 1930s – a tradition, in turn, also strongly connected to the continental-European context (Hathazy, 2020, pp. 24–27; Langer, 2007, pp. 634–636; Mira, 2020b, pp. 150–152). This is clearly visible in the case of Julio Maier, a key actor in the building of this network in the 1980s and 1990s, who had made academic stays in Germany since the mid-1960s and wrote his doctoral thesis comparing the German Criminal Procedure Ordinance of 1964 with the federal and Cordoba criminal procedure codes (Hathazy, 2020, p. 28; Langer, 2007, pp. 637–641; Mira, 2020b, pp. 139–144). In Argentina, Maier – together with a series of collaborators among whom Alberto Binder was especially prominent – was the author of a draft of the National Criminal Procedural Code presented by the National Executive Branch to the National Congress – together with other complementary legal proposals – in 1986. This project was finally not sanctioned, but implied a first reformist attempt that constituted the starting point of the processes of change in criminal justice in Latin America (Hathazy, 2020, pp. 28–30; Langer, 2007, p. 641;

---

[4]See Note 2. The absence of comparative studies at the processes of criminal justice reform in the various jurisdictions of Argentina as in broader terms in Latin America (see as an exception the comparative work between Chile and Costa Rica by González Guarda, 2018) – results in a very dramatic and striking gap that should be key in the agenda of social research in this regard (Sozzo, 2020a, 2022).

Sozzo, 2011a, pp. 6–23, 2013, pp. 204–208). These same actors – Maier and Binder – will be actively involved in the criminal justice reform in Guatemala in 1992 and thereafter – especially Binder – in a series of reforms in other Latin American countries such as Costa Rica in 1996, El Salvador in 1997, Venezuela and Paraguay in 1998, Honduras and Bolivia in 1999, and Chile in 2000 (Hathazy, 2020, pp. 30–31; Langer, 2007, pp. 643–646, 652–656; Mira, 2020b, pp. 144–145). From the mid-1990s onwards, this network of "reformers and activists" will expand and become more varied and complex.

During that decade, a greater involvement of USA actors in these processes of criminal justice reform in Latin America began. This increasing involvement involved not only governmental actors and institutions – such as the Department of Justice and the Department of State – but also academics and consultants. This movement was a consequence of certain changes in the orientation of USAID – the US government's international cooperation body – on the issue of legal reform in Latin America (Binder, 2016, p. 72; Langer, 2007, pp. 646–651, 657–659; McLeod, 2010, pp. 84–90, 116–121). Progressively, this will open the door to a stronger connection with the American tradition in criminal justice issues, generating a greater share of inspiration from it in the design of measures in the framework of criminal justice reform in Latin America, thus enabling certain doses of "Americanization" (Anitua, 2017, p. 148; González Guarda, 2015, pp. 86, 88, 2016, pp. 156–157, 2018, pp. 167–168; Langer, 2007, p. 656).[5] This has even led some observer to state, in general terms: "in the last 20 years, almost all Latin American countries have gradually transformed their penal systems through the adoption of the adversarial model of the United States of America" (Iturralde, 2019, p. 480; in a similar vein, see McLeod, 2010, pp. 87–88, 116, 119). As I have just noted, criminal justice reform processes in the region have had other influences that proved crucial, and this statement simplifies a dynamic that is more complex, but in itself constitutes evidence of the impact that, to some

---

[5]Several processes play a role in this, which still need to be investigated in detail to establish their relative weight. Important contributions in this regard have been made by Langer (2007, pp. 646–659, 664), Cooper (2008, pp. 542, 544–545), McLeod (2010, pp. 116, 131), Palacios (2011, pp. 61–62), González Guarda (2018, pp. 332–333), and Hathazy (2020, pp. 31–36). I can point out as particularly significant as fields of inquiry: a) the fact that the academic world in the United States began to become a reference for the postgraduate training of Latin American jurists – including the field of criminal law and criminal procedure law – competing with the traditional role in this regard of European scenarios; b) the existence of training programs for Latin American criminal justice actors in the United States of America financed and organized by both governmental and non-governmental actors; c) the direct financing by the USA government of various projects linked to certain facets of criminal justice reform processes in Latin America –including b); d) the more indirect influence of the USA tradition on projects financed by international organizations related to criminal justice reform in Latin America such as the Inter-American Development Bank and the United Nations Development Program.

extent, the USA tradition has indeed had in Latin American criminal justice reforms.

In this paper, I understand "Americanization" – based on the important analysis of Langer (2018a, pp. 26–33, 80–81) – as the direct inspiration in the ideas and practices built around American criminal justice to build the "what" and "how" of Latin American reforms, deliberately seeking to produce similarity. At the same time, it is crucial to recognize that there is a possible gradation in this process of Americanization between two poles, one "strong" and other "weak," which implies recognizing that it is not an all-or-nothing game, but that there are several intermediate possibilities. I also intend to distinguish in this chapter the Americanization in "the law in books" – the legal texts – from that in "the law in action" – the practices of criminal justice – two planes that in the region usually have extraordinary doses of distance (Iturralde, 2010, p. 313; Sozzo, 2011a, p. 18, 2017, pp. 8–9). Among other terrains of criminal justice reform in Latin America, I consider that the presence of this Americanization is especially visible in relation to mechanisms of conviction without oral and public trial.[6]

This is precisely the specific topic of this chapter. Around a particular case in Argentina, the Province of Santa Fe, I intend to explore the installation as dominant and legitimate of a mechanism of conviction without trial – the "abbreviated procedure." I will explore its relation to the criminal justice reform and its various programs and the balance between them. And I will discuss through this the more general the question of the "Americanization" of criminal justice, distinguishing between "weak" and "strong," "in the books" and "in action."

The Promise of "Effectiveness and Efficiency" and the "Abbreviated Procedure"

The processes of criminal justice reform in Latin America have been conveyed through new legal texts that regulate criminal procedure, as well as organizational and practical changes in criminal justice institutions. In general, it has implied the creation of new state structures, such as those resulting from the autonomization of public defense and criminal prosecution.

In the Province of Santa Fe, Argentina, the scenario to which our study refers, this trend materialized belatedly. It was only in 2007 that a new Criminal Procedure Code (Law 12734) was enacted, which sought to embody the reform against

---

[6]It must be recognized that these mechanisms already had a certain presence in the debates and proposals of the 1980s in Latin America (Langer, 2001, p. 98, 2007, p. 640, 2021, pp. 5, 8). But their sphere was imagined as limited to minor offenses. For example, in Article 371 of the draft Code of Criminal Procedure of the Nation elaborated by Maier and his team and presented in 1986 in the Congress of the Nation in Argentina, it was only available for cases with a penalty of up to 1 year of imprisonment (Ciocchini, 2018, p. 29).

the inquisitorial model identified with the precedent CPC of 1971.[7] This was followed by a series of complementary legal texts that created new state structures such as the Public Ministry for the Prosecution (Law 13013 of 2009) and the Public Defense Service (Law 13014 of 2009). The criminal courts were also restructured and the Judicial Management Offices were created (Law 13018 of 2009). An important process of appointment of new criminal justice officials was generated.[8] Finally, in February 2014, the reformed criminal justice was implemented in the entire provincial territory.

The late reform in the Province of Santa Fe – precisely because it was late – produced a very strong introduction of a large number of elements associated with the "accusatorial/adversarial model" as an "deal type," in comparison with the reform processes developed previously in most of the other Argentine jurisdictions. Moving away from the image of the "mixed model" associated with the reform produced by the 1991 enactment of the National Criminal Procedure Code, it was presented as a reform that sought to radically develop a "pure accusatory model."

In the Explanatory Memorandum of the new Criminal Procedure Code – as in other discourses produced by the actors who promoted this process of change (Taboga, 2021) – the intertwining of the three reform programs mentioned in the previous section is constantly present: a "rights-based justice," a "democratic justice" and a "managerial justice." Thus, the Explanatory Memorandum of the draft of the new CPCSF states:

> The project is oriented to the fullest and most integral respect of the principles that emanate from the Constitution and the International Treaties with the same hierarchy. It will be seen, however, that particular attention has also been paid to the realization of a procedural design that, in order to achieve social trust, is as *transparent as* possible, and, *without violating any guarantee*, is *effective*. This explains the inclusion of a series of alternatives and procedures, which were not usually found in the procedural digests in the past. (Message 3223 of the Executive Power to the Legislature of the Province of Santa Fe, November 27, 2006, emphasis added)

---

[7] Despite the fact that within the framework of the first generation of reform processes in the country, in 1993, there had already been an important attempt to draft a new Criminal Procedural Code – based on a project of a commission of legal experts in criminal procedural law from different universities based in the provincial territory – which failed after an intense public and political debate (Taboga, 2021).

[8] Although some of them had already held positions in the old criminal justice system. In the early stages of the implementation of the reform, we interviewed all judges, prosecutors and public defenders – with the exception of one judge and two prosecutors – from three of the five judicial districts, which cover the central-northern area of the Province of Santa Fe. Of 16 criminal judges interviewed, 11 had held positions in the old criminal justice system, 68% (Sozzo et al., 2016, p. 2). But this proportion was lower among prosecutors – 12 out of 23 interviewed, 52% (Sozzo et al, 2015b, p. 2) – and even lower among public defenders – 8 out of 21 interviewed, 38% (Sozzo et al., 2015, p. 2).

Regarding what this Memorandum proposes as the "conformation of a fast and efficient criminal justice system"[9] – although it is always clarified, "without detriment to the legal guarantees," reference is made explicitly as a crucial instrument to the "abbreviated procedure" together with "mediation and conciliation between the parties" (Message 3223 of the Executive Power to the Legislature of the Province of Santa Fe, November 27, 2006). The association between the specific objective of effectiveness and efficiency of the criminal justice and the incorporation of the abbreviated procedure is clearly visible in the discourses at the basis of this reform process, as it had happened before, since end of the 1990s, in this national context (Anitua, 2001, pp. 137–143, 2017, pp. 154–156). However, it should be emphasized that the space given by the various key actors involved in the reform process to argue for the inclusion of the abbreviated procedure does not turn out to be very broad. In fact, by opposition – and one might suspect that not coincidentally – much more importance is given to the reference to the oral and public trial as a crucial innovation compared to the inquisitorial model (Taboga, 2021; something similar is observed for the case of the Province of Buenos Aires by Ciocchini, 2018, p. 23).[10]

The abbreviated procedure is regulated in articles 339 to 345 of the CPCSF.[11] It provides that at any time during the Preparatory Criminal Investigation, the Prosecutor and the Defender of the accused, jointly, may request the Court of the Preparatory Investigation to open the abbreviated procedure. They have to submit a brief to the Judicial Management Office, an administrative office created in the reform process to take over the administrative tasks of the judiciary. In practice, although the regulations do not require it, this brief may be accompanied by the prosecutor's file. In order to be valid, this document must contain: (1) the personal data of the Prosecutor, the defense lawyer and the accused; (2) the description of the fact for which the accusation is made and its legal qualification; (3) the penalty requested by the Prosecutor, which must be motivated, determined according to articles 40 and 41 of the Criminal Code and in accordance with the fact under investigation; (4) the conformity of the accused and his defense with respect to the preceding requirements and the procedure chosen, as well as the admission of being guilty; (5) if applicable, the signature of the plaintiff or, failing that, the proof that the District Prosecutor has notified him of the agreement and he/she has not expressed his disagreement in due time. In case of disagree-

---

[9]In fact, "simplification" and "celerity" become principles of the new criminal process, according to Article 3 CPPSF, together with "orality," "publicity," "contradiction," "concentration" and "immediacy."

[10]The "managerial justice" program also has multiple other manifestations in this same jurisdiction, as well as in other criminal justice reform processes in Latin America. There is a whole social research agenda in this regard in the region, both in terms of discursive and practical dimensions. See in this regard, Gutiérrez (2014b, pp. 76–80), Sicardi (2019, 2020), and González Guarda (2015, 2016, 2018).

[11]These articles of the CPPSF were the subject of a legal reform, through Law 13746 of December 2017.

ment, the signature of the respective Regional Prosecutor shall be required; (6) when the agreement refers to the application of a sentence exceeding 6 years of imprisonment or the legal qualification has been modified in favor of the accused with respect to the one used in the indictment hearing, the signature of the respective Regional Prosecutor shall also be required and if the sentence exceeds 8 years of imprisonment, the signature of the General Prosecutor shall also be required.

The abbreviated procedure may be activated at any time during the criminal proceeding before the final discussion of the trial. Once the submission is declared admissible, the parties are summoned to a public hearing. If the defendant acknowledges the agreement, the Judge reads the first three points of the joint submission, explains clearly and simply to the defendant the chosen procedure and its consequences and again requires his express agreement. The presence of the Prosecutor, the defendant and his/her defense are conditions of validity of the hearing.

Subsequently, the Judge issues the sentence in strict conformity with the penalty accepted by the parties. However, if from the fact described in the agreement the Judges considers that it is not a crime or it is manifest the concurrence of any circumstance legally determining the exemption of penalty or its mitigation, they will issue a sentence acquitting or reducing the penalty in the appropriate terms.

Translation and "Weak" Americanization in "Law on the Books"

The link between this type of mechanism of conviction that avoids the oral and public trial and the "plea bargaining" of the American criminal procedural tradition is evident (Anitua, 2001, pp. 143–144, 2017, pp. 150, 156–160; Langer, 2001, pp. 98–99, 2018a, pp. 77–82, 2021, p. 3).[12] Now, as has happened before in other European and Latin American jurisdictions, the translation of "plea bargaining" into the Santa Fe Province legal text has involved a mixture of adoptions and innovations. It is not a mere "legal transplant," cutting and pasting a legal institute from a context of origin to a context of reception, but a more complex process involving a sort of "metamorphosis," which installs a "dialectic between the

---

[12] It is possible to affirm with Langer (2018a, pp. 77–82), generically, that this type of mechanism is typical of an "accusatorial model" of criminal justice, understood less in a normative sense than as a mode of its functioning that places at the center of the scene the "dispute" or "contention" between two parties – accuser and accused – on a formal footing of equality before an impartial third party – judge – who is in a relatively passive position. As the parties to the dispute or contention are its owners, the possibility of agreement between the two becomes a "logical" or "natural" alternative in its operation, unlike the "inquisitorial model" that would place at center stage the "official investigation," the ascertainment of the real truth of what happened by one or several state officials who are in a privileged position with respect to all the other actors in the criminal process – on this reconstruction of the categories of inquisitorial model and accusatorial model, see Langer (2001, pp. 114–122, 2014, 2018a, pp. 34–66).

same and the different" in the "law on the books" (Langer, 2018a, pp. 67–76).[13] I follow here for the detection of these similarities and differences the scheme proposed by Langer (2018a, pp. 82–116).[14]

On the one hand, it is possible to observe similarities with the USA tradition. First, as is usually the case in the United States – and unlike what has happened in Italy and Argentina, in the national and federal jurisdiction and in the Province of Buenos Aires (Ciocchini, 2018, p. 29) – this mechanism of conviction without trial can be applied to all criminal cases in the Santa Fe Province (Hodgson, 2015, p. 226). A timid limitation, of an administrative nature, is introduced in the framework of the Public Ministry for the Prosecution, by requiring for certain agreements – cases involving serious penalties (more than 6 years of imprisonment and more than 8 years of imprisonment) or that do not have the approval of the victim as plaintiff – the authorization of the Regional and General Prosecutors.[15]

Secondly, as in USA jurisdictions – and unlike this type of mechanisms in jurisdictions such as the Italian, German or national/federal and Province of Buenos Aires (Ciocchini, 2018, p. 33) in Argentina – in the Province of Santa Fe, the abbreviated procedure can be triggered after the indictment hearing and until the beginning of the final discussion of the trial, so that cases can be resolved through this path even when a certain amount of time has elapsed since the beginning of the process. Here, too, there is greater flexibility with respect to other scenarios in the continental European and Latin American legal tradition in which this type of mechanism of conviction without trial has recently been adopted.

Third, in the same way as in the USA – and unlike what happens in other jurisdictions such as Italy – in the Santa Fe abbreviated procedure the defendant must plead guilty to the crime. This has been explicitly incorporated by the 2017 reform of the CPCSF. Previously, the original wording gave rise to an interpretation that the conformity of the accused was only around submitting to a type of procedure and did not imply assuming guilt – in a certain sense, approximating the Italian legal rules and in relation to a concern for due process and the presumption of innocence. This interpretation has been radically displaced by the recent legal reform.

---

[13] See on this idea of translation as metamorphosis, around other issues linked to the criminal question, Sozzo (2006, 2011b).

[14] See, for an updated and more complex comparative model of analysis of the key dimensions of this mechanism of conviction without trial in Latin America at the level of the "law on the books," Langer and Sozzo (2023a).

[15] The 2017 legal reform introduced the need for the conformity of the Regional Prosecutor for cases of agreement in which the penalty to be applied was greater than 6 years of imprisonment. This can be read as an attempt to strengthen administrative controls within the Public Ministry for the Prosecution with respect to the discretion of the intervening Prosecutor. On the other hand, the reform also established that in the event of opposition by the plaintiff victim, it is the Regional Prosecutor who must decide what to do in the original wording of the CPCSF this competence was given to the General Prosecutor.

But, on the other hand, it is also possible to identify significant differences with the USA plea bargaining. First, unlike what generally happens in American jurisdictions, the prosecutor and the defendant/defender cannot negotiate the legal qualification of the occurred fact (Baclini & Schiapa Pietra, 2017, p. 374). If different from the USA context, this is basically the same as in European and other Latin American jurisdictions where this type of mechanism has been recently installed (Anitua, 2001, p. 144; Hodgson, 2015, p. 229). This constitutes a strong limit that expresses a clear legacy from the model of the official investigation – or "inquisitorial" – and its quest to determine the real truth and, in general, a conception of truth in a strong sense that moves away from the idea of relative and consensual truth of the dispute model – or "accusatorial." In Santa Fe Province, the prosecutor must respect in his exercise of legal qualification the real characteristics of the fact occurred and proven. Certainly, he can then offer the defense lawyer and the accused the imposition of a low sentence within the legally established scale for that type of crime – or a conditional execution if the legal requirements to do so are met – in order to reach an agreement. Now, as there was recognition that this legal limit does not effectively translate into criminal justice practices, the legal reform to the CPCSF in 2017 established that if there is a change in the legal qualification between the indictment hearing and the request for the abbreviated procedure that would favor the accused, the approval of the agreement by the respective Regional Prosecutor is required. This is a formal requirement that seeks to avoid extending in practice the sphere of agreement to this area, trying to reinforce this residual feature of the inquisitorial model.

Second, another important difference with respect to the USA tradition is that in the Province of Santa Fe, the defense and the accused have a right to access in the first steps of the criminal process to the evidence collected by the police and the prosecution and gathered in the prosecutor's file (Article 259 CPPSF). This has also been observed in the reception and adaptation of this type of mechanism other Latin American and European jurisdictions (Ciocchini, 2018, p. 33). This gives them – at least in formal terms – greater possibilities to negotiate an agreement with the prosecution. And it contrasts with the more limited access that defendants and defenders have in the USA criminal process to evidence produced by the police and the prosecution, subject to complex "discovery"/"disclosure" processes (Langer, 2018a, p. 85).

Third, in European and Latin American jurisdictions, the role of the judge in this type of mechanisms of conviction without trial turns out to be more active and potentially interventionist than in USA jurisdictions. This is something that happens in the German (Langer, 2018a, pp. 85–86) – with greater intensity – and Italian and Argentine cases (at the federal and Buenos Aires Province jurisdictions) – with less intensity (Ciocchini, 2018, p. 33; Langer, 2018a, pp. 97–98, 105–106). In the Province of Santa Fe, it is possible to detect elements in this interventionist direction in the legal text. The judge has a wide capacity of formally adjudicated control, not only over the free consent given by the defendant to the agreement but also over the contents of the agreement (Baclini & Schiapa Pietra, 2017, p. 374). On the one hand, in extreme cases, it can acquit the accused, despite the agreement and the declaration of guilt that it implies, if the fact lacks criminal typicity or the concurrence of any other circumstance legally determining the exemption from punishment is manifest. And as judges can do more, they can also do less, that is, reduce – or change the modality of – the penalty agreed by the parties (Baclini & Schiapa Pietra, 2017, pp. 388–393).

Thus, it is evident that in terms of the "law in the books" the Province of Santa Fe abbreviated procedure has involved, in any case, a relatively "weak" Americanization since it presents a series of important peculiarities that distance it from the American "plea bargaining." The local translators – the reformers in charge of drafting the CPCSF – have transported this legal institution from the American tradition to this new context of reception, but they have also modified it, making its identity with that of the original context at least partially problematic.

However, as Langer has argued:

> even when reformers try to imitate a legal idea or practice as faithfully as possible, this new idea can still be transformed by the structure(s) of meaning, individual dispositions, institutional and power mechanisms and frameworks, incentive systems, etc., that are present in the receiving legal system. (Langer, 2018a, p. 70)

That is to say that a legal text resulting from a translation, which is even intended to be literal, may in praxis undergo a whole series of transformations by the judicial actors in charge of its application (Langer, 2018a, p. 75). Has this "weak" Americanization that articulates the Province of Santa Fe abbreviated procedure "in the books" also occurred in "law in action"? In the next section, I turn precisely to that dimension, trying to observe whether or not the similarities of reformed criminal justice practices in this context are strengthened with respect to those observed in the American plea bargaining.

A Dominant and Legitimized Mode of Sentencing: "Strong" Americanization in "Law in Action"?

Social research on the programs, practices, and effects of these criminal justice reform processes in Latin America is still in its infancy (Sozzo, 2020a, 2022). In some countries of the región, there has been a certain growth of interest in this direction. This has occurred to a still very moderate extent in Argentina. In this framework, in general, mechanisms of conviction without trial have not been the privileged target of these explorations (Langer & Sozzo, 2023b). In the Province of Buenos Aires, three studies can be highlighted as exceptions: the master's thesis by Castorina (2014); the interviews and court observations by Ciocchini (2018); and the sentencing analysis by Bessone et al. (2020).[16] Also, in the city of Buenos

---

[16]There is also a brief reference to empirical data on this issue in this jurisdiction in Ciocchini's thesis (2013, pp. 239–240) and an interesting work referring to juvenile justice (Taddeo, 2019).

Aires, there is the work of Sicardi (2019, 2020), based on interviews with criminal justice actors and official data.[17] Finally, a research team coordinated by me conducted a first approach to the topic in the Province of Santa Fe, based on semi-structured interviews with prosecutors, public defenders, and criminal judges at the beginning of the implementation of the criminal justice reform (Sozzo et al., 2015a, pp. 45–47, 2015b, pp. 59–62, 2016, pp. 59–63).

Since 2018, trying to overcome the exploratory nature of this first approach, we have started an empirical research that seeks to describe and understand the extension and dynamics of the abbreviated procedure within the reformed criminal justice system in the Province of Santa Fe.[18]

Unfortunately, despite all the rhetoric of modernization and transparency that has accompanied the criminal justice reform in this context, no basic official data have been generated regarding the functioning and weight of the abbreviated procedure. This huge deficit does not happen only here, but occurs frequently in Argentine jurisdictions (Anitua, 2017, p. 169; see also, Sozzo, 2020a, 2022). Thus, it is not even possible to get the institutions of the new criminal justice system to publicly report how many of the people convicted in a given period have been convicted in a public trial and how many have been convicted, instead, through an abbreviated procedure. Much less, of course, is it feasible to provide more detailed information on the characteristics of the crime and the convicted person. To alleviate this enormous shortcoming, we have carried out an articulated series of fieldwork over three years. On the one hand, we have collected and analyzed all the convictions produced between 2014 and 2019 filed in the Judicial Management Office of the First Judicial District of the Province of Santa Fe.[19] The analysis has allowed the construction of a whole series of crucial quantitative data, both on the dynamics and the outcome of the abbreviated procedure. On the other hand, 47 semi-structured interviews were carried out with criminal justice actors in this First Judicial District. Twenty-one out of 28 existing prosecutors, 15 out of 16 existing public defenders, and 11 out of 15 existing criminal judges were interviewed.[20] These semi-structured interviews make it possible to reconstruct, from the voices of criminal justice actors, the dynamics and outcomes of abbreviated

---

[17] On the "national" criminal justice of the City of Buenos Aires, a brief analysis is made in this regard, in a more general study, by Bergman et al. (2017, pp. 56, 63).
[18] Sabrina Rivas, Guillermina Barukel, Angelina Rabufetti, Yamila Toller, Juan Saba, Julieta Rodeles, Antonella Zambon, Federico Blanche, and Fabricio Mándola participated in the various stages of this fieldwork. All of them were part of the team of the Observatory on Criminal Justice Reform and the Crime and Society Program of the National University of Litoral.
[19] It is one of the five areas into which the provincial territory is divided, comprising 29% of its population and based in the city of Santa Fe.
[20] The actors who were not interviewed were those who directly refused or, without doing so, evaded this possibility in various ways for several months during which requests were made to them in different ways.

procedures, as well as to explore the interpretations they construct around this mechanism.[21]

From this empirical exploration, it is possible to affirm with certainty that "in fact" the abbreviated procedure is the dominant mode of conviction in the reformed criminal justice system in the Province of Santa Fe. The oral and public trial, with all its symbolic weight in relation to the ideals of "rights-based justice" and "democratic justice" in the rhetoric of reformers in this – as in other contexts (Langer & Sozzo, 2023b) – is an absolute rarity.

The analysis of convictions in the first Judicial District of the Province of Santa Fe over this 6-year period, between 2014[22] and 2019, allows us to reconstruct the percentage of people convicted by type of procedure, differentiating between abbreviated and oral and public trial. For the entire period, the percentage of those convicted without trial is overwhelming, 98%.

This enormous weight of those convicted without trial, when analyzing its annual evolution, seems to decrease slightly in the last two years of this period, but always on an extremely high platform (see Fig. 3.1). In the comparative research carried out by Langer (2021, p. 27), of 26 jurisdictions in different regions of the world – using various years of the 2010s – the 98% that is registered in 3 years of the Province of Santa Fe series – 2015, 2016, and 2017 – is the maximum existing and only occurs in two jurisdictions, the United States (2014) and New Zealand (2017/2018). On the other hand, the 93% that results the lowest in the Province of Santa Fe series, in 2019, would only be slightly

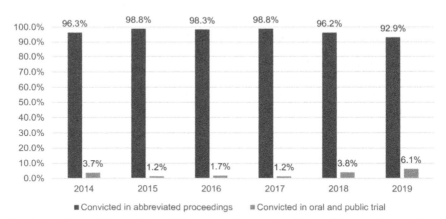

Fig. 3.1. Annual Evolution of Convicted Persons by Type of Proceeding – C1 PSF – 2014–2019. *Source*: Author's own empiric research.

---

[21] All the abbreviated procedure hearings that took place in the First Judicial District during 2018 were also observed and analyzed. These data are not used in this chapter but is the subject of other recently published (Sozzo, 2023) and future work.

[22] The criminal justice reform implementation process began on February 10, 2014.

lower than those two aforementioned cases, as well as Israel (2014: 95%) and Australia (2017/2018: 94%). The lower annual level would exceed that of all Latin American jurisdictions included in Langer's benchmarking exercise. In turn, it would be extraordinarily higher than the one reported in that study for the federal/national jurisdiction in Argentina for 2013: 65%.[23]

Reflecting this marked prevalence, in the interviews with criminal justice actors we recorded a strong consensus at the descriptive level, on the extraordinary diffusion of the abbreviated procedure in the new criminal justice, accounting for its "normalized" character (Ciocchini, 2018, p. 33). But there is also a strong coincidence – despite their different institutional belongings and procedural roles – in terms of legitimacy. The abbreviated procedure is not only recognized, in factual terms, as the dominant sentencing mechanism but is also justified as such in terms of what should be. All the interviewees affirm, in one way or another, that this mechanism is key for the new criminal justice system to function because it is impossible to resolve all cases through an oral and public trial. In general, a "pragmatic" legitimization predominates, which is frequently connected to the fact of the limitations of human and material resources. In some cases, the discourse of criminal justice actors acquires a certain "disenchanted" tone since they do not consider the abbreviated procedure as an "ideal" instrument, but only as a "possible" one. Among many statements in this direction, I can provide examples given by different types of actors:

> *PD (Public Defender) 1 (2018)*: A tool without which this system would not be possible ... otherwise it would collapse.
>
> *P (Prosecutor) 6 (2018)*: I think it is very important that this figure is in the code because it makes the possibility of the functioning and sustainability of the system, it is necessary as a tool, as a possibility for the solution of a case. ... It would be impossible to sustain the system as a whole, if the solution were only the oral trial, it would be impossible to be sustained. ... It is a tool that I think we all value and use, to the extent that it is possible, the procedure is abbreviated because it is a solution, as I said at the beginning, which is necessary and makes possible the vitality of the system. It is not possible to function, the system is not prepared to

---

[23]On the other hand, in the judicial department of Mar del Plata in the Province of Buenos Aires, Bessone, Bombini and Rajuan (2020) have shown both for 2001 and 2016 a percentage of convictions for this type of mechanism similar to that of the Province of Santa Fe case, but on a sample of cases by type of crime around simple thefts and robberies. Before them, Castorina (2014, 73), working on the same judicial department, but analyzing all types of cases from 2012, had presented a somewhat lower percentage of 82%. And Ciocchini (2013, 240), presented data regarding three judicial departments of that same jurisdiction referring to 2010, which revealed 72% of convictions without trial.

function without abbreviating cases, in a proper way, of course. It is what balances the system.

J (Judge) 2 (2018): It is rational and necessary that most of the issues are resolved by abbreviated procedure, it is impossible to substantiate all the cases that enter into the system by a trial, it is impossible without this alternative being available.

But also present in some criminal justice actors is a praise for the ability of this mechanism to "expedite" the resolution of cases. This is explicitly related to the search for effectiveness and efficiency as a crucial objective of criminal justice reform. It implies a more "enthusiastic" attitude toward the abbreviated procedure. This is especially visible – not surprisingly – in the voices of prosecutors. For example:

P3 (2018): I think it is an institute that is the one that best suits the adversarial system, although the oral and public trial is constitutionally established. But this is a way to solve the conflict faster … I think it has a positive impact … I think it is positive because it is more agile. It has streamlined the new criminal justice.

P11 (2018): It seems to me that it is a new opportunity, a new tool that is introduced from the reform that has to do with the new paradigm of the new system […]. It has to do with another way to carry out the criminal process, to streamline and make it more efficient, which is the new paradigm, I insist on the new system […]. The truth is that they have sold it badly, they speak badly of the abbreviated procedure, and for me, I say again what I said at the beginning, I reiterate and insist, it is a great tool that allows us to give more efficient and faster answers to criminal conflicts, to the victim and the accused, it avoids a waste of resources, of stress for the operators, witnesses, victims, everything. I think it has not been well clarified, it has not been well communicated to society, I think it has not been well publicized, it has not been well communicated what the abbreviated procedure implies and means, so when abbreviated procedures are agreed upon it is like a news … like people want blood, they want the circus, they want the coliseum, they want to see how they kill each other in a trial, and it seems to me that we have evolved as a society and we are not up to the circumstances, we do not end up understanding the tool we have created to respond to the conflict in a faster way.

P15 (2018): I think it allows to reach a higher level of efficiency. If it is, let's say, well used by the prosecution and the defense it allows a more efficient management of resources, allows to obtain convictions, decrease the impunity rate of certain crimes and is largely the only way out of many cases or criminal acts.[24]

Interestingly for our argument about Americanization, there appears spontaneously in the discourse of many criminal justice actors interviewed, an explicit reference to the case of the United States of America in the construction of the justification for the enormous prevalence of the abbreviated procedure in the Province of Santa Fe. In some interviewees, this occurs within the framework of the type of rhetoric of legitimization that I have identified as "senchanted." For example:

> *P17 (2018)*: To try to go to trial with everything is impossible, only 2% should go to trial. I always say, New York has so many prosecutors per district, they have everything and they can only go to trial in 2% of the cases. If they wanted to raise that level, let's say to 4% of the crimes that are committed, they would have to double the whole structure they have, in other words it should be huge, because it is already huge, if they wanted to reach a level of double the number of trials, imagine ... only 2% can go to trial.

> *PD 4 (2018)*: By abbreviated, maybe 80% of the cases are resolved, minimum. Which I understand is not a statistic that is very different from what the United States of America has. With all the human and material resources they have, they also do not take all the cases to trial .... But I repeat, it is impossible for all the cases to go to oral and public trial. This does not happen even in the most developed countries in the world. The United States of America has much more human and material resources than we do, and it abbreviates more than 90% of the cases. We are not going to pretend, with what we have, that there will be more trials here.[25]

---

[24]This attitude is also present, although almost always in a more circumspect manner, in the voices of some criminal judges. For example: "The advantage is speed, more time is gained and the system is decongested without the deployment of human resources that the oral and public trial takes" (J2, 2018).

[25]Other public defenders interviewed evoked negatively the USA model, differentiating the Province of Santa Fe experience of the abbreviated procedure from that of plea bargaining. For example, one public defender pointed out that this mechanism only exceptionally could acquire an "extortive" character "[...]but even in those cases, I guess, it is not as extortive as in the USA plea bargaining, I guess it is not like that" (DP1, 2018). Another public defender explicitly referred to the importation of this legal institution from the USA scenario with a critical tone: "It is an importation of a procedure that has its development in the United States of America and here it was brought and we still do not know very well how to use it or how to make it work" (DP13, 2019).

But in other cases, this happens within the framework of the type of rhetoric I identify as "enthusiastic." For example:

> *P1 (2018)*: I believe that prosecutors should be given more capacity and powers. More American style, a broader abbreviated, not so limited and with high requirements, because otherwise the system does not work. That is to say, an agile abbreviated procedure within the legal parameters, within the legal minimums and maximums of course, but with fewer provisions that, in my opinion, tend to cover the legislator but do not benefit the system.

> *J3 (2018)*: There is a prejudice with respect to this that has to do with educating the society about what an abbreviated procedure means. It is a success all over the world, most of the countries have it, those that have an accusatory system, it is the natural instrument to solve criminal conflicts. In fact, in the United States 2% of the cases go to public trial, most of them are resolved much earlier, with much more extensive negotiations than ours.

In response to a specific closed question on whether the extent to which the abbreviated procedure is used in the current criminal justice system in the Province of Santa Fe is adequate or not, more than half of the criminal justice actors interviewed agree that it is used to an adequate extent (64%). However, 16% (composed of prosecutors and judges) argued that it should be used to an even greater extent than it is currently used. Only 20% of them, consider more critically its use to be "excessive." This percentage is much higher among public defenders (40%). Only two prosecutors and one judge opted for this response. In other words, one out of every five criminal justice actors are concerned about the degree of diffusion of this mechanism of conviction without trial in the reformed criminal justice. However, when answering the open question as to why this is so, few interviewees elaborate on the matter and even in these cases the legitimacy of this legal institution is not explicitly questioned.[26] A few examples in this regard:

> *PD13 (2018)*: As it is the most important way out, as we said at the beginning, as it can no longer be denied, it practically denatures the expectations, or the promises of the criminal process .... If the process ends in an abbreviated trial, orality is only symbolic. Unless the prosecutor gives an account of the evidence, it is not related to the values that were postulated when the system began to be implemented: "an oral, public system." Nobody goes to the abbreviated procedure hearings. What is discussed in them does not compare with what is going on in a trial, where there are other

---

[26]Ciocchini (2018, p. 34) in his fieldwork in the Province of Buenos Aires found that for the most part his interviewees argued in favor of the "abbreviated trial," although in some cases they objected to some aspect of it -perhaps approaching the "disenchanted" version I identify here. Only 3 of the 39 interviewees in his study, all of them defense attorneys, were completely opposed to this type of mechanism.

priorities and complexities. Some ideals were lost. That pattern … the logic of the abbreviated procedure is not very much in line with the postulates of the new system.

PD 2 (2018): It is regulated as an exceptional way. One would have to, as an ordinary way, resolve the conflict through the oral trial and only resort to the abbreviated procedure exceptionally. Today it works as the rule and exceptionally we go to oral trial, so I think it works more than it should … the exception became the rule, and the rule became the exception. In other words, oral trials are the exception even though they shouldn't be.[27]

The reformed criminal justice in the Province of Santa Fe, as far as sentencing is concerned, is an "abbreviated justice."[28] On this point, the similarity in practices with the American context and tradition, at least in relation to what I would call the dimension of "penal outcomes" – the proportion of convictions without oral and public trial – is very marked and allows us to argue that in this sense there has been a process of "Americanization" in a "strong" sense. This "strong Americanization" in the "law in action" in terms of "penal outcomes" may, however, hide significant differences in the dynamics that generate them, in terms of the way in which this enormous proportion of convictions without trial is achieved. There is a whole series of issues here to explore in detail. Just thinking about the differences in the "law in the books" pointed out in Section 3: (Translation and "Weak" Americanization in "Law on the Books") do the negotiations between prosecutors and defenders/defendants only effectively revolve around the sentence or do they also reach the charges and the legal qualification of the act? Do public and private defense attorneys have unrestricted access to the evidence collected by the police and the prosecution in the first steps of the criminal process and does this allow them to plan and execute a strategy for negotiating an abbreviated procedure to close the case? Do criminal judges actually carry out an active, interventionist practice on the agreements of the parties in the framework of abbreviated procedures? I have explored some of these questions in other recent works, as they have also been the target of our empirical exploration (Langer & Sozzo, 2023b; Sozzo, 2023). But in any case, on the basis of what I have analyzed here, it is possible to affirm that the weak degree of "Americanization" in "law in the books" can be perfectly combined with this strong degree in "law in action" in the dimension of "penal outcomes."

---

[27] Another public defender, who did not consider in the closed question that the abbreviated procedure was overused, however, in another moment of the interview about the impact of this mechanism, said: "[…] the new criminal justice is not prepared for the public trial, it is prepared for the abbreviated one […] I believe that everything is solved through the abbreviated procedure, the impact has been atrocious" (DP10, 2019).
[28] One prosecutor pointed out categorically: "the new system is abbreviated" (F3 2018). And another said, with laughter, with respect to his own institution, "the 'public ministry of the abbreviated" and then pointed out: "I do not know if in comparison with other provinces there is a disproportionate use of the abbreviated system. If I think there is no trial" (F10 2018).

Toward an Explanation

A crucial question is why there is this absolute predominance of this mechanism of conviction without trial in the reformed criminal justice in the Province of Santa Fe, similar to what happens in the USA tradition and context. That is, what are the conditions that generate this "strong Americanization" in "law in action" with respect to this dimension of "penal outcomes."

Returning to the analysis of the "law in the books" it could be pointed out that some of the similarities in the Province of Santa Fe legal regulation with this type of legal institution in that context of origin are stronger than those that have been present in other scenarios of the European and Latin American traditions analyzed previously by Langer (2018a, pp. 82–116). Especially the first similarity pointed out in Section 3, the extremely broad possibility of using this mechanism to convict citizens for any type of crime, would seem to open the way to a substantive impact on the actual functioning of reformed criminal justice (Hodgson, 2015, p. 227). However, Langer has recently shown empirically, by comparing numerous contexts globally, that the fact that this type of sentencing mechanism – with its wide level of variation in terms of its particular embodiments in the various settings – is available in legal texts for all criminal cases, does not necessarily translate into a very high proportion of convictions actually imposed in this way, relative to the volume of convictions imposed in a public trial – what he defined as the "rate of administratization of convictions" – pointing to various examples in this regard, including some Latin American cases such as Panama (21% in 2017) and Peru (22% in 2014). On the contrary, countries that have high rates of administratization of convictions, however, in their legal texts exclude certain cases from the possibility of using these sentencing mechanisms – such as, in our region, Chile (91% in 2018) (Langer, 2021, pp. 28–29). These observations seem to preclude drawing an automatic connection between these elements that would explain this penal outcome in the Province of Santa Fe context.

From my perspective, a key factor in explaining this absolute predominance of convictions without trial is the fact that the reform of the criminal justice in the Province of Santa Fe, although late, sought to radically embody a "pure" accusatory/adversarial model. This is strongly reflected in the legal texts with their structuring of actors and distribution of competences and powers.[29] In his recent study on the use of mechanisms of conviction without trial globally, Langer (2021, pp. 32–35) also analyzes whether the rate of sentence administratization varies according to the existence or not, in different national contexts, of an adversarial model that adopts a dispute logic, on the assumption that where this is the case,

---

[29]This is certainly a difference with respect to some of the cases Langer analyzes, such as Germany and France, although it has certain similarities with the Italian case, where he nevertheless notes that "many legal actors continue to act according to a predominantly inquisitorial set of domestic provisions" and "structures of interpretation and meaning and inquisitorial procedural powers are still present" (Langer, 2018a, p. 94). It is also in stark contrast to the Argentine federal jurisdiction (Langer, 2018a, pp. 109–110).

the levels of such a rate should be higher. It shows that this is indeed the case in those settings that have long had such a criminal justice model in the common law tradition – such as, in addition to the United States of America, New Zealand, Israel, Australia, Scotland, and England and Wales. But in countries that have more recently adopted procedural legislation in line with the accusatorial/adversarial model, he finds a wide variety of levels of use of this type of mechanism. He points out as elements to consider in order to understand this diversity the degree of depth of the legal and organizational adoption of an accusatorial/adversarial model as well as the degrees or material and human resources available and of progress in the process of implementing the change. In both registers, the case of Santa Fe seems to be located at extreme levels, which could help to understand the level of use of this mechanism of conviction without trial.

This "purity" or "radicality" is also visible in the patterns of meaning and interpretation of the criminal justice actors, despite the fact that a significant part of them come, as I pointed out, from the old criminal justice.[30] This is clearly revealed, as I highlighted, in the interviews with them where there is a strong consensus – regardless of institutional affiliations and procedural roles – around the legitimacy of the abbreviated procedure and its strong affinity with the new criminal justice model. They all recognize its overwhelming practical use as a sentencing method, despite the fact that one in five judicial operators consider this level "excessive." In the justification of this mechanism, "pragmatic" arguments prevail, related to what is "possible" given the human and material resources available, but there are also more enthusiastic ones, referring to "agility" and the promise of

---

[30] A relevant role may have been played in this regard by the various training instances through which the actors of the new criminal justice in the Province of Santa Fe have passed. In a previous study based on interviews with criminal justice actors in the center and north of the province at the beginning of the implementation of the reform, we recorded the existence of training processes carried out by criminal justice institutions – but also by other instances to which the actors had access on their own – both before and once the new criminal process had begun to operate. It was noted that this presence was greater among judges and prosecutors than among public defenders, given the lack at that moment of a specific training center in the Public Defense Service like those existing in the Judiciary and the Public Ministry for the Prosecutor (for example, DP2 2015 and DP13 2015). Among judges and prosecutors, the experiences of meetings of 'colleagues' as spaces for debate and agreement on crucial elements of the practices of the new criminal justice were also especially valued. In general, a positive evaluation of the training processes carried out predominated, as well as of their results in terms of the acquisition of skills and competencies for the performance of one's own function in the new criminal justice (Sozzo et al., 2015a, pp. 14–16, 2015b, pp. 17–18, 2016, pp. 11–14). A specific inquiry into these training processes, their contents and agents may be important in order to understand more fully their role in the construction of schemes of interpretation and meaning among criminal justice actors, not only at the birth of the implementation but over time – and in terms of the constant incorporation of new prosecutors, public defenders, and criminal judges.

"efficiency and efficacy."[31] The latter in turn is connected precisely to the strong weight that the "managerial justice" program has had – as I have pointed out – in this late criminal justice reform process, both in the discourse of the reformers and in the design of their initiatives for legal and organizational change, which has also spilled over into the patterns of interpretation and meaning of judicial operators.

However, also playing a crucial role in this direction is the broader political and cultural climate on the criminal question in which the criminal justice reform process in this jurisdiction is inscribed, marked since the mid-1990s by the social and political construction of "insecurity"' as a fundamental problem of the public debate (Sozzo et al., 2020, pp. 3–8; see also Sozzo, 2005, 2007, 2016, 2020b; Sozzo & Montero, 2010). This has greatly intensified during the 2010s in the context of a strong growth of certain forms of violent crime. The province of Santa Fe has had throughout the last decade very high intentional homicide rates compared to the average for the country. It went from 8.3 per 100,000 inhabitants in 2010 to 9.6 per 100,000 inhabitants in 2019, with a peak of 14/100,000 in 2014.[32] But these levels are extraordinarily higher in the departments of its two main cities. In the Department of Rosario, it went from 9.8 intentional homicides per 100,000 inhabitants in 2010 to 13/100,000 in 2019, with a peak of 20.3/100,000 in 2014. In the Department La Capital it went from 16.4 homicides per 100,000 inhabitants in 2010 to 17.6/100,000 in 2019, with a peak of 27.9/100,000 in 2014. In relation to this high level of violent crime – and despite the relative stability of other forms of victimization (Sozzo et al., 2020, p. 3) – the public and political problematization of "insecurity" has been innovated during these past years. This innovation is mostly an alleged boom in "drug trafficking," which has in turn been linked to a series of public scandals. The most notable examples are the resignation and arrest of the provincial police chief for links to drug trafficking in 2012 and the gunfire attack on the Governor's house as an alleged retaliation for the criminal prosecution of some gangs linked to drug trafficking in 2013 (Gañan, 2019; González, 2019, pp. 349–361, 425–455; Sozzo et al., 2020, p. 7). Note that 2014, the year in which the implementation of the reformed criminal justice system began, was when the intentional homicide rate reached its highest level in this decade and, at the same time, a moment close to the public scandals of greatest impact recorded in the provincial context.

In this broader political and cultural climate, criminal justice actors perceive the existence of pressures, both "external" (whose sources they locate in the media and certain sectors of the public and politics) and "internal" (especially

---

[31] Interestingly, already with respect to the adoption of the "abbreviated trial" in the Argentine federal jurisdiction in 1997, the strong degree of acceptance of that legal institution among judicial operators was noted – despite the non-existence of empirical studies on the matter (Anitua, 2001, pp. 142–143, 2017, p. 168; Langer, 2001, p. 127, 2018a, 107–108).

[32] The national intentional homicide rate in 2010 was 5.8/100,000, and in 2019, it was 5.5/100,000. Not only are these rates much lower than those recorded in this province, but they show some stability between the beginning and the end of this decade.

related to the authorities of the respective organizations, in the case of prosecutors and public defenders) to demonstrate high levels of "effectiveness" and "efficiency," clearly associating the construction of this new form of criminal justice to the "fight against insecurity."[33] Within this framework, the volume of cases initiated by the new criminal justice system has been growing significantly. In the First Judicial District, according to official data from the Public Ministry for the Prosecution, in 2014, 26,014 prosecutorial files were initiated, while in 2019, 66,369 were initiated, an increase of 155%.[34] In this scenario, the abbreviated procedure appears for many criminal justice actors as a crucial instrument to demonstrate "effectiveness" and "efficiency" and ratify the relationship of the reformed criminal justice with the "fight against insecurity," due to its property of quickly producing convictions – in addition to, obviously, substantially reducing its workload compared to the oral and public trial (Anitua, 2017, pp. 159, 165; Langer, 2001, p. 127, 2018a, p. 107).

Therefore, this "strong" Americanization in "law in action," in the dimension of the "penal outcomes" of the new criminal justice in the Province of Santa Fe, can be read as less linked to the specific similarities in the legal regulation of the abbreviated procedure with the USA tradition, than to the more general type of change. This late reform has produced and is producing a pure version of an accusatorial/adversarial model and a strong presence of the "managerial justice" program, not only in the legal texts but also in the schemes of interpretation and meaning of criminal justice actors. This radical transformation is intertwined with a broader political and cultural climate on the criminal question, which places the problem of "insecurity" and its alleged connection with "drug trafficking" as a strong axis of public and political debate in a sustained manner over time and generates – at least in the perceptions of criminal justice actors – pressures towards decisions and actions that imply a swift and decisive use of the power to punish.

---

[33] In a previous inquiry based on interviews with criminal judges at the beginning of the implementation of the reform in this context, we explicitly addressed the existence of these "external" pressures. Interestingly, the actors interviewed acknowledged their existence, in general terms, but at the same time claimed that their decisions and actions were not shaped by them (Sozzo et al., 2016, pp. 65–68). On the relationship with the media and politics and perceptions about the existence of pressures by criminal justice actors, see Kostenwein (2015, 2016, 2019). In any case, this very relevant topic poses us a dilemma about its empirical exploration, since the interview with criminal justice actors may have limitations as a tool (Sozzo, 2020a, 2022), as many of the interviewees assume that it would be improper to acknowledge to an outsider, the interviewer, that they make decisions and perform actions based on these "external" and "internal" pressures, hence they frequently admit their existence on a general level but, at the same time, claim that it does not affect their own practice.

[34] Although it is necessary to consider that in this First Judicial District it went from 15 prosecutors in 2014 to 38 prosecutors by the end of 2019, an equivalent increase of 153%. In turn, the staff of the Public Ministry for the Prosecution – beyond prosecutors – increased in this jurisdiction from 55 employees in 2014 to 139 employees in 2019, an equivalent increase of 153%.

References

Anitua, G. I. (2001). El juicio penal abreviado como una de las reformas penales de inspiración estadounidense que posibilitan la expansión punitiva. In J. Maier & A. Bovino (Eds.), *El procedimiento abreviado* (pp. 137–160). Editores del Puerto.

Anitua, G. I. (2017). *La justicia penal en cuestión*. IUSTEL.

Baclini, J., & Schiapa Pietra, L. (2017). *Código Procesal Penal de Santa Fe Anotado, Comentado y Concordado*. Iuris.

Bergman, M., Langer, M., & Fondevilla, J. (2017). *¿A quien y como se juzga en la ciudad de Buenos Aires? Una radiografia de la Justicia Nacional en los Criminal y Correccional*. UNTREF, CELIV.

Bess one, N., Bambini, G., & Rajuan, C. (2020). El procedimiento de flagrancia, promesas reformistas y efectos reales: celeridad o severidad judicial. In M. Sozzo (Ed.), *Reforma de la justicia penal en América Latina: promesas, prácticas y efectos* (pp. 175–204). Didot.

Binder, A. (2016). La reforma de la justicia penal en América Latina como política de largo plazo. In C. Niño Guarnizo (Ed.), *La reforma a la justicia en América Latina: las lecciones aprendidas* (pp. 54–103). Friedrich-Ebert-Stiftung.

Castorina, A. (2014). *El juicio abreviado. Un análisis socio jurídico de su utilización en el Departamento Judicial Mar del Plata durante el año 2012* [Master's thesis, Facultad de Derecho, Universidad de Barcelona].

Ciocchini, P. (2012). Domando a la bestia. Las reformas en la justicia penal bonaerense para eliminar la demora judicial. *Revista de Derecho y Ciencias Sociales, 7*, 202–223.

Ciocchini, P. (2013). *Tiempo de Justicia. Un análisis de los cambios ocurridos en pos de erradicar la demora judicial en la Provincia de Buenos Aires* [Doctoral thesis, Universidad del Pais Vasco, Oñati].

Ciocchini, P. (2017). Cambiando todo para no cambiar nada. Las reformas al proceso penal bonaerense. In E. Kostenwein (Ed.), *Sociología de la Justicia Penal. Interrogantes actuales sobe la administación del castigo* (pp. 307–366). Ediar.

Ciocchini, P. (2018). Reformers' unfulfilled promises: Accountability deficits in Argentinean criminal courts. *International Journal of Law in Context, 14*(1), 22–42.

Cooper, J. M. (2008) Competing legal cultures and legal reform: The battle of Chile. *Michigan Journal of International Law, 29*(3), 501–562.

Fuchs, M. C., Fandiño, M., & Gonzalez, L. (Eds.). (2018). *La justicia penal adversarial en América Latina. Hacia la gestión del conflicto y la fortaleza de la ley*. CEJA y Konrad Adenauer.

Gañan, J. (2019). Entre la negación histérica y la adaptación. La política pública del Ministerio de Sgeuridad de la Provincia de Santa Fe en relación al narcomenudeo a partir del caso Los Monos. Rosario, 2012–2015. *Perspectivas. Revista de Ciencias Sociales, 4*(8), 267–286.

Ganón, G. (2007). La Macdonaldización del Sistema de Justicia? Nuevo Orden o Nuevo Derecho en la globalidad de la sociedad excluyente. In I. Rivera, H. C. Silveira, E. Bodelón, & A. Recasens (Eds.), *Contornos y Pliegues del Derecho. Homenaje al Profesor Roberto Bergalli* (pp. 439–457). Antrophos.

Garland, D. (2018). *Castigar y Asistir. Una historia de las estrategias penales y sociales del siglo XX*. Siglo XXI Editores.

González Guarda, C. (2015). El New Public Management en las reformas del sistema de justicia criminal en Latinomérica. El caso de Chile. *Actas Coloquios Ech Francia, 79*.

González Guarda, C. (2016). Hacia un modelo organizacional del sistema de justicia penal en Latinoamérica. La influencia del management y del gerencialismo en esta configuración. *Nova Criminis, 7*, 135–170.

González Guarda, C. (2018). *Gestión, gerencialismo y justicia penal*. BDF.

González, G. (2019). *La trama vincular político-policial: una exploración de las relaciones de interdependencia entre política y policía en la Provincia de Santa Fe 1995–2015* [Doctoral Thesis, Universidad Nacional de Rosario].

Gutiérrez, M. (2014a). Acusatorio y Punitivismo: la triste historia de nuestras victorias garantistas (parte 1). *Revista de Derecho Penal y Criminología, IV*(8), 70–84.

Gutiérrez, M. (2014b). Acusatorio y Punitivismo: la triste historia de nuestras victorias garantistas (parte 2). *Revista de Derecho Penal y Criminología, IV*(9), 75–99.

Gutiérrez, M. (2016). Sobre las ideologías actuales en las reformas penales. *Revista de Derecho Penal y Criminología, VI*(5), 154–168.

Gutiérrez, M. (2017). Coyuntura y frentes de tormenta. La política criminal de la Provincia de Buenos Aires 1996–2014. In E. Kostenwein (Ed.), *Sociología de la Justicia Penal. Interrogantes actuales sobe la administración del castigo* (pp. 261–303). Ediar.

Hathazy, P. (2020). Revoluciones en los campos de la justicia penal: estrategias internacionales de reformadores y cambios en la justicia penal en Argentina, Chile y más allá. In M. Sozzo (Ed.), *Reforma de la justicia penal en América Latina: promesas, prácticas y efectos* (pp. 21–40). Didot.

Hodgson, J. (2015). Plea bargaining. A comparative analysis. In J. Wright (Ed.), *International encyclopedia of the social & behavioural sciences* (2nd ed., Vol. 18, pp. 226–231). Elsevier.

Iturralde, M. (2010). Democracies without citizenships: Crime and punishment in Latin America. *New Criminal Law Review, 13*(2), 309–322.

Iturralde, M. (2019). Neoliberalism and its impact in crime control fields in Latin America. *Theoretical Criminology, 23*(4), 471–490.

Kostenwein, E. (2012). La velocidad y las formas jurídicas: prisión preventiva en tiempos de flagrancia. *Revista Pensamiento Penal*, 1–48.

Kostenwein, E. (2015). Prisión preventiva: Entre los medios de comunicación y las autoridades políticas. *Revista Direito e Práxis, 6*, 54–79.

Kostenwein, E. (2016). *La cuestion cautelar*. Ediar.

Kostenwein, E. (2017). Apresurando decisiones. La justicia penal ante las exigencias de celeridad. In E. Kostenwein (Ed.), *Sociología de la Justicia Penal. Interrogantes actuales sobe la administación del castigo* (pp. 367–412). Ediar.

Kostenwein, E. (2019). Pánicos morales y demonios judiciales. Prensa, opinión pública y justicia penal. *Estudios Socio-Jurídicos, 21*, 15–49.

Kostenwein, E. (2020a). Respuesta judicial a la demanda de celeridad: la flagrancia en la Provincia de Buenos Aires. *Temas Sociológicos, 26*, 163–195.

Kostenwein, E. (2020b). El imperativo de la celeridad para la justicia penal. In E. Kostenwein (Ed.), *El imperio de castigar. Contribuciones desde la sociología de la justicia penal* (pp. 359–389). Editores del Sur.

Langer, M. (2001). La dicotomía inquisitivo-acusatorio y la importación de mecanismos procesales de la tradición jurídica anglosajona. Algunas reflexiones a partir del procedimiento abreviado. In J. B. J. Maier & A. Bovino (Eds.), *El procedimiento abreviado* (pp. 97–133). Editores del Puerto.

Langer, M. (2007). Revolution in Latin American criminal procedure: Diffusion of legal ideas from the periphery. *The American Journal of Comparative Law, 55*, 617–676.

Langer, M. (2014). La larga sombra de las categorías acusatorio-inquisitorio. *Revista de Derecho Público, 32*, 1–34.

Langer, M. (2018a). De los transplantes legales a las traducciones legales: la globalización del 'plea bargaining' y la tesis de la americanización del proceso penal. *Discusiones, 1*, 25–134.

Langer, M. (2018b). Quince años después: traducciones legales, globalización del 'plea bargaining' y americanización del proceso penal. *Discusiones, 1*, 213–232.

Langer, M. (2021). Plea bargaining, trial-avoiding conviction mechanisms, and the global administratization of criminal convictions. *Annual Review of Criminology 4*, 377–411.

Langer, M., & Sozzo, M. (2023a). Introducción. Reforma de la justicia penal y mecanismos de imposición de condenas sin juicio en América Latina. In M. Langer & M. Sozzo (Eds.), *Justicia penal y mecanismos de condena sin juicio. Estudios sobre América Latina* (pp. 15–71). Marcial Pons.

Langer, M., & Sozzo, M. (2023b). Conclusión: Mecanismos de imposición de condena sin Juicio y sistemas acusatorios en América Latina. Balance y perspectivas. In M. Langer & M. Sozzo (Eds.), *Justicia penal y mecanismos de condena sin juicio. Estudios sobre América Latina* (pp. 383–415). Marcial Pons.

McLeod, A. (2010). Exporting US criminal justice. *Yale Law & Policy Review, 29*(1), 83–164.

Mira, J. (2020a). Humanizar la justicia penal. Cosmologías por la reforma procesal penal en la Argentina (1986–2010). In M. Sozzo (Ed.), *Reforma de la justicia penal en América Latina: promesas, prácticas y efectos* (pp. 41–56). Didot.

Mira, J. (2020b). Juristas que dicen el derecho. Levene y Maier reformadores de la justicia penal Argentina. *Temas sociológicos 26*, 121–162.

Museri, A. (2019). *El impacto del sistema de flagrancia en las prácticas judiciales sobre el uso de la prisión preventiva en la provincia de Buenos Aires* [Master's thesis, Universidad Nacional del Litoral].

Palacios, M. D. (2011). La reforma procesal en Chile: Nuevos agentes, sus trayectorias y la reestructuración de un campo. *Revista Política, 49*(1), 43–70.

Sicardi, M. (2019). *El juicio abreviado como mecanismo de gestión de casos. Una mirada a partir de las prácticas del Ministerio Público Fiscal porteño* [Master's thesis, Universidad Nacional del Litoral].

Sicardi, M. (2020). Reformas del proceso penal en Latinoamerica, gerencialismo y juicio abreviado. Aproximaciones desde la ciudad de Buenos Aires. In E. Kostenwein (Ed.), *El imperio de castigar. Contribuciones desde la sociología de la justicia penal* (pp. 303–321). Editores del Sur.

Sozzo, M. (Ed.). (2005). *Policía, violencia y democracia*. UNL Ediciones.

Sozzo, M. (2006). "Traduttore Traditore." Traducción, importación cultural e historia del presente de la criminología en América Latina. In M. Sozzo (Ed.), *Reconstruyendo las criminologías críticas* (pp. 353–431). Ad-Hoc.

Sozzo, M. (2007). ¿Metamorfosis de la prisión? Proyecto normalizador, populismo punitivo y "prisión-depósito" en Argentina. *URVIO Revista Latinoamericana de seguridad ciudadana, 1*, 88–116.

Sozzo, M. (2011a). *Transition to democracy and penal policy. The case of Argentina* [Paper Series 03/11, Straus Institute Working].

Sozzo, M. (2011b). Cultural travels and crime prevention in Argentina. In R. Sparks, D. Melossi, & M. Sozzo (Eds.), *The travels of the criminal question* (pp. 185–215). Oxford.

Sozzo, M. (2013). Transición a la democracia, política y castigo legal en Argentina. In B. Amaral Machado (Coord.), *Justicia criminal y Democracia* (pp. 195–238). Marcial Pons.

Sozzo, M. (2015a). *La reformat de la justicia penal. Las voces de los defensores públicos. Primer Informe*. Observatorio sobre la Reforma de la Justicia Penal, Facultad de Ciencias Jurídicas y Sociales, Universidad Nacional del Litoral.

Sozzo, M. (2015b). *La reforma de la justicia penal. Las voces de los fiscales. Segundo Informe* Observatorio sobre la Reforma de la Justicia Penal, Facultad de Ciencias Jurídicas y Sociales, Universidad Nacional del Litoral.

Sozzo, M. (2016). *La reforma de la justicia penal. Las voces de los jueces penales. Tercer Informe*. Observatorio sobre la Reforma de la Justicia Penal, Facultad de Ciencias Jurídicas y Sociales, Universidad Nacional del Litoral.

Sozzo, M. (2016). Democratization, politics and punishment in Argentina. *Punishment and Society, 18*(3), 301–324.

Sozzo, M. (2017). *La inflación punitiva. Un análisis comparativo de las mutaciones del derecho penal en América Latina (1990/2015)*. FLACSO-IDRC/CRDI.

Sozzo, M. (2018). Beyond the neoliberal penality thesis? Punitive turn and political change in South America. In K. Carrington, R. Hogg, J. Scott, & M. Sozzo (Eds.), *The Palgrave handbook of criminology and the global south* (pp. 659–686) Palgrave.

Sozzo, M. (2020a). Reforma de la justicia penal en América Latina: promesas, prácticas y efectos. A modo de introducción. In M. Sozzo (Ed.), *Reforma de la justicia penal en América Latina: promesas, prácticas y efectos* (pp. 9–20). Didot.

Sozzo, M. (2020b). Reforma de la justicia penal e imagen y confianza pública. In E. Kostenwein (Ed.), *El imperio de castigar. Contribuciones desde la sociología de la justicia penal* (pp. 323–358). Editores del Sur.

Sozzo, M. (2022). Reforma de la justicia penal e investigación social en América latina. Problemas y desafíos. *Revista Jurídica de la Universidad de Palomo, 2*, 217–238.

Sozzo, M. (2023) ¿Más allá de la 'angustia de juzgar'? Reforma de la justicia penal, condena sin juicio y mutaciones del rol del juez penal." In E. Kostenwein (Ed.), *Mundo judiciales y dinamicas sociales . Aproximaciones al funcionamiento de la justicia penal* (pp. 149–183). Di Placido.

Sozzo, M., & Montero, A. (2010). *Delito, sensación de inseguridad y sistema penal*. UNL Ediciones.

Sozzo, M., Montero, A, Puyol, M. V., & Bulgarella, E. (2020). Contactos entre policía y ciudadanía. Tipos, distribución social y valoraciones específicas y generales. *Delito y Sociedad, 29*(50), 87–149.

Sozzo, M., Somaglia, M., & Truchet, R. (2019). Cautela negociada. Acuerdos entre fiscales y defensores en torno a las medidas cuatelares en la justicia penal reformada. *Revista de Derecho Penal y Criminología, IX*(3), 63–81.

Taboga, J. (2021). *Rediseñando el campo de la justicia penal. Una exploración sobre las transformaciones del proceso penal en la provincia de Santa Fe* [Master thesis, Universidad Nacional del Litoral].

Taddeo, N. (2019) Justicia penal juvenil: justicia negociada vs justicia restaurativa. *Revista de Derecho Penal y Criminología, IX*(3), 173–193.

Section 2

Prison Order and Prison Life

Chapter 4

Contemporary Prison Management in Chile: Disputes About Order

Olga Espinoza M.

University of Chile, Chile

Abstract

Prison constitutes one of the main forms of managing punishment in penal systems (Dammert & Zúñiga, 2008; Garland, 2001; Sozzo, 2016). However, the study of prisons presents different emphases and scenarios depending on the context of observation. In this chapter, we analyse one of the most solid and structured prison systems in Latin America, the Chilean system, which aims to regulate all aspects of prison life, from those related to basic needs to those related to social reintegration. However, its intention of control clashes with the actual functioning of the prisons, producing tensions that are addressed by the staff under different strategies: some with a more punitive profile and others under more consensual margins. In order to explore this scenario, a documentary review of institutional reports on the Chilean prison system is carried out, which is combined with a descriptive qualitative study that, through in-depth and semi-structured interviews. The work carried out allows us to conclude that although order can be achieved through control and surveillance, that is, by imposing rules vertically, without listening to the people involved, demanding only the fulfilment of tasks, isolating and neutralising inmates in the event of any misconduct, this position creates a perception of injustice, which cumulatively can lead to violence (Byrne & Hummer, 2008). However, it is also possible to achieve order through legitimacy, that is, through relational mechanisms through which the problems of the people affected are identified and small agreements are reached, making them participants in the search for solutions.

Keywords: Violence; prison management; order; control; prison policy; qualitative methods

Prison is one of the main instruments for meting out punishment in criminal justice systems (Dammert & Zúñiga, 2008; Garland, 2001; Sozzo, 2016). The study of prisons, however, presents different emphases and scenarios, which significantly depend on their own local context. In the present work, we analyse the Chilean prison system, one of the most solid and structured prison systems in Latin America aimed at regulating all aspects of prison life, from basic needs to social reintegration. Those who manage prisons have to deal with how they actually function,[1] resulting in tensions that staff addresses with different strategies that range from the punitive to the more consensual. To explore this scenario, a documentary analysis of institutional reports about the Chilean penitentiary system was conducted, combined with a descriptive qualitative study that engages more deeply with the complexities of this research object.

The first sociological studies on incarceration (Clemmer, 1940; Sykes, 1958/2017) sought to identify what aspects prisons had in common and how their work and routines were organised, without considering management as a specific variable (Crewe et al., 2014; Drake et al., 2015). Clemmer (1940), one of the first to analyse this topic in the 1930s, proposed the existence of a prison social order, a prison subculture that gives rise to a peculiar order in which inmates become 'prisoned,' that is, they assimilate the customs, usages, and general culture of the penitentiary world. Years later, Sykes (1958/2017) analysed the role of each of the actors in the prison context and the relationships they build. He argued that prison dynamics reflect a functionally integrated social system, consisting of parts with interrelated functions that serve the system as a whole. The system, then, is composed of two large groups, inmates and prison officers; the first group, the inmates, must deal with the pains of imprisonment, the lack of dignity and deprivation, the coexistence with people of whom they are afraid; the second group, the officers, are in charge of keeping control over a conflictive population far exceeding them in number, often by the use of force. According to Sykes (1958/2017), this special social system emerges as a form of adaptation to the particular problems that accompany imprisonment: the suffering of the imprisoned and the need to maintain control with insufficient means and power. In this context, leaders emerge from both groups who are adapted and functional to the system itself (Sozzo, 2022).

---

[1] Various reports and studies have revealed the challenges faced by the Chilean prison system: serious problems of violence, deficient infrastructure and other defects that threaten the integrity and life of inmates (INDH, 2021; Sanhueza et al., 2020).

While maintaining the emphasis on structural elements,[2] other studies gave greater prominence to a more institutionally envisaged concept of management[3] (DiIulio, 1987), highlighting the key role of formal actors in determining order inside prisons. What kind of prison management maximises order and efficient organisation? According to DiIulio (1987), a management model based on control and a paramilitary bureaucracy aimed primarily at guaranteeing security are more effective in establishing order and making prison a calm and productive space (Crewe et al., 2014). However, this position is contested in other works that point out that, although the manner in which prisons are administered and power is exercised generate changes that affect the security of people deprived of liberty and the structure of social relations inside prisons, it cannot be confirmed that rigid and strict application of the rules, the impersonal implementation of procedures, are the only alternatives to avoid chaos inside prisons (Jacobs, 1977; Sparks et al., 1996).

The aim of this work is to analyse how management is understood and configured in the Chilean prison system, with special emphasis on the formal and institutional aspects adopted by the Chilean prison service (*Gendarmería de Chile*), which is responsible for the execution of sentences as well as implementation of these regulations in the daily life of prison. To this effect, the regulations governing penitentiary institutions are analysed and the experience and opinions sought of actors in charge of their application, as well as of their users or recipients. From the results, we are able to identify different ways of establishing a prison order, some with a more punitive emphasis and others with more permissive or reward-based dynamics. Next, the concept of prison order in criminological literature is reviewed, providing a theoretical focus for an analysis of the Chilean case and how prison is managed in order to comply with the institutional penitentiary mandate.

The Management of Order

The management of order within prison contexts is one of the main tasks of any prison system (Sparks et al., 1996), and it can be said that the preservation of order is the main aspiration, explicit or implicit, of prison administration.

---

[2]Apart from structural factors, some studies have highlighted the social role of inmates before their incarceration and how this role influences the prison culture, which is neither uniform nor permanent, as it adjusts to contingent social trends (Drake et al., 2015; Irwin & Cressey, 1962).

[3]Prison management will be understood as the different ways in which prisons are organised and administered to serve their primary purposes: to guarantee compliance with criminal sanctions, facilitate security and respect for the integrity of inmates, and promote reintegration into the community. From other disciplinary perspectives, it may have different emphases, including organisational aspects linked to the institutional work of the entity in charge of prisons: human resources, financial resources, infrastructure, classification of prisoners and segmentation of the prison, among others (Espinoza, 2022).

When reference is made to order, it is understood as a structured, stable, and predictable context that allows the people who coexist and conduct themselves within it to accept its rules[4] (Liebling, 2004).

While the concept of order is often linked and confused with that of control and the two terms are related, it is important to highlight the differences between them. Control is a means of maintaining order, either to impose it when it has been lost or to prevent disorder and violence from occurring (Drake, 2016). Thus, order can be achieved using different strategies, and can be based on control, that is, on the intent to control all possible aspects with the aim of reducing or neutralising any risk that may affect it. But, on the other hand, order can also be obtained by more consensual strategies, by aiming to establish minimum agreements that lead to observation of the rules and, consequently, to securing the order desired (Drake, 2016). In other words, order can be obtained by focussing on personal well-being, cooperation, and long-term compliance with rules. But it can also be established through coercive and impersonal dynamics, exclusively prioritising security (Tyler, 2003).[5]

According to Tyler (2003), the most stable way of generating adherence to norms is by promoting systems that are recognised as legitimate. Thus, a management model based solely on control would be deficient since it would not pay attention to how authority is exercised, that is, to what extent that exercise is respectful of those who submit to it and of their dignity and rights (Crewe et al., 2014). But, on the other hand, models based only on consensus among all actors, that is, on more relaxed management dynamics, are not exempt from potentially problematic situations, as they may allow the emergence of informal economies, the establishment of abusive inmate hierarchies that mainly affect those considered weaker or perverse,[6] and the outbreak of greater degrees of hidden violence (Sparks et al., 1996).

In Chile, prison management or the problematisation of prison order has generally been quite limited in its development, which explains why there are few studies on the subject (Espinoza, 2022). The works closest to this topic come from the fields of law and criminology and place special emphasis on penitentiary

---

[4]Sparks et al. (1996) propose a complementary definition of order. For these authors, a state of order is any lasting pattern of social relations, which is based on a minimum respect for people, and in which the expectations of the participants about others are usually met. The fulfilment of expectations suggests the existence of a tacit agreement, a kind of social contract that inmates and staff have implicitly accepted, but, at the same time, a relational component of exchange of positions, of rational and respectful interaction in which each person complies with and adheres to the role they are expected to assume (Drake, 2016).

[5]An example of this type of order can be observed in maximum security or 'supermax' prisons. However, it is likely that this order is obtained at the expense of the personal well-being of the people subjected to it (Liebling 2004), limiting the possibilities of spontaneous cooperation among the actors affected (Crewe et al., 2014).

[6]Such as inmates whose crimes are strongly condemned by society (as is usually the case of crimes against children, or sexual crimes).

policy (Dammert & Zúñiga, 2008; Espinoza et al., 2014; Morales et al., 2012; Stippel, 2006;; Villagra, 2008; Wilenmann, 2020, among others), with sparser discussion about the more operational functioning of prisons.[7]

In summary, it can be said that order is an aspiration that facilitates achievement of the objectives of the penitentiary system. In order to gain a deeper understanding of the Chilean case, a formal description of the Chilean prison service (*Gendarmería de Chile*) is presented below. We then explore the daily practices that put its institutional objectives into practice. First, we explain the methodology adopted.

Methodology

This work is based on a segment of the research conducted as part of the doctoral thesis 'Management and Violence: How Prisons Work in Chile.'[8] Specifically, official documents reporting on the objectives, goals, and results of prison service management were analysed, and this analysis was contrasted with the inputs obtained in semi-structured interviews carried out in four Chilean prisons during the months of February and March 2021.[9] In total, 31 interviews were carried out: 19 with uniformed prison staff (including officials with managerial roles, operational personnel, and professionals) and 12 with people deprived of their liberty, referred to here as 'inmates.'

The four prisons selected for fieldwork are located in three regions in the centre of the country (Valparaíso, O'Higgins, and the Metropolitan Region), which together comprise close to 50% of the total incarcerated population in Chile (two were semi-private prisons and the other two were public prisons). Content analysis was used to examine the information collected, since this technique allows the compilation of messages and meanings that express content that is both manifest and latent, while based on data, documents, or texts (Duarte, 2021). To this end, analytical categories were devised that were based on the theoretical framework and adjusted to the objectives of the doctoral research. This process was conducted using the Atlas-ti programme, which allowed the interviews to be organised according to the categories previously constructed.

---

[7]Nevertheless, there are various studies that have analysed more deeply different aspects of the organisation of a specific type of unit, as has been the case of semi-private prisons (Arriagada, 2013; Fundación Paz Ciudadana – FPC, 2015; Martínez & Espinoza, 2009; Sanhueza & Pérez, 2017; Sanhueza et al., 2020, cited in Espinoza, 2022).
[8]The objective of the thesis was to understand the forms of prison management and their relationship with violence, with special emphasis on inmate participation. This study was conducted with a mixed methodology, using institutional statistical data as secondary sources, and applying in-depth and semi-structured interviews to different relevant actors in the national penitentiary system.
[9]The field work was approved by the Ethics Committee of the Faculty of Social Sciences of the University of Chile and all interviews had Informed consent.

Prison Management in Chile

Gendarmería de Chile is the institution in charge of the Chilean prison system. Its mission is to guarantee that the sentences handed down by the courts are carried out and to prevent conduct and situations that place this mandate at risk. To fulfil its mission, the institution has defined some strategic objectives that aim to ensure the supervision and active and permanent control of the population deprived of liberty. These objectives must, in addition, be achieved with the use of procedures that respect human rights standards (DIPRES, 2020; Gendarmería de Chile, 2022).

Apart from its focus on the prison context, Gendarmería is also in charge of executing non-custodial sentences, that is, sentences that are alternatives to prison (known in Chile as alternative sentences[10] or measures[11]). It is also responsible for post-release support, which includes the supervision of people who are serving their sentence after release on parole, have received a pardon commuting their sentence, or are expunging criminal records.[12]

Since its formation, Gendarmería de Chile has been an entity associated with a military format. When the 'Prison Gendarmería Corps'[13] was first formed, the institution adhered to the military structure of the armed forces, which were initially in charge of the country's first prisons.[14] Gendarmería's military formation is established in its organic law, which in its second article states that 'Gendarmería de Chile, due to its purposes and nature, is a hierarchical, disciplined, obedient institution and its personnel will be subject to the norms that establish its respective legal status [...]' (CESC-FPC, 2018; Vergara, 2021).

A military format is one of the background characteristics of the bodies in charge of prisons and is especially common in totalitarian regimes. However, in democratic contexts, this responsibility usually falls on civilian institutions, as has been recommended on different occasions (Coyle, 2003; ICPS, 2016), due to the advantages of maintaining professional leadership strongly related to national

---

[10]Law No. 20,603 (2014).

[11]Law No. 18,216 (1983).

[12]Gendarmería de Chile, Resolution No. 4478 of 8 May 2012, which changed the internal organisation of Gendarmería, creating a Post-release Department.

[13]The 'Prison Gendarmería Corps' was created in 1911 (Decree No. 214), to serve functions at the national level, allowing the different local entities to be unified into a single service in charge of prisons (Gendarmería de Chile, 2016). This institutional unification, combined with the establishment of centralised regulation, coincided with the need to adhere to the developmentalist ideas of the beginning of the 20th century, which aimed to show 'progress in administration, which would improve the supervision and coordination of penal facilities' (León, 2019, p. 173).

[14]Although in the 19th century, the body in charge of prisons (not yet called Gendarmería) was separated from the army, it did not discard military forms nor adhere to the principles of a civilian structure but maintained a functionality and structure similar to that of the armed forces (Vergara, 2021).

welfare systems (in health, education, work, housing, etc.), and with strong local links to assist with social reintegration (Coyle & Fair, 2018).[15]

The enhanced profile of uniformed officers in the operational structure of Gendarmería has raised questions about the effective role of social reintegration in the institution's responsibilities. The issue is even more controversial given that the institutional body in charge of training new recruits, the School of Gendarmería, only trains uniformed personnel and is without explicit responsibility for the training of professionals and administrative staff (art. 10, Organic Law of Gendarmería). While it is true that Gendarmería has incorporated professionals during its operations to perform tasks associated with the reintegration of convicted people, the level of involvement and participation of this group in relevant institutional decisions is extremely limited, leaving leadership in these tasks mainly to uniformed personnel (Bennett, 2014).

Among the substantive innovations introduced after Chile's return to democracy in 1990, one of the prison policies with the greatest impact on Gendarmería de Chile – not only because of the resources involved but also its impact on institutional dynamics – has been the incorporation into the penitentiary system of semi-private prisons. This prison format responds to a new style of public administration (the 'new public management'), based on a series of neoliberal[16] and managerialist[17] policies introduced in Chile in recent decades (González, 2018; Hathazy, 2016; Ross & Barraza Uribe, 2020; Wilenmann, 2020) that have had an important impact on prison organisation.

---

[15]As observed in different Latin American countries whose penitentiary systems depend on civilian bodies, with training in security and reintegration issues: Uruguay (National Rehabilitation Institute – INR), Panama (General Directorate of the Penitentiary System), Peru (National Penitentiary Institute), Costa Rica (General Directorate of Social Adaptation), among others.

[16]Neoliberal policies are not only observable in the economic sphere, but also in criminal matters, having manifested themselves in the proliferation of coercive norms (especially with the increase in penalties) and in the expanding powers of police systems (Hathazy, 2013). In Chile, '[...] the government and party experts decided to strengthen the police, courts and prisons, increasing their budgets and staff, but also retraining inefficient penal service providers. National police forces shifted from being guardians of national security to security service providers to citizen-consumers (Dammert, 2006; Frühling 2009). Within the criminal justice system, the Concertación administrations [the coalition of centre-left parties] led the reforms of due process and efficiency in criminal procedure (Langer, 2007). The prisons were privatised following the recommendations of experts of the Lagos administration [the former president]' (Hathazy, 2013, p. 13).

[17]This concept can be understood as the most radical expression of new management or public management principles (known in English as *new public management*). Managerialism introduces various models and principles associated with business administration into public governance, such as decentralisation, mission fulfilment, client-user orientation, accountability, cost-effectiveness assessment, among others (González, 2018).

These new prisons were installed with the promise that they would adhere to private enterprise values (flexibility, profitability, efficiency, higher quality, and lower cost of services, among others) modernise prison management and provide a solution to the lack of infrastructure and the need to promote better social reintegration of people deprived of their liberty (Martínez & Espinoza, 2009; Sanhueza & Pérez, 2017).

These prisons are licenced to private operators in a mixed format, in which the licensee is responsible for the construction and operation of various services in the prisons, but Gendarmería de Chile retains overall administration of the facilities. Currently, there are eight semi-private prisons in the country that house a third of the total population deprived of liberty in Chile (Ramírez & Sánchez, 2021).[18]

Operationalising Prison Order

The aspects described above serve as background in analysing Gendarmería's performance in serving its public function, a performance that has been problematised given the need to guarantee order in the prison system, an issue that has ramifications both internal and external to the system. Internally, order is needed to promote conditions that guarantee the safe coexistence of those who live and work within prisons, that is, the prison population and prison staff. Externally, order is about the importance of cultivating habits and behaviours that allow the successful return of those who pass through prison and the ability to use profitably the time serving their sentences. Order in this sense is associated with Gendarmería's official mandate.

As set out in its Organic Law, Gendarmería's mission is to:

> contribute to a safer society, guaranteeing effective compliance with preventive detention and with the custodial or restrictive sentences determined by the courts, providing those affected with conditions and benefits in accordance with their quality as a person and human rights standards, developing social reintegration programs that tend to reduce the probabilities of criminal recidivism and promoting the elimination of criminal records as part of the reintegration process.[19] (Decree Law No. 2,859, 1979)

---

[18] According to Gendarmería, as of January 2022, 37% of the incarcerated population was held in semi-private prisons (Gendarmería de Chile, 2022).

[19] The institutional vision is 'to become a Service highly valued by society for its contribution to public security, through the fulfilment of its institutional mission to monitor, care for and intervene in the prison population, with strict respect for Human Rights in accordance with international standards, and the contribution of the social reintegration of the people placed at its disposal, through the action of its personnel who have the appropriate skills to achieve it'. Accessed at: https://www.gendarmeria.gob.cl/historia.html [02/17/2022].

Several elements emerge from this mission. The first is the obligation to enforce the criminal justice policy as defined by public actors. To do this, it must implement court decisions regarding preventive measures or the criminal sanctions that the courts determine. A second element refers to the circumstances under which this institutional task must be carried out, that is, guaranteeing human rights standards, providing adequate living conditions and delivering the benefits necessary to promote the reduction of criminal recidivism. As can be seen, two tasks follow from this second element: the first is to guarantee decent prison conditions and access to basic benefits, and the second is to promote participation in reintegration programmes.[20]

This second element of the institutional mission has provoked the most adverse comment, as various actors have denounced a failure to comply with living conditions adjusted to respect for inmates' dignity and life, in addition to highlighting the system's inability to offer reintegration programmes in a sufficient and appropriate manner (Espinoza et al., 2014; INDH, 2020, 2021; Sánchez & Piñol, 2015). To provide an example, some reports (PRI, 2022; UNODC, 2019) have revealed the homicide rate inside prisons, which is approximately 18 times higher than the national rate of less than five homicides for every 100,000 inhabitants (UNODC, 2019). This result positions Chile as one of the countries with the highest prison homicide rates in the world, according to the report of the United Nations Office on Drugs and Crime (UNODC, 2019).

Some Findings on Daily Life in Prisons

The state's responses to the need to manage imprisonment, enforce judicial decisions, guarantee security, and promote rehabilitation aim to maintain the required order by exercising control and also dialogue.

Despite the formality imposed by Gendarmería, in practice formal actors (prison staff, ranging from prison authorities or officers, junior officers or gendarmes and security professionals) join forces with informal actors (such as interns) in managing prisons. The participation of the latter group is due to the practical impossibility of Gendarmería officials maintaining centralised control of all prison management.[21]

At the institutional level, during the field work, it became evident that prison staff, as the front-line actors in prison management, try to avoid disorders and use various strategies to prevent episodes of violence. Among the most recurrent

---

[20] An additional element is the mention of the expunging of criminal records as a stage in achieving reintegration. Since this work is focussed on what happens inside prisons it will not be considered here, as it refers to the post-prison stage.
[21] Several interviewees recognised that interns exercise control over various spaces, especially in contexts in which staff are absent, such as, for example, during the period of confinement in their cells (which can last between 15 and 17 hours a day). Although this chapter does not analyse the role of inmates in prison management, Espinoza (2023), Weegels et al. (2021) and Stippel (2018) are recommended to address this topic.

actions are those that prioritise the surveillance and control of the prison population. One of the actions that staff highlighted is that of classifying and segmenting the prison population, a job that can be carried out more easily in prison units that are not overcrowded. They also referred to prison intelligence, that is, observation of the prison population in order to understand the dynamics of inmate interaction. This type of activity can be carried out by human perception or through closed-circuit television (CCTV).

Within the scope of control, raids and confiscations were also highlighted, which involve the entry of personnel into the cells or dormitories to check the existence of prohibited items, which are confiscated when found. Some of those interviewed said that in units where staff conduct more controls or searches, there will be fewer weapons, so fights will be settled more frequently through blows and lethal violence reduced. Another group of interviewees said that raids, especially when conducted by guards with excessive violence, generate a feeling of abuse and injustice that strains coexistence within the sector affected.

Transfers are another preventive institutional response to violence, especially of troublesome inmates.[22] These transfers may be to another sector within the same prison or to another prison. Although the transfer may solve the immediate problem in the prison or sector of origin, the situation of risk may be transferred to the inmate's new destination, given that the person in question usually retains a belligerent attitude and may provoke new violent incidents. The more unfair the inmates perceive the transfer to be, the greater the risk of the transferee acting with violence in their new destination.

But in addition to control, prison officials also prevent disorders through actions that occupy the time of people deprived of liberty. The profitable use of time is a need recognised by the majority of people interviewed; it can be promoted by managing the organisation of cultural, sports or recreational activities, among others, as well as encouraging implementation of specialised interventions by the technical area (whether psychological or social assistance). These kinds of action, added to the occupation of time in work and educational activities, enable inmates to obtain favourable evaluations of their conduct, a fundamental requirement for accessing intra-penitentiary benefits which may lead to a reduction in the sentence served.

Other actions perceived positively by different actors are those of assistance and attention to basic needs. Among those most often mentioned was health care, especially verification of inmates' physical condition in the event of an illness or accident. In second place, reference was made to religious attendance, especially given the recognised pacifying effect of those spaces in which the presence

---

[22] According to the interviewees, a conflictive person is one who has negative leadership, that is, inmates who arrive at the unit without any interest in bringing about changes in their lives but intending to extend their criminal activity within the prison. However, some of the interviewees specified that for the penitentiary institution a negative leader can also be a person who seeks to promote changes that lead to collective benefits which could alter the order of the prison (Espinoza, 2022).

of churches is allowed.[23] In these sectors, the religious leader establishes specific rules of conduct, which respond to the church's own objectives of spirituality and evangelisation, as well as the particular considerations that each leader determines (Marín, 2013). Last, the people interviewed also mentioned the opening of spaces for communication with inmates and family members as a strategy that allows conflictive situations to be addressed[24] and helps relieve tensions.

Between Rewards and Punishment[25]

In response to questions about how prisons are managed, several interviewees revealed that management will vary depending on the type of penal unit, highlighting mainly how services are provided (whether by public or semi-private prisons) and the size of the units (whether prison complexes or smaller units). However, another group of interviewees stressed the importance of staff management styles, observing dynamics associated with a reward-based management in some cases, and others with more punitive characteristics (Huebner, 2003).

While prisons are organised according to institutional norms laid down by the state, in practice there are margins for interpretation that allow unit leaders to install forms of management that prioritise reintegration or, on the contrary, emphasise security and the maintenance of order by punishing any disruptive behaviour (Crewe et al., 2014; Sparks et al., 1996). Organisational dynamics that prioritise access to basic services as well as reintegrative interventions can be identified as reward-based management.

When a prison authority implements a management style focussed on reintegration, it usually gives greater prominence to the professionals who work within the unit. However, the presence of civilian officials within an institution that aspires to military status generates various frictions that manifest themselves in greater or lesser ways, depending on the perspective of the warden or authority on duty in a prison. Thus, uniformed officials can be found who work jointly and collaboratively with professionals in the technical area, promoting a management

---

[23] Although in the fieldwork the people interviewed did not specify whether they were referring to the evangelical church or other denominations, when describing the religious group in question they mentioned characteristics specific to the evangelical community (pastors, reference to 'brothers,' etc.).

[24] In general terms, the people interviewed pointed out that generating regular channels for official communication with family members can be beneficial to prevent disorders. However, such channels are particularly important when large-scale episodes occur, whether generalised catastrophes (such as the COVID-19 pandemic) or specific ones affecting the prison, like an earthquake.

[25] Huebner (2003) analyses the different types of control exercised by staff, distinguishing remunerative control (linked to access to intra-penitentiary benefits) and punitive control (associated with the application of sanctions). In the fieldwork, interviewees did not refer explicitly to the terms reward or punishment-based; however, taking as reference the literature studied, the empirical record, and the researcher's experience, it was possible to establish this distinction as a basis for the analysis.

logic that prioritises reinsertion. Others can be found who organise the unit by prioritising security over any other consideration, disregarding the work of professionals, or limiting themselves to requesting their specific collaboration in discrete actions.

According to some interviewees, the different management styles practised will have effects on inmate behaviour, generating more tension when prison dynamics are based on compliance with orders and priority is assigned to security alone, or reducing it when dynamics of respect are introduced, and the positive use of time is encouraged.[26]

It is also pointed out that management focussed on reintegration will help reduce disorder and violence. For regardless of whether the changes undergone by participants in reintegration activities are genuine or only apparent, if in a prison people stay busy, they will learn a trade, be able to improve their quality of life by attending workshops, be evaluated with good or very good behaviour, be able to access opportunities for partial release, and, in short, have their sentence remitted. Most interns value these opportunities highly.

> Sometimes there are years that are very good for getting leave outside [...]. So people say, ok, that prison 'is stabilised', in quotes, because no one gets into trouble, everyone wants to get back on the street. And that reduces the violence. But when we are in a prison where I know that I'm going to do ten years and the possibility of leaving completed [serving my whole sentence, without benefits] is what I've got to do, then one's not going to have the choice of studying or doing anything, because it makes no difference. (Intern 4)

By the same logic, officials who take decisions on the participation of subordinates in procedures involving inmates can also choose to insist that their staff act with respect but not tolerating that they act with slackness, understanding that this is the first condition for promoting social reintegration.

> I got rid of the violence [of my subordinates], the ill-treatment and all of that. And what did that mean for me? Getting a lot of people on my back, that what. I mean, to see someone who is there and I go 'Hey, no!'. 'What'? 'Right, that's enough', 'No!', 'Hey!'. Or I get right in there, pull them away, shove, even have to get into a loud argument .... (Official 2)

---

[26] A limitation of this work is that it was not possible to distinguish the profile or work origin of the prison officers who had a reward or punishment-based stance. However, several interviewees indicated that it was more common to find a position more committed to reintegration among professional staff. In the case of uniformed personnel, it is not possible to establish any tendency, but it is more common to identify this group with a more punitive stance, associated with control (Espinoza, 2022).

As the officer interviewed points out, this position of insisting on respect for the inmates will not necessarily be valued by the staff, above all by someone who assumes that order is kept only by force and violence. Officials like this are seen as 'pro-convict' and are not well regarded by their colleagues.

In contrast to the above, some chiefs impose authority over others by exercising power permanently, that is, without giving in to any request raised by those in their charge, especially by inmates. This intransigent attitude is based on the need to exhibit firmness and strength in the decisions they make, since they believe that only in this way can they keep control over the penal unit and maintain order. We have defined this type of management as punishment-based (Huebner, 2003).

> There is also an issue of power, [since some officers] are not inclined to accede also to inmate demands. It's like, 'we are not going to change you, if that means that you are going to die because you are going to hang yourself, go hang yourself. We are not going to change you because we can't change you ..., because we can't transfer you [to the sector] that you want', for example, 'because there is no space or because you don't have the right profile', that is the other thing. (Officer/a 16)

As can be seen, this attitude is not always based on intransigence, but also on an operational rationale. However, apart from the justification, how the message is transmitted is also important in generating or not a perception of unfair treatment.

Another element that reflects a punitive stance at the institutional level is the excessive value attached to the inmate's criminal record over their ability to change. An officer with this attitude considers previous crimes and misdemeanours more important than the reintegration process, the former carrying greater weight in evaluations and decisions made by institution staff. Seen from this angle, an inmate's past can be a stigma, a stain difficult to remove, making it difficult for them to take a distance from criminality.

> I get here, they see my form (criminal record) and they want to send me to the maximum-security module. And I am no longer like I was when I was twenty or twenty-five years old, or maybe even thirty. I'm going to be different. But here they say: 'red' [for dangerous] and 'red goes here' [on the card]. (Inmate 6)

The lower value given to reintegration is also evident when the weight given to professional staff decisions is considered. Thus, it is common for security criteria defined by uniformed officers to be prioritised over requests for intervention made by civilian staff. This preference becomes visible in different circumstances in which the position of both officials clash, such as when the professional staff member calls for an inmate and he or she is not referred because the gendarme considers that the conditions to do so are not met. This may be because of a security issue, or because there are no staff available to transfer the inmate to the technical area, or because the officer simply refuses to make the referral, without giving a reason.

> Here in [this unit] the technical area is incompetent [...], because they allow Gendarmería to tell them what to do. If you, as a professional, go to look for me in the module, the officer [gendarme] has no reason to say no. Because he is there to open and lock doors, that's his job. That's not yours, yours is dealing with people. (Inmate 5)

Some interviewees suggested that this emphasis on security does not necessarily aim to prevent violence but is mainly to avoid any incident that might draw public attention to the prison or to Gendarmería. According to this logic, some prison authorities will only consider professionals in the technical area as actors who are merely instrumental in carrying out designated tasks, but not as key interlocutors in the performance of one of the main functions of the penitentiary system, such as social reintegration.

> Gendarmería is concerned with control, but not with prevention [...]. In reality, my impression is that officers don't know very well the work that is carried out in the technical area, what the purpose of having a technical area is. But the technical area sees it as: 'listen, this inmate needs to contact his family, I need a social worker' or 'this inmate is babbling', as they say, 'why doesn't a psychologist see him?' But that's it. (Official 16)

Finally, using punishment to keep order is part of the operating dynamics of many institutions, prison being no exception. However, the consequences in these spaces can be greater. Punishments or disciplinary sanctions range from the very severe (such as detention in solitary confinement) to the mildest (such as a reprimand). In Gendarmería, various periods can be identified in which the punishment regime has been to use isolation cells preferentially for various types of offences (INDH, 2017; Nash et al., 2013). However, in 2013, the Ministry of Justice issued an edict that restricts the use of this sanction, requiring that it be used only as an exceptional measure of last resort, when no other less harmful way can be found. Despite this resolution, according to reports of the National Institute of Human Rights, this type of sanction is still routinely used in different penal units (INDH, 2020, 2021).

As has been seen, two positions can be identified: one tending towards reintegration (reward-based) and another prioritising security (punishment-based). Officers of the first group are usually identified as 'pro-convicts' *(pro-reos)*, a pejorative nickname that implicitly connotes criticism of their attitude. But these positions are not necessarily antagonistic, and officers can be observed who, while being 'pro-convicts', do not abandon the role of authority within the units; they are open to dialogue but also insist on limits when inmate requests breach the norms or harm the general well-being. In the same sense, officers can be recognised who place emphasis on security (exercising a legitimate monopoly of force) but do not trample on or undermine inmates' dignity.[27]

In the opposite sense, one of the interviewees remarked that these positions did not have a single perspective. Thus, both positions, both the 'pro-con' and the security-conscious, can have negative effects when those who presume such positions engage in practices of corruption and/or are inefficient in carrying out their tasks. Under such circumstances, whoever is 'pro-con' will be recognised as weak and permissive, while those who have a more security-conscious stance will be identified as violent and abusive.

Final Considerations

As seen in this analysis, the prison system in Chile rests on an institution (Gendarmería de Chile) with a long track record, whose mission is to ensure decent treatment and respect for the human rights of people deprived of their freedom, as well as to execute judicial decisions and promote social reintegration. Therefore, the incidents of aggression observed in official records and reported in interviews violate the institution's aspiration to guarantee prison order.

Prison staff manage the penal unit and constantly have to deal with different manifestations of disorder. However, the way the staff perform their duties is far from uniform.[28] Even though they may comply with prison regulations, there is a margin of interpretation that gives room for discretion; officers can be identified as who carry out their work according to a reward-based management rationale, and others who do so based on a more punitive logic. The former are more likely to listen to inmates' opinions and are concerned to develop different activities that promote positive use of inmates' time in prison, as well as reintegration processes on their release. The latter are officers who do not recognise the voice of those imprisoned and pay special attention to control and surveillance. A question that must arise is whether these approaches are necessarily in conflict or whether a position that harmonises both perspectives can be adopted. The literature tells us that it is possible for the objectives of security and reintegration

---

[27] As already noted, it is not possible to identify tendencies among uniformed officers given that both the 'pro-convicts' profile and the more punitive profile are recognised in those who hold leadership roles and those who perform executive tasks. However, those who do fall into the first category are professional civil servants. This difficulty is also observed when analysing the different types of prisons (whether public or semi-private, penitentiary complexes or small prisons).

[28] Although Gendarmería claims to control all areas of prison life, in practice this control is not manifested in the same way in all prisons, and informal and discretionary organisational logic can be identified that, in many cases, incorporates inmates in these tasks (Espinoza, 2023).

to converge in a coordinated and coherent way.[29] But for this to be achieved, we consider that a series of conditions need to be met, involving substantial changes at the institutional level. These include modifications that begin in the training stages of aspiring officers and gendarmes and extend to on-job capacity building for the staff (both uniformed and professionals) who are currently operating the prisons. However, changes in the operational management of prisons will be more likely to occur if the indicators considered to evaluate officers, as well as incentives and goals that they must meet, are also changed, giving equal priority to control and reintegration requirements.

It can be concluded from this work that although order can be achieved through control and surveillance – that is, by vertically imposing rules without listening to the people involved, by demanding only that tasks be fulfilled, by isolating and neutralising inmates in the presence of any fault – this position creates a perception of injustice which may cumulatively lead to violence (Byrne & Hummer, 2008). Our view is that order can also be achieved through legitimacy – that is, via relational mechanisms that enable the problems of those affected to be identified and small agreements reached, thus involving inmates in the search for solutions. Both paths aspire order, but the first can feed anger and a perception of abuse, while the second promotes adherence to the rules, is based on dignity and stimulates the exercise of citizenship (the opportunity to participate in the problems of a community). This latter scheme for order not only has direct ramifications by improving basic security conditions, but also collateral ones by connecting better with people's probabilities of change (Byrne & Hummer, 2008; Drake, 2016; Liebling, 2004), leading us to believe that it is more effective.

References

Arriagada, I. (2013). Cárceles privadas: La superación del debate costo-beneficio. *Política Criminal*, *8*(15), 210–248.

Bennett, J. (2014). Las claves para un sistema penitenciario moderno: Una entrevista con Peter Bennett. Fundación Paz Ciudadana, Conceptos, (31).

Byrne, J., & Hummer, D. (2008). Examining the impact of institutional culture on prison violence and disorder: An evidence-based review, prison culture and offender change. In J. Byrne, F. Taxman, & D. Hummer (Eds.), *The culture of prison violence* (pp. 40–90). Pearson Education.

Centro de Estudios en Seguridad Ciudadana – CESC y Fundación Paz Ciudadana – FPC. (2018). *Una propuesta de modelo integral de reinserción social para infractores de ley.* Santiago. Documento de trabajo.

Clemmer, D. (1940). *The prison community*. Holt, Rinehart and Winston.

---

[29] The concept of 'dynamic security' has the same sense, in that it emphasises the relational dimension, promotes the development of human relationship skills and highlights the importance of having leaders who use authority appropriately (Santorso, 2021; UNODC, 2019; Vigna et al., 2017).

Coyle, A. (2003). *A human rights approach to prison management.* International Center for Prison Studies, King's College.
Coyle, A., & Fair, F. (2018). *A human right approach to prison management. Handbook for prison staff.* Institute for Criminal Policy Research, University of London.
Crewe, B., Liebling, A., & Hulley, S. (2014). Staff–prisoner relationships, staff professionalism, and the use of authority in public and private-sector prisons. *Law & Social Inquiry, 40*(2), 309–344.
Dammert, L., & Zúñiga, L. (2008). *La cárcel: problemas y desafíos para las Américas.* FLACSO – Chile.
DiIulio, J. (1987). *Governing prisons. A comparative study of correctional management.* The Free Press.
DIPRES – Dirección de Presupuestos. (2020). *Información de Gestión.* Ministerio de Hacienda. http://www.dipres.gob.cl/597/articles-193508_doc_pdf.pdf
Drake, D. (2016). La contribución del personal de prisiones al mantenimiento del orden. *InDret, 3,* 1–15 (texto original: Drake, D. H. (2007), Staff and order in prisons en Jamie BENNETT, Ben CREWE & Azrini WAHIDIN (Editores), Understanding prison staff, Willan, pp. 153–167).
Drake, D., Darke, S., & Earle, R. (2015). Prison life, sociology of: Recent perspectives from the United Kingdom. In J. Wright (Ed.), *International Encyclopaedia of social and behavioural sciences* (pp. 924–929). Elsevier.
Duarte, C. (2021). *Análisis cualitativo de contenidos.* Manuscrito.
Espinoza, O. (2019). *Violencia y gestión carcelaria. Funcionamiento de la cárcel en Chile* [Proyecto de tesis. Doctorado en Ciencias Sociales, FACSO, Universidad de Chile].
Espinoza, O. (2022). *Violencia y gestión carcelaria. Funcionamiento de la cárcel en Chile* [Tesis doctoral, Facultad de Ciencias Sociales, Universidad de Chile].
Espinoza, O. (2023). Participación y orden en cárceles chilenas. In E. Pizarro, B. Olivares, O. Espinoza, N. Mancilla & H. Sir (Eds.), *Chile desbordado: tensiones, resistencias y construcciones colectivas en el siglo XXI* (pp. 40–58). Astrolab ediciones. https://doi.org/10.34720/k46h-xr92
Espinoza, O., Martínez, F., & Sanhueza, G. (2014). El impacto de los Derechos Humanos en el sistema penitenciario: La percepción de las personas privadas de libertad. *Informe Anual de Derechos Humanos en Chile 2014* (pp. 243–287). Ediciones Universidad Diego Portales.
Fundación Paz Ciudadana – FPC. (2015). Estudio sobre nivel de reincidencia del sistema de cárceles concesionadas. Informe final, 19 de junio de 2015.
Garland, D. (2001). Introduction: The meaning of mass imprisonment. In D. Garland (Ed.), *Mass imprisonment: Social causes and consequences* (pp. 1–3). Sage Publications.
Gendarmería de Chile. (2016). *Antecedentes históricos y legales sobre el origen institucional.* https://html.gendarmeria.gob.cl/doc/escuela/Gendarmeria_Chile_105.pdf
Gendarmería de Chile. (2022). *Objetivos y Productos estratégicos.* Disponible en Internet February 20, 2022, https://www.gendarmeria.gob.cl/historia.html
González, C. (2018). *Gestión, Gerencialismo y Sistema Penal.* Argentina. Editorial BdeF.
Hathazy, P. (2013). (Re)Shaping the neoliberal leviathans: The politics of penality and welfare in Argentina, Chile and Peru. *European Review of Latin American and Caribbean Studies, 95*(October), 5–25.
Hathazy, P. (2016). Remaking the prisons of the market democracies: New experts, old guards and politics in the carceral fields of Argentina and Chile. *Crime, Law and Social Change, 65*(3), 163–193.
Huebner, E. (2003). Administrative determinants of inmate violence: A multilevel analysis. *Journal of Criminal Justice, 31*(2), 107–117. https://doi.org/10.1016/S0047-2352(02)00218-0

International Center for Prison Studies – ICPS. (2016). *World prison brief*. http://www.prisonstudies.org/world-prison-brief-data

Instituto Nacional de Derechos Humanos. (2017). *Estudio de las Condiciones Carcelarias en Chile 2014–2015: Seguimiento de Recomendaciones y Cumplimiento de Estándares Internacionales sobre el Derecho a la Integridad Personal*. Instituto Nacional de Derechos Humanos.

Instituto Nacional de Derechos Humanos (INDH). (2020). *Estudio de las Condiciones Carcelarias en Chile 2018: Diagnóstico del cumplimiento de los estándares internacionales de Derechos Humanos en la privación de libertad*. Santiago.

Instituto Nacional de Derechos Humanos (INDH). (2021). *Estudio de las Condiciones Carcelarias en Chile 2019: Diagnóstico del cumplimiento de los estándares internacionales de Derechos Humanos en la privación de libertad*. Santiago.

Irwin, J., & Cressey, D. (1962). Thieves, convicts and the inmate culture. *Social Problems*, *10*(2), 142–155.

Jacobs. (1977). *Stateville. The penitenciary in mass society*. University Chicago Press.

León, M. (2019). El derrotero de una eterna reforma. Prisiones, estado y sociedad durante el Chile desarrollista (1920–1970). In J. Cesano, J. Núñez, & L. González (Eds.), *Historia de las prisiones sudamericanas. entre experiencias locales e historia comparada: siglos XIX y XX* (pp. 173–223). Universidad Nacional de Tucumán.

Liebling, A. (2004). *Prison and their moral performance. A study of values, quality and prison life*. Oxford University.

Marín, N. (2013). Religión y cárcel: reflexiones a partir del evangelismo pentecostal en Chile. In L. Bahamondes (Ed.), *Transformaciones y alternativas religiosas de América Latina* (pp. 153–173). Santiago de Chile. CISOC – Centro de Estudios Judaicos.

Martínez, F., & Espinoza, O. (2009). Cárceles concesionadas en Chile: ¿El camino a la privatización?. *Debates Penitenciarios*, *9*, 3–15.

Morales, A., Muñoz, N., Welsch, G., & Fábrega, J. (2012). *La Reincidencia en el Sistema Penitenciario Chileno*. Fundación Paz Ciudadana y Universidad Adolfo Ibáñez.

Nash, C., Milos, C., & Aguiló, P. (2013). *Personas privadas de libertad y medidas disciplinarias en Chile*. Facultad de Derecho - Universidad de Chile, Santiago.

PRI – Penal Reform International. (2022). *Deaths in prison: Examining causes, responses, and prevention of deaths in prison worldwide*. University of Nottingham. https://cdn.penalreform.org/wp-content/uploads/2022/12/Deaths-in-prison-briefing.pdf

Ramírez, A., & Sánchez, M. (2021). Ejecución penal y sistema penitenciario en Chile. In M. Fuch & L. González (directores), *Sistemas penitenciarios y ejecución penal en América Latina. Una mirada regional y opciones de abordaje* (pp. 243–283). Tirant lo Blanch.

Ross, J. I., & Barraza Uribe, B. (2019). The Chilean government's attempt to reform and close cárcel ex- penitenciaría (CDP Santiago Sur): ¿Mientras más cambian las cosas, más se mantienen igual? *International Criminal Justice Review*, *29*(1), 59–89.

Sánchez, M., & Piñol, D. (2016). *Condiciones de vida en los centros de privación de libertad en Chile. Análisis a partir de una encuesta aplicada a seis países de Latinoamérica*. Centro de Estudios en Seguridad Ciudadana.

Sanhueza, G., & Pérez, F. (2017). Cárceles concesionadas en Chile: Evidencia empírica y perspectivas futuras a 10 años de su creación. *Política Criminal*, *12*(24), 1066–1084.

Sanhueza, G., Pérez, F., Candia, J., & Urquieta, M. (2020). Inmate-on-inmate prison violence in Chile: The importance of the institutional context and proper supervision. *Journal of Interpersonal Violence*, *36*, 1–24

Santorso, S. (2021). Rehabilitation and dynamic security in the Italian prison: Challenges in transforming prison officers' roles. *The British Journal of Criminology*, *XX*, 1–18.

Sozzo, M. (2022). Introduction: Inmate governance in Latin America. Context, trends and conditions. In *Prison, inmates and governance in Latin America* (pp. 1–34). Palgrave Macmillan.

Sozzo, M. (2016). Postneoliberalismo y penalidad en América del Sur. A modo de introducción. In *Postneoliberalismo y penalidad en América del Sur. Buenos Aires, CLACSO* (pp. 9–28).

Sparks, R., Bottoms, A., & Hay, W. (1996). *Prisons and the problem of order.* Clarendon Press.

Stippel, J. (2006). *Las cárceles y la búsqueda de una política criminal para Chile.* Santiago Editorial LOM.

Stippel, J. (2018). Acerca del "autogobierno" en las cárceles. *en Nova criminis: visiones criminológicas de la justicia penal, 16,* 1–25.

Sykes, G. (1958–2017). La sociedad de los cautivos. *Estudio de una cárcel de máxima seguridad.* Siglo XXI Editores.

Tyler, T. (2003). Procedural justice, legitimacy, and the effective rule of law. *Crime and Justice, 30,* 283–357.

UNODC – Oficina de las Naciones Unidas contra la Droga y el Delito. (2019). *Estudio Mundial sobre Homicidio 2019.* Naciones Unidas. Viena, Austria.

Vergara, L. (2021). *La militarización penitenciaria: Un fenómeno que afecta la eficacia de la fase ejecutiva de la pena.* Manuscrito.

Villagra, C. (2008). Reinserción: Lecciones para una política pública. Revista electrónica Debates Penitenciarios, n. 6. Centro de Estudios en Seguridad Ciudadana. http://www.cesc.uchile.cl/publicaciones/debates_penitenciarios_06.pdf

Vigna, A., Cardeillac, J., & Trajtenberg, N. (2017). Estilos de trabajo de los funcionarios penitenciarios: orientaciones hacia el trabajo relacional con la población privada de libertad en Uruguay. Manuscrito, preparado para el Congreso de la Asociación Latinoamericana de Ciencias Sociales, mayo 2017.

Weegels, J., Gual, R., & Espinoza, O. (2021). Compartiendo el poder. Experiencias de cogobierno entre reclusos y autoridades en las cárceles latinoamericanas. In N. Hernández (Ed.), *Temas Criminológicos Latinoamericanos. Teoría, evidencia empírica y ejecución penal.* Bogotá. Tirant lo Blanch.

Wilenmann, J. (2020). Neoliberal politics and state modernization in Chilean penal evolution. *Punishment & Society, 22*(3), 259–280.

Chapter 5

In/Out: Revisiting the Relationships Between Prisons and Slums in Latin America

Andrés Antillano

Central University of Venezuela, Venezuela

Abstract

We propose to see, regarding the Venezuelan context and at the same time in dialogue with the literature on Latin American prisons, the prison through the prison-neighborhood correspondence. This includes, for example, looking at how the prison organizes crime outside, attributes social and reputational capital, extracts and redistributes illegal profits, export/ import modes and logics of action and domination. The purpose is to (a) discuss the "hydraulic" theses on prison gangs, dominant in North American literature, which explain their emergence through conditions endogenous of the prison, and instead put the emphasis on the dynamics of exclusion and the "lumpen economies" in which the poor subsist, and (b) nuance the perspectives on the relations between prison and community from the point of view of the peripheral South, marked by high rates of exclusion, informality, and an economy strongly dependent on commodities and a significant labor surplus population, in contrast to the industrial economies of the Global North.

Keywords: Prison; neighborhood; slums; families; informality; exclusion; illegal economies; Venezuela

Most literature on the Global North postulates a sharp and clear separation between the prison and the outside world, considering the latter as a closed system, disconnected from other extramural orders. The prison order is understood as an effect of endogenous factors that shape it, and its correspondences with society are usually reduced to abstract functional relationships, aimed at governing and containing the popular classes.

Discussions on prison interactions and disadvantaged social groups, from which it recruits its "clientele," have recently returned in literature, although the focus has been on the deleterious effects of mass incarceration for communities and families of convicts in the core countries. Instead, in light of the recent literature on prisons in the region and our own fieldwork in Venezuela, we propose that, in contexts of mass incarceration, high levels of poverty, and large underground economies that absorb a significant part of those excluded from the formal sector, the prison becomes porous, multiplying the flows, exchanges and correspondence between this space of confinement, and the impoverished contexts where the prisoners come from, organizing and regulating these contexts of exclusion and the illegal and informal economies.

Within this framework, the social order that operates inside the prison can be understood in its relationship with those flows and returns between the space of confinement and its exterior, and not as a mere effect of endogenous conditions; while this social order born in the inside extends and reshapes illegal social interactions and economies in poor communities.

The seminal works on the sociology of the prison privileged the notion of a closed, self-contained, and disconnected space, severed from society outside. Goffman considers that the barriers that separate the inmate's world from the exterior world condition the nature of total institutions. In them, the inmates submit to a single authority that manages their lives and satisfies their needs. Exchanges with the outside, symbolized by impassable walls and severely controlled access doors, function as a strategic leverage for management (Goffman, 2001). This approximation to the prison as an environment closed in on itself and isolated from the influences of the external environment will be consolidated with the discussion about the origin of the prison subculture, in the antagonism between the hypothesis of deprivation and the hypothesis of importation. The first, of which Sykes' thesis will be the most complete expression, presumes that the social order of inmates is a consequence of adaptation to the structural conditions of confinement (Sykes, 1974). An example of its continuity and sophistication is Skarbek's explanation of the prison gang. He explains its emergence because of the lack of control and regulation of the inmate's life by the administration (Skarbek, 2014, 2020). The opposite hypothesis, which supposes that the prison order is shaped to different degrees by street codes and criminal gangs (Irwin & Cressey, 1962; Schwartz, 1971, more recently, see Mitchell et al., 2021) still maintains the idea of a sharp separation between street crime's world and the inmate's world. Additionally, it incurs the risk of circular causality, in that it is difficult to discern whether street gangs influence prison gangs or prison gangs shape streets. In addition, many of the arguments that explain the internal order by endogenous factors admit the importance of some variables prior to prison, such as social differentiation (Clemmer, 1958), or racial homogeneity and the previous reputation of the inmates (Skarbek, 2014, 2020).

The skyrocketing prison population during the last decades has increased the interest in the effects of the prison beyond its walls. The main research highlights the impact on the family and communities (Clear, 2007; Comfort, 2007; Cunha, 2008); the conditions and effects of the return of released prisoners to their communities (Morenoff & Harding, 2014); the paradoxical effects of mass imprisonment on crime, by generating social disorganization (Clear, 2007; Drakulich et al., 2012; Kirk, 2021); or strengthening street gangs (Pyrooz, 2021; Skarbek, 2014), and other collateral consequences of punishment (Huebner & Frost, 2019; Kirk & Wakefield, 2018; Sampson, 2011). Different works coincide in pointing out that mass incarceration accentuates suffering and social disadvantages among prisoners, their families, communities, and social networks, perpetuating their exclusion, and at the same time, their containment and control (Wacquant, 2001, 2010).

However, these models, linking the prison to the social spaces where most of its inmates come from, are not adequate or, at least, appear as insufficient to account for the complexity of relationships and exchanges between such spaces of confinement and exclusion in the Latin American context.

As we will try to demonstrate, more than import relations, endogenous production, or externalization of the effects of the prison, the carceral order and the social order of the poor are mutually determined. Different works shed light on this interdependence by highlighting the porosity of Latin American prisons which goes beyond the simple undesired effect of mass incarceration since these exchanges help to sustain both the life inside prisons and to constitute criminal social orders in disenfranchised communities. Some works point out the importance of the family not only as emotional support and in modulating the experience of confinement but also as a key vector in the support of inmates, including the forms of sociability and organization that occur inside, as well as communication channels that allow the transfer of information, relationships, and resources abroad (Ferreccio, 2015; Fisher-Hoffman, 2020; Godoi, 2015). Others attend to the illegal economies, particularly those linked to drugs, which not only allow prisoners to survive but also shape the internal social order and redefine relationships, practices, and norms that regulate collective life within the prison (Ariza & Iturralde, 2022; Carter, 2017; Fontes & O'Neill, 2019; Nuñez, 2007). Also, the contexts of origin, criminal careers, reputations, and expectations of those who enter prison can operate by grouping and serializing inmates, while functioning as a management mechanism for internal social order (Drybread, 2021; Fontes, 2021; Pérez Guadalupe, 2000).

In a different sense, some research shows the role of mass incarceration in the expansion of criminal networks and street gangs in poor communities in Latin America (Antillano, 2023a, 2023b; Biondi, 2018, 2021; Feltran, 2018; Lessing, 2010, 2017). The neighborhood "imitates" the prison: devices and culture are copied, the "prison gang-form" are exported to society outside walls; and crime and street criminal organizations are regulated and governed from a distance by bosses of prison gangs. The carceral social order becomes a code with the potential to expand and become universal, while prison provides men, knowledge, and relationships that are incorporated into crime and alter life outside the walls (see Antillano et al., 2020; Biondi, 2018, 2021; Lessing, 2017; Dias & Darke, 2016). In the shadow of the prison, crime, illicit markets, and criminal networks grow, change, and organize. The carceral is infused into the veins of society.

Our hypothesis is that in the Latin-American context, the prison does not operate so much as a device to control and contain the surplus population, as in central countries, but rather as disciplining; articulating, organizing, and regulating the world of crime; governing the economy and the lives of the poor.

In what follows, we identify specific mechanisms that sustain the prison-slum continuum. First, we describe the dynamics that make poor neighborhoods contribute to shaping the prison order. We then describe the conditions that favor this order, born behind bars, and extending its influence into illegal economies and excluded groups. Although these exchanges occur with different intensities and effects in Latin American countries (the proliferation of the prison gangs in Venezuela and Brazil, the powerful street gangs led from prison in Central America, the greater state control and treatment in the prisons of the south, etc.), these different fluxes and circulations and the reciprocal effects between the prison social order and the world of the poor that they generate are present in a good part of the region.

Our hypotheses and most of the data come from extensive fieldwork in prisons, poor neighborhoods, illegal markets, and criminal economies in Caracas and other places in Venezuela. In this sense, our argument refers fundamentally, to the Venezuelan case. However, a comparative reading with the literature on prisons from the rest of Latin America allows them to be applied to varying degrees in other regional contexts.

How the Slum Shapes the Prison

Contemporary North American literature on the social order of the prison maintains the deprivation hypothesis but turns to a new source of stress: internal disorder. They replace the previous pains of prison to focus on the inability of the formal administration to offer protection and governance. The society of captives will no longer be understood as a mechanism for the protection of inmates against the administration but as its substitute. However, by supporting endogenous factors as the only, or at least the main cause of prison social order, these explanations are insufficient to account for the nature of the social organization of inmates in Latin American penitentiaries, clearly determined by an interrelation with the outside. But the thesis of *importation* would not be enough either. It is not about the transfer of cultural values and social and criminal trajectories from the outside to the inside, although this can also happen, but how these flows modulate, regulate and even make possible the prison social order, its structures, codes, and practices. We will discuss five of these fluxes: the continuing supply of new inmates, the expectations of newcomers, their trajectories, family relationships, and economies. These different flows intersect and overlap: population, family networks and economies condition each other, expectations reproduce *outside* what trajectories bring *inside*, etc. While for Goffman the closure of the prison and the blockage of exchanges with the outside would be the strategic lever for the management of total institutions, instead in many Latin American prison contexts the management of these exchanges (flow of new prisoners, expectations, reputations, family relationships, and money) become a central mechanism for the government of the inmates.

The Continuous Flow of the Incarcerated Population

There is an indisputable relationship between mass incarceration and changes in the organization of prisoners, particularly the emergence of different self-government structures. As Skarbek and Freire point out, "prison gangs are interpreted as an unintentional consequence of the massive demographic shift that has taken place in American prisons in the last years. This shift has made the previous system of norms, the convict code, insufficient to meet the prisoners' demands for social order. Gangs provide security and facilitate trade in a diverse penal system by using effective enforcement mechanisms and transmitting reliable information to inmates. Prison gangs are therefore not a cause, but a solution to many of the inmates' problems" (Skarbek & Freire, 2016, p. 404).

Latin America has some of the highest incarceration rates in the world, which has impacted the social order of its prisons. The combination of massive social exclusion, institutional abandonment of excluded populations, and *mano dura* (hard hand) policies have contributed to a continuous flow of young men to prisons in the region.

Massive social exclusion is redoubled with the institutional exclusion of disadvantaged groups, who are abandoned by the state to their fate, unprotected both from poverty and from the threats of other poor people. Social destitution and erosion of the state's regulatory capacity lead to an increase in conflicts, intraclass crimes, and punitive demands in excluded communities, to which Latin American states, permeated by neoliberalism, offer punitive responses (instead of the welfarist and penal-welfarist policies of the past) in an effort (generally unsuccessful) to contain the surplus population and achieve political gains, while the jails are filled with poor youth.

This continuous flow of poor young people into Latin American prisons overwhelms the precarious institutional capacity in such a magnitude, that it has no comparison to the phenomenon in northern countries. Only taking into account its existing physical capacity, without considering the chronic lack of budget to cover the needs of inmates and understaffing, the incarcerated population in Latin America surpasses by almost 20% the number of places available; while more than half of such population exceeds the limits by up to 150% (Nuñovero, 2019). This level of overcrowding makes the problems of order, security, and provision of the essential goods faced by US prisons, more pressing and complex for Latin American prisons.

This expansion of the incarcerated population in the region not only affects the internal social order by breaking the previous forms of regulation or state control (Skarbek, 2014), but above all, it implies the permanent supply of soldiers, manpower to be subjected and exploitable population by the self-government structures arising in its interior, at least in the case of Venezuela prison. *Soldiers*, frequently tested in the context of confrontations between gangs and violent criminal trajectories, are used by the structures that govern the prisons against the other prisoners to impose order and punish the rebels, confront rival gangs and armed incursions by the authorities, and then extend their power outside the prison walls. *Labor* that, in conditions of overexploitation, allows the operation of underfunded prisons, self-government, and the creation of businesses inside (and outside) the prison. Finally, the existence of the groups controlling the prison and the reproduction of the internal social order depend on a biopolitical economy based on the exploitation and extraction of revenues from the captive population, through extortion, the control of goods and services, and the lucrative drug market. The larger the population, the more chances of increasing profits. The increase in the incarcerated population is not only an occasion for the existence of these structures, legitimizing their emergence to the extent that they offer order and protection, but also an opportunity, since it offers bodies and income that allow the reproduction of the internal social order which increase the power and business of those who govern it.

Expectations

The relationship between the experience before prison and the internal social order is not that of an empty field nor that of simple causality, at least in the case of Venezuela, and surely in many other Latin American prisons. The prison does not behave like a *tabula rasa* or like clay that can be molded by external forces. Prison becomes a central experience for the poor, not just those who have been or those who know they will be, but for family members, friends, and entire communities whose lives gravitate, to a large extent, around the imprisonment of loved ones and acquaintances.

But this importance of prison is not only explained by mass incarceration, which means that the prison experience is directly or indirectly present, current or future, in broad sectors of the poor. In a context marked by social exclusion and lack of protection, prison can become a source of reputational capital, social relations, cultural capital, economies, and protection against the violence that hits excluded communities. Many violent young men from the poor neighborhoods where we do our fieldwork in Caracas, consider that going to prison is not so much a punishment but an opportunity to gain respect and acquire the necessary capital (social relations, cultural norms) for a successful criminal career. Young girls came to the prison hoping to find a partner among the prisoners (if it was a boss, even better) and to see themselves rewarded with prestige and gifts that they would hardly get on the street (Antillano, 2023a). For the family, the prison can be a place for protection and survival for a loved one too involved in violent dynamics (Ferreccio, 2015), while relatives and friends go to the bosses to ask for protection against threats from other criminals or seek to resolve disputes in their home communities.

This centrality of the prison experience for excluded groups has practical effects. The expectations of obtaining recognition and accreditation for adjusting to the prison order make newcomers to Venezuelan prisons accept without much opposition regulations and practices that they would reject in another context: blind obedience to a fierce and rigid hierarchy, submission to draconian and invasive regulations, denigrating and destructive practices. Couples and family members play a fundamental role in the financial support of the prison and become a transmission belt with the outside, and the demands for intervention by the prison gangs favor their extension toward the impoverished peripheries that demand order and regulation. Above all, this presence of the prison in the everyday world of the poor redefines its meaning and lends legitimacy and support to the prison social order. As Godoi shows, prison among the Latin American poor does not necessarily acquire the stigmatizing effect of other latitudes and, on the contrary, is often covered with a positive function, articulating and mobilizing external social networks (Godoi, 2015, 2017). Ferreccio, in his acute discussion on the use of the concept of "less eligibility," in contexts of exclusion and violence, such as those in Santa Fe (Argentina), concludes that for many poor people, being in prison is not necessarily worse than being free (Ferreccio, 2017. See also Cunha, 2014).

Trajectories

The social and criminal trajectories before imprisonment inform and help the functioning of the prison social order. The places of origin, belonging to certain criminal groups, networks, or social positions distribute and modulate the new arrivals in complex and serial structures. In the case of Venezuela, given the role played by the State in recent times, the relationship with the State, or even with the world of formal work, operated as a cleavage that distributed the inmates into opposing or subordinate groups (Antillano, 2015). Participation in one gang or the social networks and communities to which they belong determine their destinations within the prison. In most Latin American prisons, certain crimes, such as rape or parricide, carry stigma and exclusion, if not the punishment by those who govern the prison (Biondi, 2018; Drybread, 2021; Fontes & O'Neill, 2019). On the other hand, those who have prestige in the criminal world or maintain good relations with the boss of the prison, secure relevant positions. In his investigation at the end of the last century in the Lurigancho Prison, Pérez Guadalupe describes how the neighborhood of origin, the type of crime, and the previous reputation of the prisoner will define his position within the prison (Pérez Guadalupe, 2000). The admission of prisoners for drug offenses, generally with greater economic power and a more pragmatic sense that clashes with the old values that governed the world of crime, also redefines social positions and places in prison structures (see Feltran, 2018 on the displacement within the First Command of Capital, or PCC, of the bank robber by the drug trafficker as a figure of greater reputation and authority).

Reputation plays a strategic role in prison order management. In Venezuelan prisons, the prisoner who enters must give a detailed account of his criminal history to the prison gang, to play his fate during his stay in prison. Social networks are also fundamental: an older prisoner who knows him must "rescue" the newcomer, prove his career and take care of his behavior during the early days. In case of serious violations of the prisoner's codes, the defendant may defend himself by giving references to known criminals on the street who can attest to his good behavior. But the conduct that precedes entering prison is only considered about the codes and values that regulate the life of prisoners (not having collaborated with the police, not having betrayed, etc.) while disputes and blood debts (called "*culebras*") are canceled, which makes it possible to build a shared social order among criminals with violent trajectories, an extra-legal order that nonetheless requires and regulates violence.

Closing the circle, the value acquired in the prison social order by previous trajectories and reputations and the anticipation of rewards and punishments means that the prison can model the behavior of delinquents even before setting foot in jail.

Family Networks

Various works have reported the effects of mass incarceration in the region on the relatives of the detainees, in accordance with what Comfort calls "secondary prisonization": family breakdown, suffering, and overloading of the relatives who take care of the prisoner (Comfort, 2008. See also Ferreccio, 2015; Fisher-Hoffman, 2020). Although less attended to, the effect in the opposite direction is particularly important in Latin American prisons: family networks sustain, reproduce, and partially determine the internal social order. In addition to the role of emotional support, connection with the outside world, and modulator of the confinement experience, the family has, in the case of Latin American prisons where the State has resigned from its role as the provider of the necessary means for subsistence, a key place in the economic and material support of the inmates. It is usually the main, if not the only source of basic goods, money, and even illegal goods inside the prison, which implies an economic, physical, and emotional burden, and even, in the case of the entry of illegal goods, the risk for their freedom (Fontes & O'Neill, 2019; Fisher-Hoffman, 2020). This gives family members and visitors a central role in the prison economy, which conditions relationships, practices, and informal norms. On the other hand, family members are the main link to maintain communication with the outside world, be it with the lawyers, employers, the neighborhood, friends, or the criminal group they belong to, allowing the inmate to restore relations with the outside world that the prison intended to suspend (Biondi, 2018; Godoi, 2015). A particular case is that of the San Pedro penitentiary, in La Paz, Bolivia, where the family moves with the prisoner to provide support (while resolving the problem of family accommodation) inside the prison (Cerbini, 2012).

The supplies provided by the prisoner's relatives contribute to structuring forms of sociality and networks of mutual support and protection both among inmates and family members, as in the case of the paulista *jumbo* (Godoi, 2015) and the Argentinian *rancho* (Ferreccio, 2015). On the other hand, the smuggling of drugs and prohibited goods by some relatives encourages illicit markets within the prison that allow some inmate's survival and at the same time support self-government structures. Family networks also allow communication and transactions with key external actors for the reproduction of prison order and the prison gang economy, as well as mobilize resources against the state and the administration. In Venezuela, the protests of the relatives have been key to obtaining demands from the prisoners or defending them from any government measure that harms them. On occasions, the prison chiefs organize "self-kidnappings" of relatives as a measure of pressure against the threat of transfers or inspections.

But at the same time, the family becomes leverage for the management of prison orders by the state. Ferreccio (2015) has documented how the family reproduces the prison and treatment discourse despite the situation of their own loved ones. The suspension of visits is one of the measures most feared by the prisoners that the administration uses strategically to press for concessions. In Venezuela, the prison protests at the beginning of the century gave rise to an undeclared concession, the family overnight stay (*la pernocta*), which authorizes partners and family members to remain in the facilities under the control of the prisoners throughout the weekend, but at the same time, this measure makes it possible to avoid conflicts and maintain peace in prisons at the risk of losing this privilege or endangering their loved ones.

The importance of family members and visits for the maintenance and reproduction of the internal social order is expressed in strict codes that ensure their integrity. In the Venezuelan jailhouses controlled by prison gangs, a set of severe dress code rules (be decently dressed in the presence of women, avoid wearing dark glasses, never show your torso), relationships (do not address another prisoner's partner directly or communicate with her by other means, do not flirt with another's person relative, do not spy on a couple while they are in private, etc.), activity (do not carry weapons or fight while there are visits, protect at all costs the life and integrity of the family during the visit), and of honor (not to desire, nor talk with, and even less try to steal another prisoner's partner) regulate the relations between the prisoners and the family and the development of the visit. Assaulting a family member during the visit, even if it is the partner, can cost an inmate his life. The unequal social structure of the captive society is expressed in the position of women and family members. Having a young and pretty woman as a partner, *portar una fresa*, is a status symbol that is often associated with positions of power within the structures that govern the prison. The wives and relatives of the kingpins of the prison have privileges when entering the prison and during the body searches that compound it, and frequently lead the other women in protests and mobilizations (for the role of relatives of prisoners and members of the PCC in São Paulo prisons, see Biondi, 2010, 2018).

Economies

In chronically defunded and overcrowded prison systems that overwhelm management capacities, the reproduction of inmates' lives and the reproduction of their social order will depend on the external economies in which they and their families are enrolled, and on financial flows generated from outside. The prisoners survive thanks to the economic and affective circuits supported by their relatives, who provide them with food, clothing, medicine, and other goods for daily consumption. But in addition, these popular economies allow life in prison to be sustained, and finance the prison social order and the groups that govern it. Most explanations of prison gangs attribute their existence to a functional response to prison strain, forgetting that they are above all profitable enterprises based on the extortion of prisoners and the control of drug and illicit goods markets within the prison.

The growth of commodities in Latin America during the first decade of the century, and the redistributive policies that some governments implemented, paradoxically could have financed self-government structures in a context of mass incarceration and monetization of the poor (Antillano, 2023b). However, it will be the extensive and often thriving illegal economies in which the poor are forced to survive, particularly the drug economies, that will have the greatest impact on an expanded reproduction of the prison social order. So much so that its financial flows make possible the material reproduction of the incarcerated population abandoned by an underfunded administration; they finance the structures controlling this internal order and allow its expansion toward deregulated economies.

The conditions of exclusion in which most of the Latin American population lives mean that, for many poor people, economies outside the law represent the only option for survival. These informal and illegal economies proliferate precisely because of Latin America's place in the international order, as a supplier of cheap raw materials, which condemns the countries of the region to have primary economies and very small formal labor markets and to be sources of illegal merchandise which, in turn, take advantage of the high volume of available labor. In the case of Venezuela, after the drop in oil revenues that had sustained the illusion of social inclusion for historically excluded sectors, illegal economies flourished in which many poor people sought to replace their declining incomes. In a context of recession and impoverishment, in which a family could live with less than 20 dollars a month in formal income, the extortion "taxes" of the prison gangs doubled and, in the case of prisons that received a greater volume of prisoners for drugs, increased by up to 400%, paying inmates to prison bosses much more than what an average family receives as formal income. Illegal economies allow the poor to subsist both outside and inside prison.

The flows of money, illegal goods, and men from illicit economies to prison reshape and sustain the internal social order. In deficit-budgeted prisons and insufficient and underpaid staff, financial flows from illegal economies to prison redefine relations with the state. By surpassing the dwindling budget of an underfunded administration and covering maintenance costs that the state cannot absorb (see, in the case of Honduras, Carter, 2017; for Guatemala, Fontes & O'Neill, 2019), they increase the ability to bribe and co-opt the state bureaucracy, while inequality deepens within the prison social order, accentuating the privileges and fattening the coffers of self-government structures. While the majority of the prisoners barely survive with the scarce resources provided by their impoverished relatives, those who control these flows lead a life of luxury and excesses (Ariza & Iturralde, 2022; Carter, 2017; Fontes, 2021; Fontes & O'Neill, 2019).

A source both of survival for the prisoners and, above all of accumulation of large surpluses for those who govern the penitentiary (and their institutional allies), is the control of the markets of illegal goods that enter the prison. Although some poor inmates survive inside by selling these products on a small scale, in the case of Venezuela's self-governing prisons, those who govern the prison reserve a monopoly on the most profitable merchandise, such as drugs, which increases their economies and strengthens their position of power. In his early ethnography inside a Peruvian prison, Pérez Guadalupe demonstrates that control of the internal drug market defines the group that controls prison life (Pérez Guadalupe, 2000).

Finally, the anti-drug policies of the region's countries, subordinated to the US agenda of the War on Drugs, have stuffed the prisons with prisoners from local and international drug trafficking networks, reconfiguring the social order of the prisons. Especially with the entry of drug barons, who buy privileged positions within the prison, the previous social order, based on relatively horizontal relationships and on reputation and violence-display capacity, is replaced by more hierarchical and unequal relationships with exuberant privileges and luxury inside the prison (Ariza & Iturralde, 2022) and a more pragmatic rationality typical of business, as opposed to the previous expressive rationality.

How the Prison Shapes the Slum

The Latin American prison casts its long shadow over poor neighborhoods and the illegal economies in which its inhabitants survive. Although some works discuss the relationship between prison gangs and crime outside of prison, most of the Anglo-Saxon literature on the prison-neighborhood continuum focuses on the deleterious effects of prison and the export of its logic to poor neighborhoods. These works would coincide with the Foucauldian thesis of the carceral archipelago (Cohen, 1979; Foucault, 1978), according to which the prison would extend its effects of discipline, surveillance, and containment beyond its walls. However, Foucault outlines in his work another generally neglected thesis, which he attributes to prison, as an unexpected effect, creating and organizing criminality. The social order that flourishes in overcrowded prisons abandoned by the state, characterized by extra-legal governance, the regulation of a violent and motley population, the imposition of hierarchical forms of authority, and the disciplining of prisoners, would facilitate the mutation of expressive and violent delinquency in an organized and efficient crime, articulating the world of crime, pacifying the poor neighborhoods and regulating the illegal markets on which it is projected.

Discipline

Venezuelan prisons are fed predominantly by young people excluded from the urban peripheries linked to violent crimes and predatory crimes of little complexity. It is a fundamentally expressive, violent, disorganized, and opportunistic crime, governed by codes of honor, respect, and masculinity. However, when they set foot in a prison under the control of a prison gang, they face a social order comprised of rules, hierarchies, and orders that cannot be disobeyed, a hyper-coded and overcontrolled space, where there is no place for autonomy and expressiveness and, on the contrary, they must learn to regulate their behavior and submit to rules and hierarchies. Similar to the disciplinary prison, the prisoner-ruled prison imposes a rigorous set of controls over spatial distribution, time, body, and activity, but this time from the prisoners themselves.

The *irmaos* (brothers) who enter the PCC in Brazilian jails must carry out similar work on themselves (Biondi, 2010, see also Dias & Darke, 2016). The inmates "[...] absorb theories of prison life [...] everyday practices and come to understand the importance of the Command" (Biondi, 2010, p. 46). Camila Nunes Días discusses how the conditions of the prisons of the Sao Paulo penitentiary system made it easier for the PCC to become a centralizing instance for the elaboration of norms, and with prerogatives to judge and punish, producing a process of social reconfiguration among the prisoners, allowing the expansion and control of the PCC over all the prisons in São Paulo, the pacification of life inside the prisons (and later outside it, in the areas under the influence of the PCC) and the discipline and self-regulation of the prisoners. The pacification and control imposed by the PCC in Brazilian prisons translate into self-control of the prisoners themselves (Dias, 2011; Dias & Darke, 2016). For Feltran, the government of the PCC over the São Paulo prisons could be explained by the substitution of violent relations for pacified ways of resolving conflicts. PCC members act as mediators and arbitrators, relying on judicial mechanisms to settle disputes and assign responsibilities (Feltran, 2018). Pérez Guadalupe describes a complex system, with prosecutors and judges, inside the Lurigancho prison in Peru in the 1990s, through which the prisoners judge and punish those who break informal regulations (Pérez Guadalupe, 2000). Other ethnographies within Latin American prisons highlight the capacity of the informal organization to discipline inmates and punish those who break the rules (see, for Bolivia, Cerbini, 2012; for Dominican Republic, Peirce, 2022). A similar role has been played by the evangelical churches that control areas and prison populations in Latin America (see Duno-Gottberg, 2020; Manchado, 2015; Navarro & Sozzo, 2022). Paradoxically, these informal and often illegal organizations achieve what prison administration has never achieved in Latin America: maintaining order and peace inside prisons and governing the incarcerated population (Antillano, 2021).

This displacement process that imposes the modification of the wayward and violent behavior of the prisoners who enter prison, transforming them into subjects with the capacity for self-containment and self-regulation, subordinated to norms and criminal hierarchies, pacifies both social life in overcrowded prisons and in chronically violent slums once convicts return to their communities, while producing a disciplined and obedient reserve army that feeds the world of crime. Similar to the original prison reformer's pretension of turning a shapeless and wayward mass into obedient and disciplined workers, the prison transforms excluded and violent youth into disciplined and self-contained soldiers, functionals for organized crime networks, and the expansion of illegal economies.

Regulation

The social order that rules the interior of Latin American prisons expands its government outside of them, contributing to the ordering, regulation, and organization of crime, illegal economies, and excluded populations beyond their walls. On the one hand, the return of ex-convicts to their communities of origin, taking with them the cultural and social capital acquired in prison, contributes to the decline of violence and expressive crime, favoring instead an instrumental crime, based on more pragmatic rationality. At the same time, it opens them to a universe of relationships that complicates activities more than the narrow local limits in which the old gangs operated. The return to Los Girasoles (a poor neighborhood in southwestern Caracas) of the gang leaders, after serving sentences, brought an end to the incessant violence that had rocked the community for more than a decade and helped the gang escalate into more sophisticated and profitable criminal activities, leveraging the relationships with criminal networks and skills that the ex-convicts had gained in prison, while imposing control over the neighborhood, much like that of the groups that control the prison.

On the other hand, prison controls life outside the walls due to the expectations of administering rewards and punishments for those who eventually end up in it (see Lessing, 2017). For criminals, prison is a destination and an expectation. The prospect of being punished once inside for not behaving in accordance with the rules imposed from the prison or for disobeying an express instruction from the prison bosses, or on the contrary, of being accepted as someone with merits for their conduct on the street, determines the courses of action. The greater the probability of going to prison, the stronger the expectations and the more power prison gangs have over behavior outside. Mass incarceration not only creates conditions for the rise of prison gangs within the prison but also strengthens their power over crime outside its walls.

Third, the prison projects its logic, codes and structures into poor neighborhoods and illegal markets. Different works indicate how prison gangs control street gangs both in the USA (Skarbek, 2014, 2020) and in Latin American countries (Lessing, 2010, 2017). In the case of the PCC in Brazil (Biondi, 2018, 2021), this process is facilitated, according to Lessing, by the consolidation of prison gangs and their extension to other prisons, in such a way that they use the expectations of punishments and rewards inside as leverage to control crime outside, allowing more extortion and recruitment of new members. In the case of many Latin American countries, with prison gangs expanding and achieving almost unchallenged control of the prison system and street gangs becoming the main, if not the only, available source of economic opportunity and social recognition, the interactions between each other would be much more intense (Biondi, 2018; Feltran, 2020; Lessing, 2010, 2017).

The correspondences between the prison and the criminal social order outside are not necessarily reduced to these relationships of subordination and command. In Venezuela, perhaps because the expansion phase proposed by Lessing (2010) did not take place, few street gangs have a clear organic relationship with prison gangs. However, at least since 2014, at the height of mass incarceration and the worsening of the economic recession, the poor peripheries of Caracas began to copy forms of regulation and structures more typical of prisons controlled by the prisoners themselves: the gangs, until then embroiled in endless vendettas against other local gangs, dropped the old disputes and established alliances between them, imposed severe regulations on the neighborhood's criminals and later on the local organizations and the neighbors in general. They established restrictions for the entrance to the slums under its control and for those who had to live there, and so began an extortive collection of economic activities. Although the opinion of the prison gangs could be important (especially when it came to negotiating some kind of agreement with other gangs), their role, with a few exceptions, is to serve as a political and cultural model.

These different possibilities of correspondence between the prison and the dynamics of the socially excluded sectors suggest that the projection of the prison gang not only responds to organizational factors such as their ability to directly control crime outside, but also to the structural equivalence between prisons and poor neighborhoods so that conditions that favor similar logics, forms, and codes are duplicated in one context and in another (see Wacquant, 2001; for Venezuela, see Antillano 2023b). Three types of conditions present in prisons and poor neighborhoods in Latin America could explain this correspondence: social exclusion, lack of protection from the state, and outlaw economies. The poor youths who feed the prisons find copying their forms and codes a vicarious source of respect and reputation, but also participating in structures that replicate the prison gangs in the neighborhood offers them economic and material advantages that improve their position in a context of exclusion and lack of opportunities. Faced with the lack of protection by the state, criminal governance structures such as prison gangs and street gangs allow the regulation of collective life and the pacification of violent contexts, both inside and outside prison. Finally, the illegal economies, in which a large part of the poor survive, finance these structures and at the same time demand their existence as a means of regulating economic transactions that do not have the formal mechanisms to function and arbitrate conflicts.

Coordination

The prison favors the articulation and coordination of the underworld, generally marked by local conflicts and violent competition, allowing escalation in its operations and scope. The prison is *cosmopolitan*: it imposes on the prisoners the coexistence with other prisoners who come from different contexts and trajectories, in the face of locally confined crime and the limited social capital of small gangs dedicated to expressive violence or small-scale crime. Prisoners diversify their social capital through incarceration, and expand their relational universe, accessing far-reaching criminal alliances and networks that allow them to act beyond their original community.

This same cosmopolitanism allows the kingpins of the prison gangs to build relationships with criminals scattered in different places and activities. This allows for building effective information and communication networks with poor communities where the ex-convicts are inserted, and at the same time, coordinate dispersed groups that, without prison bosses, would make it more difficult to communicate. This task is reinforced by different "services" that the prison gangs can provide based on their relationships (sending men, offering contacts, solving problems) or using the prison facilities. In Venezuela, prison gangs allow their allies to take refuge in prison for some time if they are at risk of police persecution. In the case of particularly complex illegal operations, such as drug trafficking, involving coordination between international actors, local criminals and state agents, it is crucial to develop such relationships to gain access to privileged information and resources, thus allowing to influence and coordinate with different groups.

Prison not only involves interactions and relationships between criminals of different origins and activities but also serves as an interface with state actors, directly involved in crime: guards, prison administration, police, judges, and prosecutors, favoring negotiations, pacts and co-optations necessary for criminal activities to prosper.

The prison offers a safe "business room" to agree on deals and coordinate operations, a privileged observatory of crime and society, and an impregnable headquarters to articulate different actors and processes. To the extent that those involved, when serving sentences in prisons under the control of the prisoners themselves, are ironically outside the reach of the law and its possible reprisals.

Conclusions

Most work on the subject has studied the prison as a closed order; and those forms of social organization emerging from within, have been seen as the exclusive effect of endogenous factors. In the case of the prison gangs, the most common explanation relies on what we could call the "hydraulic hypothesis": the space left by the retraction of state control is occupied by the prison gangs and forms of extralegal governance as if they were opposing forces colliding within a closed system (Skarbek, 2014). Although, on the surface, this type of explanation would seem to account for the Latin American context, with the growth and expansion of powerful prison gangs within overcrowded, underfunded, and understaffed prison systems, these same factors would suggest an alternative explanation, nevertheless. A weak administration, without resources, with corruptible underpaid staff, is incompetent to prevent and even to regulate movement between the prison and the outside. On the other hand, the survival of the prisoners, and life in prison in general, often including supplements to staff salaries and infrastructure works, depend on the money and support that flows from outside. These external fluxes shape the prison social order and offer opportunities for gangs to accumulate profit and power, both, inside and outside prison. At the same time, these structures not only govern the internal order but also manage and regulate these exchanges. They oversee and control the money and the merchandise that enter into the penitentiary (which, although essential for the reproduction of the internal order and the power of gangs, can also generate distortions and conflicts). They also modulate and order the flows of new prisoners; organize and protect visits; manage businesses abroad; and supervise subordinates to whom diverse functions are delegated outside (the "principal-agent problem," see Miller, 2005).

They manage branches and regulate violence and crime in the contexts over which they influence. They arrange alliances. They take care of ex-convicts who return to their communities. They meet various demands to intervene, mediate or resolve conflicts between criminal groups, etc. The functioning of Latin American prisons is shaped and sustained by multiple circulations, by the continuous supply of bodies, legitimacies and money on which the lives of inmates depend, their social organization, the structures that govern them, even the income of the staff and the essential operations that would correspond to the state. At the same time, prisons radiate power, relationships, and cultural codes toward the territories under their influence. The prison would be both stock and flow.

This continuum is only partially explained by factors pertaining specifically to the prison and its management. Above all, the correspondences and exchanges between the prison and the impoverished peripheries of Latin America are better explained through the isomorphisms between such spaces of double exclusion (social and institutional) and lumpen economies. As such, the prison acquires a singular capacity to pacify excluded communities and to order, regulate and articulate crime. The exclusion and lack of protection by the state induce social disorganization and violence in poor neighborhoods, as well as in prisons. This contributes to the emergence of extralegal forms of governance as a means of solving the problem of order. At the same time, in this context of chronic violence and predatory crimes of the poor against the poor and through state policies that, far from protecting, criminalize poverty, a continuous supply of young people nourishes and saturates the penitentiary systems. On the other hand, the prison social order that thrives in different penitentiaries in the region becomes a source of reputation, relationships, and power for excluded young people. They know their "destiny" is to end up incarcerated; while their relatives and other members of disadvantaged communities will seek the protection of those groups that control the prison. Something the state cannot offer.

Groups that fill the vacuum of state regulation and impose their control over the population would find favorable conditions first within prisons but then radiate into the poor neighborhoods where the inmates come from and the illegal economies in which they are involved, taking advantage of conditions similar to those that gave rise to them in prison. The prison order, shaped by exclusion and popular informal economies, contributes to the reordering of excluded groups, pacifying collective life, regulating interactions, providing protection to illegal economies and offering symbolic and material alternatives to the most disadvantaged sectors. Poor communities provide excluded youth, legitimacy and capital, prison returns disciplined and self-regulated subjects, governance and the conditions for the expanded reproduction of a lumpen economy.

Although some of these factors may be present in central countries (see, e.g., Wacquant, 2001), their magnitude and scope define different configurations of the government of the poor and the role of the prison. The inability of the regional economies, extractivist, and highly dependent on the fickle international raw material markets, to absorb large volumes of labor implies a chronic surplus population excluded by the labor markets that overwhelms the diminished capacities of underfunded states to establish an effective regulation on it, be it through prison and the penal system or clearly deficient social policies. The state, rather than controlling or disciplining, manages the subaltern classes, alternating violent repression and overcriminalization with tolerance and abandonment of the poor to their fate (Auyero, 2000; Auyero & Sobering, 2021). This same logic, which combines exclusion, institutional violence and abandonment, is reproduced inside the prison, a failed symbol of the modernization attempts of the Latin American elites (Salvatore & Aguirre, 1996).

In these contexts of exclusion and state withdrawal, the poor become a reserve army of labor for illegal economies, many of them articulated with legal and global economies, such as drug trafficking, whose lower links (those in which excluded young people are recruited to the most dangerous tasks and the most morally damaging) are plagued by violence, fragmentation, and uncertainty. These popular economies (finance the maintenance and reproduction of the prison social order) and export cultural devices (codes, knowledge, and values) and organizational devices (structures, relationships, and disciplined men) that mitigate violence and dislocation both in popular sectors and in illicit markets.

It is difficult to understand these relationships without considering the colonial dimension and the effects of neoliberalism on this prison-neighborhood continuum. The countries of Latin America have been relegated since colonization to a peripheral place as a supplier of raw materials for the colonial metropolises, through primary and extractive local economies with little capacity to absorb labor and that impose deregulated labor regimes (unlike the disciplinary order of labor in industrial economies), implying a secularly excluded and deregulated population that feeds recurring cycles of violence, crime, and repression. In recent times, the global peripheries also supply illegal commodities (drugs, illegal migration, sex work, counterfeits, etc.) spurred on by the demands of global markets, deepening violence and deregulation (what Philippe Bourgois calls "predatory accumulation," see Bourgois, 2018). Latin American states, marked by fragility and authoritarianism, a legacy of their colonial origins, face this picture through excessive violence and tolerance (and reutilization) of zones of exception, deregulation, and disorder.

The insertion of the region in neoliberal globalization meant revamping some old colonial devices: accentuating the focus on the primary economy; which reversed the timid attempts at the industrialization of previous decades); increasing social exclusion; defunding and dismantling some aspects of the State (especially, the precarious welfare structures that offered some protection to the poor against the ups and downs of the economy); increasing authoritarianism that privileged punitive responses, the massive use of prison, and police violence in the face of poverty and precariousness. The effects of the war against drugs, promoted by Washington and assumed as a motto by the neoliberal governments of the region, had the paradoxical effect of growing a shadow economy, fueled by the infinite demand for narcotics in core countries, which gave shelter to many poor people who could not find opportunities in the legal economy. In an ironic twist, this mixture of exclusion, abandonment of the state, and illegal markets, makes the social order preached by the neoliberal creed, flourish in the prisons and poor neighborhoods of Latin America, but as a monstrous parody (Antillano, 2022).

Acknowledgments

This work involves different investigations carried out over the last ten years in prisons, poor neighborhoods of Caracas, and illegal economies. For this reason, I cannot but thank those who accompanied me in these investigations, such as Chelina Sepúlveda, Verónica Zubillaga, Iván Pojomovsky, Keymer Ávila, José Luís Fernández-Shaw, Desmond Arias, Benjamin Lessing, Alberto Alvarado, Francisco Sánchez, Rebecca Hanson, Amarylis Hidalgo and Luz Ortiz. Also, I want to thank UNICEF, the Ministerio del Poder Popular para el Servicio Penitenciario, the Corporación Andina de Fomento (CAF), and the Red de Activismo e Investigación para la Convivencia (Reacin). I thank Ivan Pojomovsky, Jennifer Martinez, and Luis Duno-Gottberg for their comments and suggestions.

References

Antillano, A. (2015). Cuando los presos mandan: Control informal dentro de una cárcel venezolana. *Espacio Abierto*, *24*(4), 16–39.

Antillano, A. (2021). When to punish is not to discipline. In S. Darke, C. Garces, L. Duno, & A. Antillano (Eds.), *Carceral communities in Latin America: Troubling prison worlds in the 21st century* (pp. 39–60). Palgrave Macmillan.

Antillano, A. (2022). The carceral reproduction of Neoliberal order: Power, ideology and economy in Venezuelan prison. In M. Sozzo (Ed.), *Prisons, inmates and governance in Latin America* (pp. 159–154). Palgrave Macmillan.

Antillano, A. (2023a). Galaxia-Prisión: Cómo la cárcel remodela la vida de las clases populares en Venezuela. *Prisiones*, *3*(2), 29–46.

Antillano, A. (2023b). The lights of Peonía: Violence and prison order in Venezuela. In D. Smilde, V. Zubillaga, & R. Hanson (Eds.), *The paradox of violence in Venezuela: Revolution, crime and policing during Chavismo* (pp. 95–113). University of Pittsburgh Press.

Antillano, A., Arias, D., & V. Zubillaga. (2020). Violence and territorial order in Caracas, Venezuela. *Political Geography*, *82*, 102221.

Ariza, L., & Iturralde, M. (2022). Tales from *La Catedral*: The *Narco* and the reconfiguration of prison social order in Colombia. In M. Sozzo (Ed.), *Prisons, inmates and governance in Latin America* (pp. 63–92). Palgrave Macmillan.

Auyero, J. (2000). The hyper-shantytown: Neo-liberal violence(s) in the Argentine slum. *Ethnography*, *1*(1), 93–116.

Auyero, J., & Sobering, K. (2021). *Entre narcos y policías: Las relaciones clandestinas entre el Estado y el delito, y su impacto violento en la vida de las personas*. Siglo XXI Editores.

Biondi, K. (2010). *Junto e misturado, uma etnografia do PCC*. Terceiro Nome.

Biondi, K. (2018). *Proibido roubar na quebrada: Território, hierarquia e lei no PCC*. Terceiro Nome.

Biondi, K. (2021). Facing the first command of capital (PCC): Regarding ethnography of Brazil's "Biggest Prison Gang." In S. Darke, Ch. Garces, L. Duno, & A. Antillano (Eds.), *Carceral communities in Latin America: Troubling prison worlds in the 21st century* (pp. 357–374). Palgrave Macmillan.

Bourgois, P. (2018). Decolonising drug studies in an era of predatory accumulation. *Third World Quarterly*, *39*(2), 385–398.

Carter, J. (2017). Neoliberal penology and criminal finance in Honduras. *Prison Service Journal*, *229*, 10–14.

Cerbini, F. (2012). *La casa de jabó: Etnografía de una cárcel boliviana*. Edicions Bellaterra.
Clear, T. (2007). *Imprisoning communities: How mass incarceration makes disadvantaged neighborhood worse*. Oxford University Press.
Clemmer, D. (1958). *The prison community*. Rinehart.
Cohen, S. (1979). The punitive city: Notes on the dispersal of social control. *Contemporary Crises*, *3*, 339–363.
Comfort, M. (2007). Punishment beyond the legal offender. *The Annual Review of Law and Social Science*, *3*, 271–296.
Comfort, M. (2008). *Doing time together: Love and family in the shadow of the prison*. University of Chicago Press.
Cunha, M. (2008). Closed circuits: Kinship, neighborhood and incarceration in urban Portugal. *Ethnography*, *9*(3), 325–350.
Cunha, M. (2014). The ethnography of prisons and penal confinement. *Annual Review of Anthropology*, *43*, 217–233.
Dias, C. C. N. (2011). *Da pulverização ao monopólio da violência: Expansão e consolidação do Primeiro Comando da Capital (PCC) no sistema carcerário paulista* [Doctoral dissertation, Universidade de São Paulo].
Dias, C. N., & Darke, S. (2016). From dispersed to monopolized violence: Expansion and consolidation of the Primeiro Comando da Capital's Hegemony in São Paulo's prisons. *Crime Law Social Change*, *65*, 213–225.
Drakulich, K. M., Crutchfield, R. D., Matsueda, R.L., & Rose, K. (2012). Instability, informal control, and criminogenic situations: Community effects of returning prisoners. *Crime, Law and Social Change*, *57*, 493–519.
Drybread, K. (2021). The extrajudicial punishment of rapist imprisoned in Brazil. In S. Darke, Ch. Garces, L. Duno, & A. Antillano (Eds.), *Carceral communities in Latin America: Troubling prison worlds in the 21st century* (pp. 89–108). Palgrave Macmillan.
Duno-Gottberg, L. (2020). Spiritual life and the rationalization of violence: The state within the state and the Evangelical order in a Venezuelan prison. In S. Darke, C. Garces, L. Duno-Gottberg, & A. Antillano (Eds.), *Carceral communities in Latin America: Troubling prison worlds in 21st. century* (pp. 321–338). Palgrave Macmillan.
Feltran, G. (2018). *Irmaos: Uma história do PCC*. Companhia das Letras.
Feltran, G. (2020). *The entangled city: Crime as urban fabric in São Paulo*. Manchester University Press.
Ferreccio, V. (2015). Familiares de detenidos: Exploraciones en torno a prácticas de equilibrio institucional en las prisiones de Santa Fe. *Argentina: Espacio Abierto*, *24*(1), 113–145.
Ferreccio, V. (2017). Lo prefiero vivo en la cárcel que libre en el cementerio: Nuevas versiones de la less eligibility en el contexto santafesino. *Actas XXXI Congreso ALAS 2017, Montevideo, Uruguay*. https://www.easyplanners.net/alas2017/opc/tl/5471_vanina_ferreccio.pdf
Fisher-Hoffman, C. (2020). The quadruple burden: Reproductive labor & prison visitation in Venezuela. *Punishment and Society*, *24*(229), 95–115.
Foucault, M. (1978). *Vigilar y castigar: Nacimiento de la prisión* (3rd ed.). Siglo XXI.
Fontes, A. (2021). Border, Ghetto, prison: Cocaine and social orders in Guatemala. In D. Arias, & T. Grisaffi (Eds.), *Cocaine: From Coca Fields to the streets* (pp. 139–164). Duke University Press.
Fontes, A., & O'Neill, K. (2019). La visita: Prisons and survival in Guatemala. *Journal of Latin American Studies*, *51*(1), 85–107.
Godoi, R. (2015). Vasos comunicantes, fluxos penitenciários. *Entre dentro e fora das prisoes de Sao Paulo: Vivencia*, *46*, 131–142.

Godoi, R. (2017). *Fluxos em cadeia: As prisões em São Paulo na virada dos tempos*. Boitempo Editorial.
Goffman. E. (2001). *Internados*. Amorrortu.
Huebner, B. M., & Frost, N. A. (2019). *Handbook on the consequences of sentencing and punishment decisions*. Routledge.
Irwin, J., & Cressey, D. (1962). Thieves, convicts and the inmate culture. *Social Problems*, *10*(2), 142–155.
Kirk, E. (2021). Community consequences of mass incarceration: Sparking neighborhood social problems and violent crime. *Journal of Crime & Justice*, *45*(3), 1–17.
Kirk, D. S., & Wakefield, S. (2018). Collateral consequences of punishment: A critical review and path forward. *Annual Review of Criminology*, *1*(1), 171–194.
Lessing, B. (2010). The dangers of dungeons: Prison gangs and incarcerated militant group. In *Small arms survey 2010*. Cambridge University Press.
Lessing, B. (2017). Counterproductive punishment: How prison gangs undermine state authority. *Ration Society*, *29*(3), 257–297.
Manchado, M. (2015). Dispositivo religioso y encierro: Sobre la gubernamentalidad carcelaria en Argentina. *Revista Mexicana de Sociología*, *77*(2), 275–300.
Miller, G. (2005). The political evolution of principal-agent models. *Annual Review of Political Science*, *8*, 203–225.
Mitchell, M., Pyrooz, D., & Decker, S. (2021). Culture in prison, culture on the street: The convergence between the convict code and code of the street. *Journal of Crime and Justice*, *44*(2), 145–164.
Morenoff, J. D., & Harding, D. J. (2014). Incarceration, prisoner reentry, and communities. *Annual Review of Sociology*, *40*, 411–429.
Navarro, L., & Sozzo, M. (2022). Evangelical wings and prison governance in Argentina. In M. Sozzo (Ed.), *Prisons, inmates and governance in Latin America* (pp. 259–293). Palgrave Macmillan.
Nuñez, J. (2007). Las cárceles en la época del narcotráfico: Una mirada etnográfica. *Nueva Sociedad*, *208*, 103–117.
Nuñovero, L. (2019). *Cárceles en América Latina 2000–2018: Tendencias y desafíos*. Pontifical Catholic University of Peru.
Pérez Guadalupe, J. L. (2000). *La construcción social de la realidad carcelaria: Los alcance de la organización informal en cinco cárceles latinoamericana: Perú, Chile, Argentina, Brasil y Bolivia*. Fondo Editorial de la Pontificia Universidad Católica de Perú.
Peirce, J. (2022). Provós, representantes, agentes: The evolution of prison governance arrangements in the Dominican Republic's prison reform process. In M. Sozzo (Ed.), *Prisons, inmates and governance in Latin America* (pp. 93–126). Macmillan Palgrave.
Pyrooz, D. C. (2021). The prison and the gang. *Crime and Justice*, *51*, 237–306.
Salvatore, R., & Aguirre, C. (1996). The birth of the penitentiary in Latin America: Toward an interpretive social history of prisons. In R. D. Salvatore & C. Aguirre (Eds.), *The birth of the penitentiary in Latin America: Essays on criminology, prison reform, and social control, 1830–1940*. University of Texas Press.
Sampson, R. (2011). The incarceration ledger: Toward a new era in assessing societal consequences. *Criminology and Public Policy*, *10*, 819–828.
Schwartz, B. (1971). Pre-institutional vs. situational influence in a correctional community. *The Journal of Criminal Law, Criminology, and Police Science*, *62*(4), 532–542.
Skarbek, D. (2014). *The social order of the underworld: How prison gangs govern the American penal system*. Oxford University Press.
Skarbek, D. (2020). *The puzzle of prison order: Why life behind bars varies around the world*. Oxford University Press.

Skarbek, D., & Freire, D. (2016). Prison gangs. In H. Griffin & V. Woodward (Eds.), *Handbook of corrections in the United States* (pp. 399–408). Routledge.
Sykes, G. (1974). *The society of captives: A study of a maximum security prison.* Princeton University Press.
Wacquant, L. (2001). Deadly simbiosis: When Ghetto and Prison meet and mesh. *Punishment & Society*, 3(1), 95–133.
Wacquant, L. (2010). *Castigar a los pobres*. Gedisa.

Chapter 6

The Arrival of the Risk Paradigm to Prison Management in Uruguay

Ana Vigna[a] and Santiago Sosa Barón[b]

[a]*University of the Republic, Uruguay*
[b]*Office of the Parliamentary Commissioner for Prisons, Uruguay*

Abstract

This chapter examines the context in which the risk model began to permeate prison management in Uruguay during the prison reform that took place from 2010 to 2020. Based on the general debate surrounding the introduction of the risk paradigm in prison policy, we focus on the particularities of importing a specific model and its associated assessment tools into a Latin American prison system. This chapter draws on interviews conducted with authorities and experts involved in the importation of this risk-based model, as well as with staff responsible for the implementation of risk assessment tools in Uruguayan prisons. The findings highlight the importance of the "intangible" aspects of prison policy, as well as the limitations of transferring programs and tools developed in the Global North to the Global South.

Keywords: Prison management; risk model; risk assessment; RNR model; policy transfer; prison reform

Introduction[1]

The history of debates about the (overt and covert) purposes of incarceration is almost as long as the history of the prison itself (Foucault, 1975; Garland, 1999). Within this debate, while there is considerable academic discussion of the concept of "prison management" (Bottoms & McWilliams, 1979; McNeill, 2006) and the various models and programs associated with it (Andrews et al., 2006, 2011; Redondo, 2017; Redondo et al., 2002; Ward & Maruna, 2007), there is not as much background focused on the specific implementation procedures of such programmatic proposals. Even more limited is the discussion of the challenges of transferring such models (generally developed in the Anglo-Saxon world) to other contexts. This discussion becomes particularly relevant in light of recent developments aimed at decolonizing criminological concepts, theories, and methods by challenging the uncritical importation by the South of policies developed in the global North (Blaustein, 2016; Carrington et al., 2016).

This chapter centers on the Uruguayan prison system's adoption of the Risk-Need-Responsiveness (RNR) model and the Offender Assessment System (OASys), an assessment tool built to forecast recidivism rates and used to design individualized treatment. The Uruguayan government adopted the RNR model as part of a prison reform initiative that took place from 2010 to 2020. This prison reform was consistent with the government's progressive agenda, aligned with the "pink tide" movement that spread throughout several Latin American countries in the early 21st century. The goal of the reform was to end the inhuman living conditions in prisons, and create a human rights-centered approach, under the administration of the recently created National Institute of Rehabilitation (INR). This transformation strives to include civilian officers to reduce police control in managing prisons. The following stage of this process was the incorporation of programs and practices into a coherent model based on politically legitimated technical criteria, with the intention to overcome the historical lack of a unified prison policy (González et al., 2015). The subsequent period (2015–2020) was aimed at introducing a rationale to guide prison management after these institutional changes: the rationale of rehabilitation.

The chapter is divided into five sections. After this brief introduction, we present an outline of the fundamental components of the risk model and the accompanying assessment instruments. The third section furnishes details on our methodology. The following section presents and analyzes the primary outcomes of this study, while the concluding section examines the paradoxes that emanate from the transfer of concepts and programs from the Global North to the Global South.

---

[1]This chapter is based on the dissertation of the Certification on Public Policy on Crime and Insecurity, elaborated by Sosa Barón (2021) and entitled "Desafíos de la implementación del OASys en el Uruguay" (Challenges of the implementation of the OASys in Uruguay).

The Risk Model and the Use of Diagnostic Tools

After a period dominated by skepticism about rehabilitation, the 1980s witnessed the emergence of what Feeley and Simon (1992) termed a "new penology" in the northern hemisphere. This new paradigm redefines the goals of crime control through a new vocabulary that emphasizes the centrality of rationality and efficiency in penal intervention. This shift is closely linked to the replacement of the notion of "dangerousness" with that of "risk." Within this framework, the focus shifts from concerns about individuals in need of a particular type of intervention to a view of the system as an aggregate of populations that need to be managed (Feeley & Simon, 1992). This type of approach (based on the calculation of recidivism probabilities) gains strength with the development of information systems and the sophistication of statistical analysis.

The RNR Model

Within this context, Risk-Need-Responsivity (RNR) has been one of the most popular models of correctional intervention in recent decades. It was originally developed in Canada in the 1980s by Andrews et al. (2006), and while it has evolved over time[2], its three guiding principles have remained consistent. The risk principle suggests that the intensity of intervention should be proportional to the risk of reoffending. Specifically, the model argues that interventions should focus on high-risk populations. The need principle suggests that interventions should focus on addressing "criminogenic needs" (dynamic risk factors that contribute to criminal behavior). The responsivity principle suggests that interventions should take into account the cognitive abilities and learning styles of participants. From this perspective, it is understood that the most effective way to intervene is through structured, cognitive-behavioral programs (Andrews & Bonta, 2007; Andrews et al., 2011).

The RNR model highlights the following factors as particularly relevant for predicting reoffending: (i) criminal history; (ii) antisocial personality pattern; (iii) pro-criminal attitudes; (iv) social support for crime; (v) family/marital relationships; (vi) school/work; (vii) substance abuse; and (viii) housing situation. The model distinguishes between static risks (those that cannot be changed, such as criminal history or family background) and dynamic risks (those that can be addressed through interventions, such as attitudes, thinking styles, employment, or housing). One of the major strengths of the model, according to its proponents, is its robust empirical support. Its adaptability to diverse populations (in terms of gender or race) is highlighted as a key feature that enhances the model's utility across different settings (Cullen & Gendreau, 2006).

More recently, Andrews and Bonta (2016) introduced two additional principles to the model: (i) the principle of professional discretion, which recognizes

---

[2] "Today, the RNR model includes 15 principles, that take into account not only the core principles, but also overarching and organisational principles" (Bonta, 2023).

that practitioners may deviate from standardized approaches in specific cases to effectively address particular situations and (ii) the principle of integrity, which relates to how assessment and treatment are actually conducted (Redondo, 2017). Among the most common threats to program integrity, several authors have pointed to (i) programmatic drift (when the original goals become distorted over time); (ii) programmatic inversion (when there is a direct questioning of the program's goals); and (iii) institutional disagreement (when there is a change in the hegemonic conception at the organizational level) (Hollin, 2001; McGuire et al., 2008). Among the elements highlighted to combat integrity problems are: (i) a solid theoretical foundation; (ii) an implementation manual; (iii) institutional commitment; (iv) adequate material and building resources; (v) trained and committed staff; (vi) monitoring mechanisms; and (vii) evaluation plans (Redondo, 2017; Rojido et al., 2014).

Despite its momentum, the development of this approach has not been without criticism. First, various authors perceive the risk paradigm as a new version of traditional governmental strategies of population control (O'Malley, 2000; Velásquez, 2014). Criticisms include the primacy of economic rationality associated with a neoliberal perspective on crime, and the alleged value-neutrality of this "neopositivist" approach (Brandariz, 2014). In addition, there is a strong critique of the risk paradigm because it focuses not on what the offender has done in the past, but on his or her future projections. In fact, some authors highlight that it emphasizes risk over protective factors (McNeill, 2006, 2017). Thus, while it is acknowledged that the underlying concepts are not new, they are being redefined in a new context of knowledge production (Rivera Beiras, 2016).

Assessment Instruments as Key Elements of the Model

The development of different assessment tools is closely linked to global trends in treatment models. At least three stages can be identified in this process, with unstructured clinical judgment, actuarial methods, and structured clinical judgment dominating successively.

Until about the 1970s, the preferred form of diagnosis was unstructured professional judgment (Andrews & Bonta, 2007). Several difficulties have been identified with this approach. First, it has serious reliability problems and lacks transparency in decision-making. Moreover, it often has a weak theoretical foundation that tends to reify the history of violent behavior, with little ability to distinguish between modifiable and permanent traits (Andrés-Pueyo & Echeberúa, 2010). In addition, the empirical justification of the assessments depends on the individual experience of the practitioner involved, which hinders the possibilities of systematization and replication (Andrés-Pueyo & Redondo, 2007). Finally, some studies have begun to observe high levels of error in the predictions derived from this method (Esbec & Fernández, 2003).

The second stage is identified with the introduction of actuarial methods. The development of sophisticated information systems made it possible to create models that weigh multiple variables about people who have committed crimes and estimate the probability of recidivism. Andrews and Bonta distinguish two stages in the use of these tools. In the first stage, which occurred in the 1970s and 1980s, structured "second generation" instruments were developed that could discriminate between low and high-risk offenders with some relative success. However, these instruments lacked a solid theoretical foundation and, more importantly, were insensitive to individual change. In the 1980s, a new generation of actuarial instruments began to distinguish between static and dynamic factors, providing valuable information to guide treatment. However, it was found that these instruments had problems in individualizing the diagnosis because they were based on generalizations related to groups of individuals (Andrés-Pueyo & Redondo, 2007).

The third and final stage is mixed assessment based on structured clinical judgment. Proponents argue that these instruments integrate the strengths of the previous tools and expand the dimensions of analysis and diagnostic capabilities. They are based on known risks, but at the same time offer a greater degree of flexibility based on a mix of epidemiological studies and clinical research (Andrés-Pueyo & Echeberúa, 2010). These tools identify both criminogenic needs and protective factors (Andrews et al., 2006). These developments are based on the intensive and increasingly sophisticated use of information, allowing for continuous evaluation of applications, in line with the concept of "evidence-based policy" (Cullen & Jonson, 2017). This generation of tools can be used for risk management, target selection for treatment, allocation to programs, and monitoring of outcomes (Campbell et al., 2009).

Several assessment tools are currently available. Some aim to predict the overall probability of criminal risk, while others are designed to predict risk for specific types of crime, such as sexual violence. In this regard, several authors emphasize the need to specify precisely the type of behavior to be predicted and the population for which such a prediction is expected (Andrés-Pueyo & Echeberúa, 2010; Villagra et al., 2014). Beyond treatment, the resulting information is also used for prison management, allowing for population classification, justifying decisions about security levels, and even determining early release (Kroner & Mills, 2001).

The Offender Assessment System (OASys) belongs to the third generation of instruments. It is a general risk and needs assessment scale developed by the National Offender Management Service (NOMS) in England, and has been in use since 2001 (Debidin, 2009). In addition to predicting the likelihood of reoffending (distinguishing between low, medium, and high risk), the scale also allows for the estimation of the risk of serious harm to self and others. The tool measures the following dimensions: (i) current offense; (ii) criminal history; (iii) attitudes; (iv) housing situation; (v) close relationships; (vi) education, training, and employment; (vii) financial management; (viii) lifestyle; (ix) alcohol abuse; (x) substance abuse; (xi) emotional well-being; (xii) thinking and behavior; and (xiii) health status (Morales et al., 2018).

Recommendations to ensure theoretical consistency in the implementation of these instruments include the need to test them with the target population, verify inter-rater reliability, test face validity, and ensure compatibility of requirements with available resources (Austin, 2006). When using tools developed in other regions, the process of adaptation and validation becomes crucial (Villagra et al., 2014).

It is important to take into account the specificities of the population as well as local risk factors (Folino, 2015; Villagra et al., 2014).

In addition, it is necessary to consider the link between these factors and the socioeconomic structures that characterize the application contexts. The uncritical adoption of models and assessment tools implies the possibility that these instruments may end up operationalizing social vulnerability traits as "criminogenic factors" (Feeley & Simon, 1992; Rivera Beiras, 2016). In this regard, the class bias in criminal prosecution may be reflected in the construction of risk assessment and prediction tools, which are based on the types of crimes that are more commonly pursued, thereby reinforcing the selectivity of the system (Rivera Beiras, 2015, 2016). Moreover, it has even been suggested that the use of risk assessment tools (which are highly intrusive in relation to already convicted individuals) may conflict with the fundamental rights of incarcerated individuals and may become an additional punitive component of the sentence (Rivera Beiras, 2015, 2016; McNeill, 2017).

Moreover, it should be noted that the acquisition of these instruments involves significant costs, not only for the purchase of the scales themselves, but also for other elements such as patents, application protocols, consultations, manuals, and software programs. This raises the debate about the link between industry and policy assessment in relation to potential conflicts of interest between the market, government, and academia (Eisner & Humphreys, 2012; Vose, 2021). In this regard, international financial organizations play a crucial role in the cross-national transfer of models and policies (Blaustein, 2016).

In Latin America, Chile was a pioneer in the adoption of the RNR model (Villagra, 2022) and was also the first country to adopt the OASys as an assessment tool.[3] The first version of the instrument began to be applied in 2012, and in 2013 a new version (OASys II) was implemented, modifying some items, adjusting the translation, and adapting the typology of crimes to the Chilean reality (CESC, 2017). Despite these adjustments, the instrument has not yet been validated for the Chilean population (Morales et al., 2018). A few years later, Uruguay tried to follow its neighbor by adopting the RNR and the Chilean version of the OASys as a diagnostic tool.

Methodological Strategy

In order to describe and examine the process of arrival and incorporation of the risk paradigm in prison management in Uruguay, we systematized official documents and interviewed prison officers and qualified informants. Between October 2018 and November 2019, we interviewed seven deputy technical directors, four professionals (psychologists and social workers) belonging to technical subdirectorates, and two practitioners. The interviewees were selected from those most directly involved in the management of OASys and the information it generates.

---

[3] Based on a collaboration between the British government, the Gendarmería de Chile and the Fundación Paz Ciudadana.

We tried to maximize the heterogeneity of the interviewees, taking into account the facilities in which they work in terms of size, security level, and geographical area. Specifically, interviews were conducted with staff from Units No. 3 Libertad, No. 5 Mujeres, No. 6 Punta de Rieles, No. 14 Colonia, No. 16 Paysandú, No. 19 Florida, No. 20 Salto, and No. 24 Soriano and Río Negro. Staff from the Diagnostic and Referral Intake Center, the Assisted Liberty Supervision Office, and the National Directorate for the Released were also interviewed.

The perceptions of practitioners are considered key to the implementation of the model (Moore, 2015). The interviews reveal the participants' perspectives on three key dimensions: the institutional adoption process of the risk paradigm, the assessment tool's features, and the utilization of the information it produces.

On the other hand, in order to contextualize the institutional and political process of adopting the risk paradigm, three interviews were conducted between 2018 and 2022 with the person who occupied the National Technical Subdirectorate of the INR from 2016 to 2018 and the National Directorate of the institution from 2018 to 2020. In addition, an international consultant from the Inter-American Development Bank (IADB), who played an important role in promoting the implementation of the RNR in Uruguay, was interviewed in 2022.

ADOPTION of the RNR Model by the Uruguayan Prison System

Latin American prison systems have recently begun to explore the incorporation of systematic prison intervention practices and related risk assessment tools (CESC, 2017; Folino, 2015; Villagra et al., 2014). Although it is natural that the introduction of paradigmatic change will generate resistance in any organization (Warrick, 2023), it is to be expected that this will be particularly noticeable in institutions that are traditionally resistant to change, such as prison systems (Akoensi & Amankwah-Amoah, 2023). These difficulties were evident in the Uruguayan case, where these processes had the additional challenge of contesting legitimacy in the face of police hegemony within a historically fragmented system (Vigna, 2021).

In this context, the National Institute of Rehabilitation was established in 2010 with the goal of rehabilitating prisoners. However, it was not until 2017 that the concept of "rehabilitation" gained technical and programmatic significance (Juanche, 2018). One of the initial decisions was to separate human rights-based treatment from rehabilitation (Juanche, 2018). This separation facilitated a more coherent conceptualization of ongoing experiences. After an initial search of evidence-based models from international experience, carried out in collaboration with the University of the Republic (Trajtenberg & Sánchez de Ribera, 2019), the National Technical Subdirectorate decided that the RNR model served as a comprehensive framework for organizing the intervention. The authorities highlighted the potential of the risk paradigm to tackle criminal risk factors and move beyond the traditional notion of rehabilitation solely tied to education and work. The prominent presence of the IADB in terms of citizen security in the country was crucial for this rhetoric to gain political legitimacy.

Despite this conceptual effort, the implementation of treatment programs aligned with this new paradigm was significantly limited due to the absence of a dedicated budget for technical intervention. Thus, only a limited number of intervention programs were executed, including: (i) a program for individuals who struggle with drug addiction; (ii) a program for addressing sexual aggression; (iii) a program for preventing gender-based violence; (iv) a program for promoting favorable social behavior; and (v) a program for enhancing emotional regulation. Although these initiatives demonstrated a robust institutional commitment, their coverage was very limited, and their evaluations were practically non-existent (De Ávila, 2021; Vigna & Juanche, 2022).

Given the contextual backdrop of widespread prisoner human rights violations coupled with limited material and human resources, there existed a substantial potential for the newly implemented interventions to stray from the original model (González et al., 2015; Vigna, 2021).

OASys Adoption Process, Coverage, and Use of Information

In terms of diagnostic tools, prior to 2017, INR had some scattered technical protocols to manage inmates' admissions, mainly based on their patronymic information. However, their use was neither widespread nor part of an intervention model. Especially in the interior of the country, evaluation depended on each facility. For technical reports required by judicial procedures (such as early or temporary release), the assessments were based on the idea of "dangerousness," and were carried out by professionals from the National Institute of Criminology. This procedure was very opaque since it was not possible to systematize the criteria used. Subsequently, there was a significant delay in relation to the global discussion on assessment instruments, resulting in the prevailing use of unstructured professional judgment (Barboni & Bonilla, 2018; Trajtenberg & Sánchez de Ribera, 2019). A report by the State Agency for the Evaluation of Public Policies pointed to a great dispersion in the practices and perspectives of the technicians, and the absence of a comprehensive methodological strategy, protocols, and uniform criteria for decision-making (AGEV-OPP, 2013).

Thus, the National Technical Subdirectorate began addressing the idea of adopting an assessment tool based on "empirical criminology" (Juanche, 2018). Concurrently, the IADB and the Ministry of the Interior entered into an agreement to implement violence prevention and recidivism reduction programs based on similar theoretical foundations. In this context, the Chilean experience was presented. Consequently, Uruguay became the second country in Latin America to implement the RNR model.

As previously mentioned, the process of acquiring assessment tools is extremely expensive. Due to the OASys patents belonging to the British government, incorporating this model into the Ministry of the Interior's budget posed a challenge. As a result, a replica of the Chilean form was introduced. This process encountered difficulties. The manuals were not available until several months later, and the instrument required modifications due to elements that did not align with the Uruguayan context.

A pilot test was conducted in 2017, and various aspects of the vocabulary had to be adjusted. Additionally, a summary sheet was introduced, which includes the final score for the risk of reoffending and an evaluation for the risk of serious harm (to self and to others). Finally, a qualitative assessment table was added to provide suggestions for intervention. Beyond these revisions, the INR has not yet validated the tool in the Uruguayan context.

Over time, the Offender Assessment System was gradually integrated into various penitentiary facilities, and since July 2018, it has been compulsory for all individuals entering the correctional system, including those making transfer and judicial requests such as early release, temporary permits, or other special authorizations. However, it is challenging to assess the overall coverage since there is no digital support for the resulting information. The data are simply recorded on paper, and subsequently, the summary sheet is digitized and linked to corresponding reports based on cases that come to the Diagnosis and Referral Center. This database does not encompass the entire population. In particular, numerous assessments conducted in the interior of the country are omitted. As a result, its utilization prospects are quite limited.

Evaluations by Technical Staff and Instrument Users

Human resources are crucial to implementing this type of evaluation tool and intervention model. The IADB conducted the initial training sessions on the RNR model, and based on that, the INR established a "pivot team" composed of 8 operators who were responsible for conducting training sessions with the technical teams across the country.

Although it was specified that the training should last 80 hours, in many units the applicators did not receive the full training. In general, the technicians requested training sessions with practical cases, as it is understood that there is a lack of space to discuss aspects of the application of the instrument. The interviews revealed a wide variety of application styles. While some are strongly guided by the structured questionnaire, in other cases, the interview with inmates is almost independent of it. In this context, the possible variation in scores due to differences in applicator subjectivity is seen as a clear risk. In fact, it was pointed out that, despite the degree of standardization of the instrument, its results ultimately depended on the subjectivity of the evaluator. In at least two units, the Technical Subdirectorates expressed serious doubts about the validity of the scale, preferring approaches that were more "open" and "adaptable" to the individual.

Beyond the diagnostic tool, there was resistance to the risk paradigm and, more generally, to the concept of evidence-based policy. Strong opposition to the notion of "risk" itself was present from an epistemological and even an ethical standpoint, stemming mainly from its intuitive association with the concept of "criminal dangerousness."

The time required to apply the OASys has been cited as a weakness in previous evaluations (Moore, 2015). In the case of Uruguay, the increase in the workload caused by the use of the assessment tool was another factor explaining the resistance to it. Initially, there was a feeling that a lot of time was being wasted, although application times were later reduced. However, there was considerable variation in the average time spent by practitioners, ranging from half an hour to two hours.

In some cases, it was noted that inmates have "learned" the instrument and often answer what they understand is expected of them. Another criticism that emerges from the interviews is that the assessment instrument seems to work better for certain types of crimes (such as robbery, theft, or homicide) but not for others (such as sexual or economic crimes), where the risk of reoffending is perceived to be underestimated. There is also a perception that the instrument is better at predicting male behavior than female behavior.

The most widespread criticism, however, stems from the lack of capacity to act on the information gathered. Practitioners admit that they do not have enough treatment programs or human resources to implement them. This is a source of delegitimization of the instrument. One Technical Subdirectorate directly states that the results of the OASys are of no use to them for intervention and that they only use them for management purposes.

Despite these criticisms, OASys has also raised awareness of the need to strengthen the technical teams in the units. In 2018, only 3.4% of the nearly 4,400 officers in the INR held technical positions, and only 65 worked in facilities across the country.[4]

Among the positive aspects of the implementation of OASys is the possibility to get a screenshot of the people who enter the system, as well as to improve the preparation of reports. In general, the ability to provide a qualitative basis for risk assessment, highlighting aspects to be taken into account in day-to-day management, is highly appreciated. Emphasis is placed on the tool's ability to quickly provide information that may be useful for referring cases to the appropriate teams[5] or for security aspects. However, as noted above, the tool's potential for intervention is extremely underutilized. In many units, especially some in the interior of the country and in the larger and more complex units, the possibilities for technical intervention are scarce or directly non-existent.

Final Thoughts

After a great deal of effort, the INR was able to integrate the OASys into the daily management of prisons. This has led to the training of many staff members in diagnostic assessment and to progress in the definition of a specialized role in prison intervention. Thus, one of the unexpected benefits of this process has been the empowerment of the technical teams in some facilities. The use of the tool has meant a protocolized intervention that has tangible consequences for different target groups, both inside and outside the prison system. Additionally,

---

[4]According to the data provided by the National Institute of Rehabilitation to the Office of the Parliamentary Commissioner for Prisons.
[5]For example, if there is a health condition, a disability, a psychiatric pathology, or a problematic use of drugs.

the OASys has filled a gap in terms of information that was previously scattered or non-existent.

This first step was achieved with various difficulties and leaves many challenges for the future. The way in which this risk assessment tool has been selected and introduced reflects the notorious institutional and material weakness of the INR. More in general, the discussion about the efficacy of using instruments developed abroad, which would require a substantial expenditure and availability of highly qualified staff for proper application, versus developing our own instruments tailored to local population profiles and available resources, remains open (Trajtenberg & Sánchez de Ribera, 2019).

The various actors consulted agree on the limited possibilities of responding to the criminogenic needs of prisoners resulting from the application of the assessment tool. In particular, it is noted that the main shortcoming lies in the lack of treatment programs. Thus, practitioners use the information obtained mainly for the management of daily needs. This deficiency allows the latent risk that the routinization of the application of the instrument implies the abandonment of one of its central practical purposes, which refers to the identification of needs in order to implement individualized interventions. This risk is manifested, for example, in the discourse of the practitioners, when the language of dangerousness and risk appears undifferentiated and when concerns about effective intervention for social reintegration remain absent.

On the other hand, in the context of scarce resources, it is relevant to determine whether efforts should be focused on the possibility of developing routine activities, or on implementing individualized diagnosis and intervention. Of course, this is not necessarily a dichotomy. However, given the inhuman and cruel conditions observed in at least one-third of the prison system (Parliamentary Commissioner, 2022), the question arises as to whether the structural conditions are in place for the effective implementation of a model such as the RNR.

In fact, it is possible to hypothesize a tendency toward a reversal of the risk principle. If the OASys is used as an input to segregate inmates, with a tendency to group higher-risk individuals in mega-prisons and lower-risk individuals in facilities with more open regimes and greater opportunities for intervention, the perverse effect could be that the people who need more intensive treatment are the ones who end up in the worst places and with less chance of receiving attention. This is relevant to the warnings raised by various authors about the 'collateral damage' of the use of diagnostic tools (McNeill, 2017).

Another aspect that should be noted is the dependence of the Uruguayan State on international financial organizations in the area of crime prevention and treatment policies. This mode of operation results in a lack of continuity of initiatives in the medium and long term, and is related to the danger of importing instruments and programs from abroad without adequate validation. All of this ultimately leads to a limited capacity to build our own agenda on security issues (Juanche & Palummo, 2012; Vigna & Juanche, 2022).

Ultimately, it is clear from the Uruguayan case that the "managerial narrative" (Feeley & Simon, 1992) has had little capacity to penetrate the penitentiary field. Thus, despite the impetus given to the risk paradigm in the context of prison reform, this perspective is far from hegemonic. Among the elements that explain this result are the lack of an adequate budget, the resistance of the traditional organizational culture, the weakness of technical teams and information systems, and the predominance of a punitive sensibility. This experience allows us to reflect on the mechanisms underlying the processes of conceptual and programmatic transfer from North to South, leading to results that, although they are related to those observed in the latitudes of origin, are strongly influenced by the conditions of possibility and dominant philosophies in the local context.

References

AGEV-OPP. (2013). *Instituto Nacional de Criminología—Oficina de Supervisión de Libertad Asistida (INACRI–OSLA) 2012–2013.* https://transparenciapresupuestaria.opp.gub.uy/sites/default/files/evaluacion/INACRI_OSLA.pdf

Akoensi, T. D., & Amankwah-Amoah, J. (2023). Cynicism toward change and career stage: An exploration of work environment and organizational based characteristics among prison officers in Ghana. *International Criminology, 3,* 63–76. https://doi.org/10.1007/s43576-023-00084-3

Andrés-Pueyo, A., & Echeberúa, E. (2010). Valoración del riesgo de violencia: Instrumentos disponibles e indicaciones de aplicación. *Psicothema, 22*(3), 403–409.

Andrés-Pueyo, A., & Redondo, S. (2007). Predicción de la violencia: Entre la peligrosidad y la valoración del riesgo de violencia. *Papeles del Psicólogo, 28,* 157–173.

Andrews, D., & Bonta, J. (2007). Risk-need-responsivity model for offender assessment and rehabilitation. *Rehabilitation, 6,* 1–22.

Andrews, D., & Bonta, J. (2016). *The psychology of criminal conduct* (6th ed.). Routledge.

Andrews, D., Bonta, J., & Wormith, S. (2006). The recent past and the near future of risk and/or need assessment. *Crime and Delinquency, 52,* 7–27.

Andrews, D., Bonta, J., & Wormith, S. (2011). The risk-need-responsivity (RNR) model: Does adding the good lives model contribute to effective crime prevention? *Criminal Justice and Behavior, 38,* 735–755.

Austin, J. (2006). How much risk can we take? The misuse of risk assessment in corrections. *Federal Probation, 70*(2), 58–63.

Barboni, L., & Bonilla, N. (2018). Evaluación psicológica en el ámbito forense: La libertad anticipada en el contexto uruguayo. *Ciencias Psicológicas, 12*(2), 285–292.

Blaustein, J. (2016). Exporting criminological innovation abroad: Discursive representation, 'evidence-based crime prevention' and the post-neoliberal development agenda in Latin America. *Theoretical Criminology, 20*(2), 165–184.

Bonta, A. (2023). *The Risk-Need-Responsivity model: 1990 to the Present.* HM Inspectorate of Probation. Academic Insights.

Bottoms, A., & McWilliams, W. (1979). A non-treatment paradigm for probation practice. *British Journal of Social Work, 9*(2), 160–201.

Brandariz, J. (2014). *El gobierno de la penalidad: La complejidad de la política criminal contemporánea.* Dykinson.

Campbell, M., French, S., & Gendreau, P. (2009). The prediction of violence in adult offenders: A meta-analytic comparison of instruments and methods of assessment. *Criminal Justice and Behavior, 36*(6), 567–590.

Carrington, K., Hogg, R., & Sozzo, M. (2016). Southern criminology. *British Journal of Criminology, 56,* 1–20.

CESC. (2017). *Evaluación del impacto del Programa de Reinserción Social: Centro de Estudios en Seguridad Ciudadana (CESC)*. Instituto de Asuntos Públicos, Universidad de Chile.

Parliamentary Commissioner. (2022). *Informe Anual. Situación del sistema carcelario y de medidas alternativas*. Parlamento del Uruguay. https://parlamento.gub.uy/sites/default/files/DocumentosCPP/Informe_2022_Comisionado_VF_web.pdf

Cullen, F., & Gendreau, P. (2006). Evaluación de la rehabilitación correccional: Política, práctica y perspectivas. In R. Barberet & J. Barquin (Eds.), *Justicia Penal Siglo XXI. Una selección de Criminal Justice 2000* (pp. 275–347). National Institute of Justice (U.S. Department of Justice).

Cullen, F., & Jonson, C. (2017). *Correctional theory: Context and consequences*. Sage Publications.

De Ávila, F. (2021). La evolución del tratamiento penitenciario en Uruguay. *Revista Fermentario* (Vol. 15, Issue 2). Facultad de Humanidades y Ciencias de la Educación de la UdelaR y Facultad de Educación de la UNICAMP.

Debidin, M. (2009). *A compendium of research and analysis on the offender assessment system (OASys) 2006–2009*. Ministry of Justice Research Series. https://www.cep-probation.org/wp-content/uploads/2018/10/Debdin-Compendium-of-OASys-research.pdf

Eisner, M. P., & Humphreys, D. (2012). Measuring conflict of interest in prevention and intervention research: A feasibility study. In T. Bliesener, A. Beelmann, & M. Stemmler (Eds.), *Antisocial behavior and crime: Contributions of developmental and evaluation research to prevention and intervention* (pp. 165–180). Hogrefe.

Esbec, E., & Fernández, O. (2003). Valoración de la peligrosidad criminal (Riesgo-Violencia) en Psicología forense: Instrumentos de evaluación y perspectivas. *Psicopatología Clínica Legal y Forense*, *3*(2), 65–90.

Feeley, M., & Simon, J. (1992). The new penology: Notes on the emerging strategy of corrections and its implications. *Criminology*, *449*, 449–474. http://scholarship.law.berkeley.edu/facpubs/718

Foucault, M. (1975). *Vigilar y castigar. Nacimiento de la prisión*. Siglo XXI Editores.

Folino, J. (2015). Predictive efficacy of violence risk assessment instruments in Latin-America. *The European Journal of Psychology Applied to Legal Context*, *7*, 51–58.

Garland, D. (1999). *Castigo y sociedad moderna: Un estudio de teoría social*. Siglo XXI editores.

González, V., Rojido, E., & Trajtenberg, N. (2015). Sistema penitenciario de Uruguay (1985–2014): Cambios, continuidades y desafíos. In G. Bardazano, A. Corti, N. Duffau, & N. Trajtenberg (Comps.), *Discutir la Cárcel, pensar la Sociedad. Contra el sentido común punitivo* (pp. 127–152). Ediciones Trilce.

Hollin, C. (2001). To treat or not to treat? An historical perspective. In C. Hollin (Ed.), *Offender assessment and treatment* (pp. 1–13). Wiley.

Nuance, A. (2018). *La perspectiva técnica en la privación de libertad. Breve Reseña*. Instituto Nacional de Rehabilitación, Subdirección Nacional Técnica.

Juanche, A., & Palummo, J. (2012). *Hacia una política de Estado en Privación de Libertad. Diálogo, recomendaciones y propuestas*. Servicio Paz y Justicia y OSJ.

Kroner, D. G., & Mills, J. F. (2001). The accuracy of five risk appraisal instruments in predicting institutional misconduct and new convictions. *Criminal Justice and Behavior*, *28*(4), 471–489. https://doi.org/10.1177/009385480102800405

McGuire, J., Bilby, C. A. L., Hatcher, R. M., Hollin, C. R., Hounsome, J., & Palmer, E. J. (2008). Evaluation of structured cognitive-behavioural treatment programmes in reducing criminal recidivism. *Journal of Experimental Criminology*, *4*(1), 21–40. https://doi.org/10.1007/s11292-007-9047-8

McNeill, F. (2006). A desistance paradigm for offender management. *Criminology and Criminal Justice*, *6*(1), 39–62.

McNeill, F. (2017). Las consecuencias colaterales del riesgo. In C. Trotter, G. McIvor, & F. McNeill (Eds.), *Beyond the risk paradigm in criminal justice* (pp. 143–157). Palgrave Macmillan.

Moore, R. (Ed.). (2015, December 3). *A compendium of research and analysis on the OASys.* https://assets.publishing.service.gov.uk/government/uploads/system/uploads/attachment_data/file/449357/research-analysis-offender-assessment-system.pdf

Morales, A., Pantoja, P. D., and Sánchez, M. (2018). *Una propuesta de modelo integral de reinserción social para infractores de la ley*. Fundación Paz Ciudadana. Centro de Estudios en Seguridad Ciudadana (CESC), Instituto de Asuntos Públicos, Universidad de Chile.

O'Malley, P. (2000). Risk societies and the government of crime. In M. Brown, & J. Pratt (Eds.), *Dangerous offenders: Punishment and social order* (pp. 17–34). Routledge.

Redondo, S. (2017). *Evaluación y tratamiento de delincuentes: Jóvenes y adultos*. Ediciones Pirámide.

Redondo, S., Sánchez-Meca, J., & Garrido, V. (2002). Los programas psicológicos con delincuentes y su efectividad: La situación europea. *Psicothema, 14*(1), 164–173.

Rivera Beiras, I. (2015). Actuarialismo penitenciario, su recepción en España. In Bardazano (Ed.), *Discutir la cárcel, pensar la sociedad: Contra el sentido común punitivo* (pp. 102–144). Ediciones Trilce.

Rivera Beiras, I. (2016). El actuarialismo penitenciario en España. In G. Anitua & R. Gual (Eds.), *Privación de libertad: Una violenta práctica punitiva* (pp. 133–155). Ediciones Didot.

Rojido, E., Trajtenberg, N., & Vigna, A. (2014). Problemas de integridad en programas de tratamiento: El caso del Centro Nacional de Rehabilitación. *Revista de Ciencias Sociales, 27*(34), 11–32.

Sosa Barón, S. (2021). Desafíos de la implementación del OASys en el Uruguay. *Revista Pensamiento Penal.* https://www.pensamientopenal.com.ar/doctrina/89634-desafios-implementacion-del-oasys-uruguay

Trajtenberg, N., & Sánchez de Ribera, O. (2019). *Programa de Control de la Agresión Sexual (PCAS): Evaluación de proceso y resultados clínicos en Unidad 4 Santiago Vázquez (COMCAR)*. Consejo Superior de Investigaciones Científicas y Facultad de Ciencias Sociales de la UdelaR, Instituto Nacional de Rehabilitación.

Velásquez, A. (2014). El origen del paradigma de riesgo. *Política Criminal, 9*(17), 58–117.

Vigna, A. (2021). *Funcionarios penitenciarios y ejercicio del poder: Rol ocupacional en un modelo en transición* [Tesis de Doctorado en Sociología, Facultad de Ciencias Sociales, UdelaR].

Vigna, A., & Juanche, A. (2022). The unfinished symphony: Progress and setbacks towards a rehabilitation policy in Uruguay. In M. Vanstone & Ph. Priestley (Eds.), *The Palgrave handbook of global rehabilitation and criminal justice* (pp. 651–666). Palgrave MacMillan.

Villagra, C. (2022). History and transformations of the model of rehabilitation in the criminal justice system in Chile. In M. Vanstone & Ph. Priestley (Eds.), *The Palgrave handbook of global rehabilitation and criminal justice* (pp. 71–88). Palgrave MacMillan.

Villagra, C., Espinoza, O., & Martínez, F. (2014). *La medición de la reincidencia y sus implicancias en la política criminal*. Centro de Estudios en Seguridad Ciudadana (CESC), Instituto de Asuntos Públicos, Universidad de Chile.

Vose, B. (2021). Conflict of interest. In J. Barnes & D. Forde (Eds.), *The encyclopedia of research methods in criminology and criminal justice* (pp. 233). Wiley-Blackwell. https://doi.org/10.1002/9781119111931.ch43

Ward, T., & Maruna, Sh. (2007). *Rehabilitation: Beyond the risk paradigm*. Routledge.

Warrick, D. (2023). Revisiting resistance to change and how to manage it: What has been learned and what organizations need to do. *Business Horizons, 66*(4) 433–441. https://doi.org/10.1016/j.bushor.2022.09.001

Chapter 7

The Inca's Two Bodies: The Prison Condition in Latin America

Libardo José Ariza and Fernando León Tamayo Arboleda

University of the Andes, Colombia

Abstract

In this chapter, we show how physical violence is a central part of the prison experience in Latin America. Such a violence is perceived both a legally admitted and forbidden practice. In this sense, corporal punishment appears not as an imperfection, but rather an ordinary element of punitive power in the region. This strange existence of corporal punishment as permitted and forbidden violence ends up by legitimizing the punishment of the inmates in their physical body and their existence as a subject of law. This juxtaposition places prisoners' bodies "betwixt and between" the natural world and the normative world of punishment. Thus, the life of prisoners is protected by law. Their indemnity is recognized, and their fundamental rights are guaranteed. However, at the same time, their lives are expendable.

Keywords: Prison; Latin America; violence; body; punishment; legal discourse

It seems like a sordid and strange tribute to the complex transplantation and cultural rootedness of prisons in Latin America the fact that Ecuador's main detention facility is named *El Inca*. The legacy of possibly the most fantastic Andean indigenous culture, the Inca empire is now inscribed on the entrance of one of the largest confinement centers in the region. Prison and colonization mix and mingle. Nowadays, the Inca not only remember a pre-colonial culture but also invoke penitentiary punishment with its ritualized forms of violence and exclusion.

This confusing mixture of the pre-colonial culture, the colonial past, its impact on the formation of contemporary post-colonial relations, and the adoption of European punitive modernity represented by a prison with an Amerindian name suggests two questions that contribute to an interpretation of the meaning of penal institutions from a southern perspective (Galleguillos, 2023; Sozzo, 2023). First, from a carceral anthropology perspective is an approach to the complex relationship between body and punishment as the core of the punitive experience in Latin America.

Exploring the meaning and scope of the prison condition in the global south is essential to define the traces that characterize the historical formation of punitive power beyond the history related by the philosophy of liberal criminal law (Beccaria, 2011), the political economy of punishment (Melossi & Pavarini, 1985; Rusche & Kirchheimer, 1984) or the narrative of modernization (Aguirre, 1996). In this sense, the question about the prison condition allows us to explore the subject that emerges from the interaction among discourses and symbolic and material practices deployed by the punitive powers in a given cultural space. In the heart of El Inca, the image of the Latin American prison condition is hidden in plain sight. Its heartbeat of anguish and violence also echoes in other Latin American prisons like *La Modelo* (Bogotá), *Roraima* (Brazil), *San Miguel* (Chile), and *Topo Chico* (Mexico), Unraveling such meanings is the purpose of this chapter.

The second question concerns a critique of what Garland called the problem of the body in modern state punishment (Garland, 2011), in order to reveal its deep roots in the Northern experience. Garland's approach emphasizes the always-problematic link between the body and punitive power. However, how he includes the triad of body, punitive power, and law in the occidental Global North implies a grammar of absence, failure, and incompleteness. Indeed, as we show below, it evokes classic discussions in legal anthropology about legal systems' (in)existence in non-European communities, one of the critical issues that once occupied the attention of classical legal pluralism (Merry, 1988). It also seems to evoke – albeit without explicitly analyzing it – a reading of the characterization of the "modern State" vis-á-vis "State's in the south" to point out that what could be called "failed punishment" occurs in these contexts as a correlate of "failed states." If it is assumed that what exists in Latin America are failed states, it could be said that this condition will also burden the punitive power they deploy.

As long as the model for understanding the development of punitive power and its institutions beyond the epistemological space of the global north continues to be the orthodoxy of the modern liberal history of punishment, the result will inevitably be the same. This restricted view will continue to see punitive power in Latin America as failed, unleashed in excesses, without clear legal boundaries, and plagued by violence. Incarceration will be understood only as a form of confinement (Birkbeck, 2011). Latin American punishment will thus always be the dark side of penal enlightenment. This narrow understanding of the punishment apparatus in the region prevents an adequate comprehension of the characteristics and social consequences of punitive power.

Of course, we are not saying that the "failure" of punitive power in Latin America is not a possible explanation, especially when measured in terms of its capacity to fulfill the purposes legally assigned to the penal apparatus. Nor are we intended to deny that the prisoner's body is the recipient of the state punishment or that there is overcrowding and a human rights crisis. Nevertheless, these indicators could describe the most diverse punitive systems in the global north and south. The question is how to qualify such a reality from the point of view of a culturally embedded analysis of penal institutions and, in particular, of prisons (Melossi, 2001; Sozzo, 2023).

In this chapter, we show how physical violence is a central part of the prison experience in the region, not in terms of its opposition to a legal discourse based on the abandonment of corporal punishment, but instead as a legally admitted practice and, at the same time, denied. In this sense, corporal punishment is not an imperfection, as Garland suggests, but rather a facet of punitive power that targets the subject in their abstract, legal, and material dimensions regarding the living body. This juxtaposition places prisoners' bodies "betwixt and between" the natural world and the normative world of punishment. In this space of suspension, the prison condition emerges within our context.

To do so, we will follow the next analytical route. In the first section, we present the broader debate within the liberal criminal discourse about the problem of violence and the human body in exercising punitive power. In this part, we show the discourses that criminal and constitutional law use to neutralize the problem of corporal punishment in prison. In the second part, we show that a characteristic of prison in Latin America is that the legal prohibition of corporal punishment coexists with the possibility of death, injury, and deprivation of essential goods as a central part of the prison experience.

Dying in Prison: The Inca's Two Bodies and the Liberal Discourse

On Friday, November 18, 2022, blood flowed through the corridors of El Inca (Mella, 2022). The chronicle has been craved in the recent prison history in Latin America. It tells how violence broke out after the attempt to transfer the head of "Los Lobos," one of the criminal gangs that governed the establishment, to La Roca, a maximum-security prison where hundreds of inmates belonging to the gang had already been transferred. The riot was unleashed with the virulence of an explosive device, and its horror left ten people dead. Riots had followed one after another in the previous months throughout the Ecuadorian prison system, leaving 450 dead in just one year. The relatively peaceful Ecuadorian prison system is now dominated by the specter of the massacre that haunts its establishments, as it has done in most Latin American countries for decades.

The El Inca massacre is not an isolated event in the bloody history of Latin American prisons. Similar events occurred in the Anísio Jobim prison in Manaus, in May 2019 and January 2017; as well as in Pará III, in Belém, in April 2018; and in Roraima, in Boa Vista, in January 2017 and October 2016. The total number of victims in these five massacres in Brazilian prisons exceeded two hundred people (Darke, 2018). The recent wave of prison violence in Brazil remembers the infamous massacre in the Carandiru prison in São Paulo in 1992, in which 111 prisoners were killed in a military police operation (Ferreira & Machado, 2012; Comisión Interamericana de Derechos Humanos, 2000). Such a violent scene is a feature shared by many Latin American countries (see Table 7.1).

Table 7.1. Deaths in Latin American Prison System.

Date	Prison	Country	Contexts	Deaths
18/11/2022	El Inca	Perú	Gang war. Riots	10
21/03/2020	La Modelo	Colombia	Riots	23
30/07/2019	Altamira	Brazil	Gang war. Riots	57
28/05/2019	Manaus. Complejo Penitenciario Anísio Jobim	Brazil	Gang war	57
6/01/2017	Roraima. Complejo Penitenciario	Brazil	Gang war.	33
2/01/2017	Manaus. Complejo Penitenciario Anísio Jobim	Brazil	Gang war. Riots	60
17/10/2016	Roraima. Complejo Penitenciario	Brazil	Gang war. Riots	10
27/11/1992	Retén de Catia	Venezuela	Riots	63
29/03/2018	Valencia. Comando General de la Policía de Carabobo	Venezuela	Riots	68
8/07/2010	Cárcel de Rocha	Uruguay	Conflagration	12
20/05/2001	Cárcel de Iquique	Chile	Conflagration	26
6/12/2010	Cárcel de San Miguel	Chile	Conflagration	81
15/02/2012	Granja Penal de Comayagua	Honduras	Conflagration	360
17/05/2014	San Pedro Sula	Honduras	Conflagration	104

Table 7.1. (*Continued*)

Date	Prison	Country	Contexts	Deaths
7/04/2013	El Porvernir	Honduras	Gang war. Riots	69
18/06/1986	El Frontón, San Juan de Lurigancho y Cárcel de Mujeres de Santa Bárbara	Perú	Riots	300
8/10/2017	Cadereyta	México	Riots	17
11/02/2016	Topo Chico	México	Gang war. Riots	49
02/19/2012	Centro de Readaptación Social (Cereso) de Apodaca	México	Riots	44

Source: Author's update from Ariza and Tamayo Arboleda (2021).

Statistics, which remain incomplete, on deaths and injuries in the region's prison systems show this bleak picture. In Venezuela, 3,664 inmates died violently, and 11,401 more were injured between 1999 and 2008 (Gracia, 2009). In Brazil, there are around 1,000 deaths of inmates per year (Sanhueza, 2015). In Argentina, 57% of the prison population reports having suffered different forms of physical and sexual violence (CELIV, 2014; Gual, 2019). In Chile, around 40 inmates die annually (Sanhueza, 2015), and in Honduras, 756 inmates died between 2006 and 2012 (Comisión Interamericana de Derechos Humanos, 2013).

Each event shows the special relationship between violence and the condemned's body in Latin America. In Latin American prisons, death is not, at least not exclusively, the effect of exercising power from above to "make the condemned die" (Foucault, 1995). This violence also comes from below, from the captives' society, which unleashes war in its quest for controlling the internal social order or during protests against the shameful conditions of confinement (Bergman & Fondevila, 2021). Prison punishment thus appears as the total, excessive, and borderless expression of the violence that destroys the condemned's body.

This typical violence of regional penitentiary systems seems invisible to the legal discourse. When liberal penal discourse questions contemporary forms of punishment, the narrative of humanizing punishment appears at the heart of the arguments (Ferrajoli, 2011; Hassemer, 1999). The – undoubtedly important – insistence of legal discourse on humanization contrasts with the brutality of prison systems. The legal narratives that understand punishment as a rational way of inflicting pain pale when confronted with the macabre side of the prison.

Liberal penal discourses start from a break in the moral history of punishment that could be traced back to Beccaria's text "On Crimes and Punishments" – published in 1764. According to Ferrajoli (2011), whose way of representing changes in the ways of punishment is widely extended in liberal criminal law studies, Europe before the French Revolution was characterized by the use of corporal punishment as a mechanism to reaffirm the sovereign's ability to control state violence and contribute to the expiation of the offender's soul through physical pain. Meanwhile, post-revolutionary Europe showed an abandonment of corporal punishment in response to the new conception of the human being as a subject of rights, the limitation of state powers by the people, and the rationalization of the State's use of punitive force.

Ferrajoli's narrative – with its simplicity, eurocentrism, and the romanticization of the academic and revolutionary movements of the time – shows how continental European and Latin American criminal legal discourse has understood modern penality. For criminal law, the reason for the existence of prisons is that it is more humane than the pre-modern forms of punishment that were responsible for martyring the body.

Although the causes of the reduction of corporal punishment cannot be explained, at least not exclusively, as the result of a process of humanization of punishment, as indicated by the liberal legal-criminal academy, it is possible to admit that this was a relevant part of the issue. Rusche and Kirchheimer's (1984) explanation, for example, of the disappearance of corporal punishment as a result of mutations in the labor market, as well as historical accounts of the parallel emergence of the factory and the prison (Melossi & Pavarini, 1985), pointed to this process of abandoning the body as the destination of state punitive power, in which legal forms adapted to this new configuration of the political economy of punishment (Simon, 2013). As Ignatieff (1978) points out in his description of the emergence of the penitentiary during the Industrial Revolution, pain and bodily suffering would take a back seat as an inevitable effect of a rational and humane punitive apparatus. Physical violence would not be part of the modern penitentiary project, either because of the existence of a process of humanization, or because of the emergence of a new political economy of punishment.

Although the substitution of corporal punishment can be related to different processes, two aspects seem difficult to deny: first, that the punishment of the body took a back seat, at least discursively, and second, that there was a change in terms of how punishment enforced violence. Regarding the first issue, although it is necessary to assume that prison can also be considered a physical affliction for those subjected to it, the liberal legal-criminal discourse explained prison violence as a more appropriate and benevolent way of punishing the body. The idea that punishment was humanized and criminal law worked as a limit to it served as a vehicle to move the problem of the body into the background by supplanting the idea of punishment as affliction with the discourse of the limitation of rights as the center of penalty (Foucault, 1995).

Regarding the second issue, the metaphor used by Foucault, which states that the emergence of the prison represented a substitution of the punishment of the body for that of the soul, is a simple way of understanding the problem of the replacement of how violence was exercised. The substitution of the object of penalty implies that "From being an art of unbearable sensations punishment has become an economy of suspended rights" (Foucault, 1995, p. 11). According to

Foucault, the vital issue of prison technology is that it executes less intense but more extensive violence on the condemned through a power that works both against them and through them. On the one hand, prison violence operates against the subject, forcing them to modify their behavior, subjecting them to a routine imposed on them, confining them to a closed space, and depriving them of the exercise of specific rights. On the other hand, it acts through the individual, reconfiguring his or her subjectivity and making him or her a voluntary part of the disciplinary machinery of social control. Such technical and disciplinary foundations have made "the prison seem the most immediate and civilized form of all penalties" (Foucault, 1995, p. 223).

Thus, replacing corporal punishment with imprisonment did not imply an abandonment of the punishment of the physical body but a redefinition of how punishment relates to it. It is precisely this tension that Garland (2011) denominates as the problem of the body in modern state punishment. For Garland, the neutralization of violence, which the legal discourse constructed to justify imprisonment, did not deny that this was an undesirable intervention on the body but rather the least violent of the various possible interventions.

In order to conjure up violence, the legal discourse affirms that prison reform is necessary to guarantee standards of quality of life and the fundamental rights of those imprisoned. In other words, the law recognizes the violence of the prison world and, through its narratives, reaffirms the need to transform it. Although this goal is undoubtedly a valuable ideal for states that continue to use prison as a form of punishment, the way the legal discourse poses the problem only neutralizes the suffering of the incarcerated.

The denial of pain while acknowledging its existence has been allowed through two legal figures in continental law countries. First, the constitutional law narrative that considers fundamental rights of those deprived of their liberty as directives that cannot be demanded directly and immediately but must be guaranteed to the greatest extent possible. This sacrifices the possibilities of legal defense against structural violence and also, indirectly, against various forms of daily violence allowed by the structural conditions of the penitentiary systems. Second, the legal doctrine that maintains that in addition to deprivation of liberty prisoners must endure "accidental" restrictions on their fundamental rights, legitimize structural violence to the body as an indefectible consequence of prison life.

Law and Death: The Prison Condition in Latin America

The reality of prison systems and their relationship with physical pain is relative and does not always correspond to that defended by liberal legal-criminal discourse. Moreover, one may say that the prison experience rarely is like the one described by such discourses. In the case of Latin American prison systems in recent decades, violent punishment of the body is not only present but a central part of the prison experience in the region. Although pain as a public spectacle certainly does not appear as one of the central aspects of the Latin American penalty, pain as a permanent structural factor is still part of the typical relationship between the body and the punitive systems mentioned above.

The physical suffering of bodies in the region's prisons cannot be considered simply as a normal part of the pains associated with disenfranchisement in the prison space (Sykes, 1958), but is much more widespread and brutal. In Latin America, the condemned's soul and body are punished equally, and the threat of death appears latently as a central part of the prison experience. Being in prison includes, then, the physical violence coming from different actors that manifests itself with the threat – and materialization – of death and injuries and the symbolic violence of a legal-criminal discourse that neutralizes the violent routine of prisons through the idea of punishment as a temporary loss of rights.

Much of the Global North analysis of the relationship between body and punishment has focused on the death penalty as its most precise and forceful expression (Sarat, 2001). Death by electrocution in the electric chair and lethal injection are the ultimate punitive practices, severing a person's existence in a secret and veiled ritual of execution where State's power over life is materialized. Sarat (2001) argues that a cultural analysis of the death penalty must go beyond the questions usually addressed in political and criminal debates to focus on how it expresses and constitutes the political community. In this sense, he argues, "Capital punishment is the ultimate assertion of righteous indignation, of power pretending to its own infallibility. By definition, it leaves no room for reversibility" (Sarat, 2001, p. 16). The death penalty symbolizes States' power to kill the irredeemable criminal, reaffirming through this legally ritualized act of violence the community's commitment to the rule of law. Through such a ritual, society's contempt for the criminal transmutes into a definitive and irreversible act of justice as revenge. In this act, revenge and crime are merged and confused and, as Fassin (2018) explains, therein lies the inevitability of suffering:

> The shift from an affective economy of the debt, in which the sentiments of vengeance were channeled through various forms of restitution and compensation, to a moral economy of punishment, in which committing an offense calls for a retribution supposed to redeem the offender, is the major fact to take into account when reflecting on the central place occupied by suffering in the act of punishing. (Fassin, 2018, p. 56)

The death penalty has been interpreted as a sacrificial ritual symbolizing the impossibility of redemption for the heinous offender, and State's power over life and total retribution (Harding, 2000; Smith, 2000). Despite the relevance of the death penalty as a manifestation of punitive power as a biopolitical exercise, this relationship can be grasped in other legally ritualized sacrifices. The rituals of sacrifice in exercising State's punitive power are neither limited to nor exhausted by the legally sanctioned death penalty. The relationship between punishment and sacrifice may be more subtle and present between the informal ritualization – neutralized by legal discourse – of violence in the Latin American penitentiary experience and the legal rejection of death.

Recent studies about the characterization of the prison experience in Latin America have pointed out the importance of understanding the relationship between the abstract dimension of the system of safeguards working as barriers against the excesses of punitive power and how prisoners' bodies appear on the stage of the regional punitive theater (Ariza & Tamayo, 2020). Thus, the problem of the physical body in modern state punishment would not arise from the inevitable contradiction between the system of safeguards and the undesirable corporeal dimension of punishment, as Garland (2011) argues: "The problem arises because the human body is the inescapable object of state punishment, even when it is emphatically declared that it should not be" (p. 768). Instead, the problem of the prisoner's body emerges because the prison machine, in its specific contexts of production and reproduction as a culturally embedded artifact, functions under a spatiotemporality whose inseparable mixture can produce a prisoner's death. Under the protection of constitutional law, the prison becomes a space where a legally ritualized sacrifice takes place on the immanent locus of law and the material and everyday reality of the prison world. Both the subject of rights and the body of the convicted person are sacrificed.

From this perspective, which is critical to understand the human and existential dimension of the prison condition, the prisoner's body is found in an uncertain space, protected and unprotected by law, abandoned to violence yet recognized as a subject of rights. Always waiting for a potential death, that could be found when a ritual of prison violence is unleashed. Of course, the dimension and scope of this ritual of death can vary significantly; it can be the death that results from a knife fight in a corridor, the assault of the *narco* who seeks to subvert the social hierarchy of prison society or the frenzy of bullets and fire of prison riots (Ariza & Tamayo, 2020). As Fassin (2017) points out,

> While violence between inmates is set in the context of relations between equals (in statutory terms, for of course length of time spent in the prison, physical strength, financial resources, and social networks are all sources of inequality), violence between inmates and staff is radically asymmetrical. (Fassin, 2017, p. 179)

The *sacrifice* of those deprived of their liberty is legally forbidden and accepted. That is one of the defining elements of their condition as prisoners, which deserves further explanation. In recent years, necropolitics has been used as a framework for understanding the prison experience in the region (Mbembe, 2011). From this perspective, and drawing on the broader narrative about sovereignty, the exercise of power that imprisonment entails has been characterized in the local context as an exercise of sovereignty aimed at killing and leaving the prisoner to die. As Bello and Parra state, prison must be understood "as a place where rights are suspended, and the bodies of prisoners are exposed to illness, suffering, abandonment, and murder, allowing us to trace a reading of this institution as another expression of necropolitics" (Bello & Parra, 2016, p. 368).

In the same way, De Dardel (2015) characterizes resistance to incarceration in Colombia as an arrangement of political strategies aimed at containing the *nuda vida* (bare life) within the region's prisons. Although these two analyses establish the prison question in the terrain of life, death, and power, that is, as a biopolitical and necropolitical exercise and point out the defining features of the penitentiary world in our context, they do not allow us to adequately understand the meaning that the threat of death poses for the prison condition, nor the relationship between legal forms, the abandonment toward death and the type of subject that emerges from this complex assemblage.

These difficulties are present due to two reasons. First, the characterization of prisoners' existence as a bare life assumes that they are in a place of non-right. Agamben himself indicates that prisoners' life cannot be understood as bare life because prison is not a space of exception. Instead, he points out,

> The camp – and not the prison – is the space that corresponds to this originary structure of the nomos. This is shown, among other things, by the fact that while prison law only constitutes a particular sphere of penal law and is not outside the normal order, the juridical constellation that guides the camp is (as we shall see) martial law and the state of siege. This is why it is not possible to inscribe the analysis of the camp in the trail opened by the works of Foucault, from Madness and Civilization to Discipline and Punish. As the absolute space of exception, the camp is topologically different from a simple space of confinement. (Agamben, 1998, p. 20)

Agamben makes this point because he considers that the normative legal frameworks surrounding the concentration camp and the prison are different in their links with normality insofar as penitentiary law is not outside the normal order while the legal constellation of the camp is the state of siege.

As a result of the relation of inclusion/exclusion of the living person in the abstract world of the legal system, with the political consequences that derive from this,

> [...] the realm of bare life-which is originally situated at the margins of the political order-gradually begins to coincide with the political realm, and exclusion and inclusion, outside and inside, *bios* and *zoe*, right and fact, enter into a zone of irreducible indistinction. (Agamben, 1998, p. 9)

The indistinction and confusion between the factual and the juridical world are vital to understanding the emergence of this special relationship between sovereign power and life. As Fitzpatrick states, "(t)he exceptional becomes normal, and what is extended is something other than the juridical, if not entirely the realm of the factual, at least a realm in which law cannot be distinguished from fact" (Fitzpatrick, 2015, p. 66). This relation of inclusion/exclusion supposes that the juridical existence of certain subjects is recognized as a condition for their simultaneous expulsion from the legal order. They are recognized and included for denying their existence through their juridical exclusion.

In this sense, Continental law includes prisoners within the legal world as their status is recognized through what is called the "special relationship of subjection." Such a relationship has two crucial elements. On the one hand, it creates a duty for the State to care over the physical and political life of prisoners. On the other hand, it allows the limitation of any right that should be controlled for guaranteeing order within prisons (Ariza & Romero, 2020). Such legal concept allows a wide discretion of penitentiary officers for limiting prisoners' rights.

Prison is outside and inside the constitution. The prisoner is not excluded from the legal order, but neither is fully integrated into it (Macana & Tamayo, 2023). The law protects prisoners by declaring the violation of their rights by the inhuman conditions of the Latin American prison system. However, it fails to protect prisoners while avoiding their acknowledgment as subjects of rights. In Agamben's (1998) words,

> According to the schema of the sovereign exception, law applies to him in no longer applying, and holds him in its ban in abandoning him outside itself. The open door destined only for him includes him in excluding him and excludes him in including him. And this is precisely the summit and the root of every law. (p. 50)

If Latin American prisons – despite their infamy – cannot be characterized in topological terms as a space of non-law, of the absence of legal safeguards, as Garland points out, neither can the subjects located there be automatically characterized as a manifestation of the nuda vida, as *homo sacer*. Indeed, if anything has characterized the regional penitentiary field in recent decades, it is its excessive juridification. Prisons are spaces dominated mainly by law and legal discourse. It is enough to review the enormous normative production that has attempted to limit State's punitive power and to create minimum rules for the treatment of prisoners (Ariza & Torres, 2019), as well as the enormous body of constitutional jurisprudence that shapes the content and scope of the rights of persons deprived of their liberty (Livingstone, 2000). These normative arrangements include the emergence of technical standards with which prisons must comply.

Of course, we do not mean to say that the prison world is a peaceful heaven, that there is no violence, nor that the rights of persons deprived of their liberty are respected. We want to show the complex relationship between a prison reality opposed to the law, and how the law legitimizes its existence. The law makes the inhuman prison conditions intelligible through juridical language when condemning its existence but also tolerates it by delaying the solution to the problem.

Between the prison imagined by legal discourses and the law's inability to govern prison, there is a ritual of legal sacrifice of the prisoners. Prisoners are suspended in a no-way-out situation of legal protection/non-protection. The law recognizes the violation of prisoners' rights and declares that, in the future, it will diminish their pain. However, it also legitimizes their suffering, putting them on a permanent wait for solutions. Thus, the prison condition in Latin America is a form of legal existence/non-existence that emerges in the spaces of exception that suspend the legal order by affirming prisoners' rights while denying their actual protection. The question, then, is not whether prisoners die – or could die – in prison but what the prisoners' possible death means for the legal order. Prisoners are, at the same time, recognized as subjects of protection and then abandoned to the possibility of their death. Such is the meaning of the prison condition in the region.

What legal discourse does to Latin American prisoners' condition is not just a matter of a gap between law in the books and law in practice, but a particular way of dominance allowed by how legal discourses have addressed the governance of prison. The liberal legal discourse not only fails to be a reality within Latin American prisons, but it presents itself as a form of blurring the problem of the particular violence in the region's penitentiary system and legitimizing prisoners' deaths within prisons. When the Latin American legal discourses recognize that prisoners' rights are being violated and that death is a possible outcome of prison experience but deny any legal protection to prisoners, such discourses end up admitting that extreme suffering or death is somehow legally accepted.

If we want to understand how prisoners' body is punished within the Latin American prison system and how prison condition is created in the region, it is critical to analyze how northern discourses of what punishment is – and should be – affect how Latin American countries address punishment. The liberal legal discourse has had an ambivalent role in the region, working both as a way of legal recognition and as a way for suspending prisoners' rights indefinitely, allowing their suffering and their death in collapsed penitentiary systems.

Conclusion

Physical punishment is a central aspect of the Latin American penitentiary experience. On the one hand, death, as an extreme manifestation of penitentiary violence, appears as a component of the always tense coexistence of prisoners, as well as a result of the dynamics of the penitentiary order, the intervention of the correctional officers, or the structural conditions of misery present in the penitentiary establishments. On the other hand, the harshness of living every day under violent relations, the threat of physical injury, and the subjection to subhuman conditions of confinement complement an experience in which the body is the primary target – though often incidental – of penal punishment.

These ways of punishing the condemned's bodies coexist with an abstract legal discourse that forbids interventions on their bodies, configuring a specific relationship between punishing practices and the body in the Latin American context. The body is the permanent object of punishment to the point of destruction and the object of protection of a legal discourse that fails to guarantee its indemnity. For the liberal legal-criminal and constitutional discourses, it would seem that reality exceeds the capacities of the State to provide attention to prisoners' rights. Attempts to reform the penitentiary system in the region, which recognizes the problems of the body and claims to be doing everything possible, within the legal framework, to reduce pain levels, seem to acknowledge this. However, the recognition of the violence to which the bodies of prisoners are placed in Latin America is followed by the inability to prevent the widespread violence in the region's prisons and the commitment to keep hundreds of thousands of people in prison in subhuman conditions.

The life of prisoners is protected by law. Their indemnity is recognized, and their fundamental rights are guaranteed – at least to the extent that arbitrary standards of prison life allow. However, at the same time, their lives are expendable. Their criminal actions force them, factually and legally, to endure certain levels of violence. Prisoners' obligation to endure violence blurs the line between acts like losing their rights to interact with the outside world and acts of violence like death.

Understanding the specificity of the prison condition in Latin America, its complex relationship with the social circumstances of inequality and violence, and with the penal and constitutional discourses that shape, legitimize, and seek to transform punishment in the region requires making a break with northern discourses about the meaning of the law, the body, and the punishment, which, in turn, will allow us to analyze the prison problem with new lenses. Such a task does not imply ignoring the violence and brutality of punishment in Latin America, but rather ceasing to restrict its analysis to its failure to conform to northern ideals of what punishment should be in order to try to unravel the conditions of the possibility of its existence and its effective transformation – or abolition – in the region.

References

Agamben, G. (1998). *Homo sacer. Sovereign power and bare life*. Stanford University Press.
Ariza, L. J., & Romero, E. D. R. (2020). ¿Tratamiento penitenciario a domicilio? El alcance de la Relación Especial de Sujeción en el régimen de domiciliarias en Colombia, Universitas 69.
Ariza, L. J., & Tamayo, A. F. L. (2020). El cuerpo de los condenados. Cárcel y violencia en América Latina. *Revista de Estudios Sociales*, 71(1), 83–95.
Ariza, L. J., & Tamayo Arboleda, F. L. (2021). El cuerpo de los condenados: cárcel y violencia en América Latina, *Estudios Sociales*, 73(1), 93–95.
Ariza, L. J., & Torres, G. M. (2019). Constitución y Cárcel. La judicialización del mundo penitenciario en Colombia. *Revista Direito e Práxis*, 10(1), 630–660.
Aguirre, C. (1996). The Lima penitentiary and the modernization of criminal justice in nineteenth-century Peru. In R. D. Salvatore & C. Aguirre (Eds.), *The birth of the penitentiary in Latin America* (pp. 72–108). University of Texas Press.
Beccaria, C. (2011). *De los delitos y de las penas*. Trotta.
Bello, R. J. A., & Parra, G. G. (2016). Cárceles de la muerte: necropolítica y sistema carcelario en Colombia. *Universitas Humanística*, 82, 368.
Bergman, M., & Fondevila, G. (2021). *Prisons and crime in Latin America*. Cambridge University Press.
Birkbeck, C. (2011). Imprisonment and internment: Comparing penal institutions North and South. *Punishment & Society*, 13(3), 307–332.

CELIV-Centro de Estudios Latinoamericanos sobre Inseguridad y Violencia. (2014). *Niveles de violencia y conducta dentro del penal. Delito, marginalidad y desempeño institucional en Argentina: Resultados de la encuesta de presos condenados.* Universidad de Tres de Febrero.
Comisión Interamericana de Derechos Humanos. (2000). *Informe Nº 34/00, Caso 11.291 Carandirú- Brasil.* 13 de abril de 2000.
Comisión Interamericana de Derechos Humanos. (2013). *Informe de la Comisión Interamericana de Derechos Humanos sobre la situación de las personas privadas de la libertad en Honduras.* 18 de marzo de 2013.
Darke, S. (2018). *Conviviality and survival. Co-producing Brazilian prison order.* Palgrave Macmillan.
de Dardel, J. (2015). "Resistiendo la "nuda vida": los prisioneros como agentes en la era de la Nueva Cultura Carcelaria en Colombia". *Crítica Penal y Poder, 8,* 47–65.
Fassin, D. (2017). *Prison worlds. An ethnography of the carceral condition.* Polity Press.
Fassin, D. (2018). *The will to punish.* Oxford University Press.
Fitzpatrick, P. (2015). *Homo Sacer* and the Insistence of Law. In B. Moran & C. Salzani (Eds.), *Towards the critique of violence* (pp. 49–73). Bloomsbury Press.
Ferrajoli, L. (2011). *Derecho y razón: teoría del garantismo penal.* Trotta.
Ferreira, L., & Machado, M. (2012). Massacre do Carandiru: vinte anos sem responsabilizaçã. *Novos estud. – CEBRAP, 31*(3), 5–29.
Foucault, M. (1995). *Discipline and punish.* Vintage Books.
Galleguillos, S. (2023, November 16). How southern is Southern criminology in Latin America? *Theoretical Criminology,* Online First.
Garland, D. (2011). The problem of the body in modern state punishment. *Social Research 78*(3), 767–798.
Gracia, M. M. (2009). *Situación actual de los derechos humanos en las cárceles de Venezuela.* Instituto Latinoamericano de Investigaciones Sociales.
Gual, R. (2019). La prisión irresistible. Muertes por autoagresión bajo custodia penitenciaria en Argentina. *Revista de Ciencias Sociales, 32*(45), 91–118.
Harding, R. M. (2000). Capital punishment as human sacrifice: A societal ritual as depicted in George Elito's Adam Bede. *Buffalo Law Review, 48,* 175–297.
Hassemer, W. (1999). *Persona, mundo, responsabilidad.* Temis.
Ignatieff, M. (1978). *A just measure of pain: The penitentiary in the industrial revolution, 1750–1850.* Pantheon Books.
Livingstone, S. (2000). Prisoners' rights in the context of the European convention on human rights. *Punishment & Society, 2,* 309–324.
Macana, N., & Tamayo Arboleda, F. L. (2023). Vidas prescindibles: resistencia y derecho en las cárceles colombianas. *Dikaion, 32*(1), 1–32.
Melossi, D. (2001). The cultural embeddedness of social control: Reflections on the comparison of Italian and North-American cultures concerning punishment. *Theoretical Criminology, 5*(4), 403–424.
Mella, C. (2022, November 18). *Un traslado de presos deja 10 muertos en una cárcel de Ecuador.* El País. https://elpais.com/internacional/2022-11-19/un-traslado-de-presos-deja-10-muertos-en-una-carcel-de-ecuador.html
Mbembe, A. (2011). *Necropolítica.* Melusina.
Melossi, D., & Pavarini, M. (1985). *Cárcel y fábrica. Los orígenes del sistema penitenciario (siglos XVI–XIX).* Siglo XXI.
Merry, S. E. (1988). Legal pluralism. *Law & Society Review, 22*(5), 869–896.
Parra Gallego, G., & Bello Ramírez, J. A. (2016). Cárceles de la muerte: necropolítica y sistema carcelario en Colombia. *Universitas Humanística, 82,* 365–391.
Rusche, G., & Kirchheimer, O. (1984). *Pena y estructura social.* Temis.
Sanhueza, G. E. (2015). Victimización física entre internos en cárceles chilenas: una aproximación. *Revista Trabajo Social, 88,* 61–73.

Sarat, A. (2001). *When the state kills. Capital punishment and the American condition.* Princeton University Press.

Simon, J. (2013). Punishment and the political technologies of the body. In J. Simon & R. Sparks (Eds.), *The sage handbook of punishment and society* (pp. 60–89). Sage.

Smith, B. K. (2000). Capital punishment and human sacrifice. *Journal of the American Academy of Religion, 68,* 3–25.

Sozzo, M. (2023). Reading penalty from the periphery. *Theoretical Criminology, 27*(4), 660–675.

Sykes, G. (1958). *The society of captives.* Princeton University Press.

Section 3

Theoretical Exchanges

Chapter 8

Actuarial and Managerial Justice: Theoretical and Empirical Impacts on Latin-American Criminological Realm

Mariano Sicardi[a] and Claudio González Guarda[b]

[a]*National University of José C. Paz, Argentina*
[b]*University of Chile, Chile*

Abstract

This chapter aims to trace how the theoretical frameworks of actuarialism and managerialism have been slowly introduced into the Latin–American scientific debate, focusing on the Argentinian and Chilean examples. With this objective in mind, we explore the journey of these theories in our region focusing on the work. Additionally, we address other academic contributions that highlight "actuarial techniques" of risk as central features to analyze contemporary penalty, policing tactics, or criminal court outcomes and practices (Hannah-Moffat, 2013a, 2013b; Harcourt, 2007; Marutto & Hannah-Moffat, 2006), even overlapping concepts like actuarialism and managerialism (Barker, 2009; Kohler-Hausmann, 2018). Subsequently, we describe the acclimation of these theories in Argentina and Chile, characterized for a limited impact on the scientific debate. We suggest that the main reason for this little impact is the different stages of the criminal justice system between Global North and Global South countries. While in the first one, actuarialism and managerialism were born to explain especially the field of risk analysis, and secondarily, the role of the new public management; in the case of Latin America, managerialism has been observed through the criminal justice system reform developed in the last three decades. This observation has focused especially on some

---

Punishment in Latin America: Explorations from the Margins, 163–181
Copyright © 2025 by Mariano Sicardi and Claudio González Guarda
Published under exclusive licence by Emerald Publishing Limited
doi:10.1108/978-1-83797-328-620241009

organizational transformations and, for this reason, the analysis about actuarialism and risk assessment have been marginals. We concluded that although the influence of the literature about actuarialism and managerialism from the Global North in Latin–American is real, it is not possible to extrapolate all its elements to the penal systems in the region.

Keywords: Actuarialism; managerialism; criminal justice system; Latin America; punishment; criminal justice

Introduction

In the first edition of the Dictionary of Criminology, McLaughlin (2001a, p. 5) defines actuarialism as risk assessment techniques that underpin correctional policies and are closely related to new penology ideas, a term coined by Feeley and Simon (1992). In another entry, McLaughlin (2001b, p. 169) characterizes managerialism as a "set of techniques and practices which aim to fracture and realign relations of power within the criminal justice system in order to transform the structures and reorganize the processes for both funding and delivering 'criminal justice.'"[1]

Despite McLaughlin's distinction between the two concepts, criminal justice system scholars overlap them and use them as an interchangeable ideas, considering actuarialism as a general trend and managerialism as a specific one or, as McLaughlin conceives, two different processes and practices within the criminal justice system. Cohen (1994), for instance, suggests that the most influential variant of managerialism is the increasing trend to population control, framed by an actuarial regime where "risks are calculated by statistical probability rather than referring to an actual person" (pp. 72–73). Recently, Kohler-Hausmann (2018) argues that New York City's criminal courts in the era of Broken Windows shifted from an *adjudicative model of criminal law* administration to a *managerial* one, where, in a similar way as Feeley and Simon described,

> the practical orientation of criminal court actors and their regular operations are largely organized around the supervision and regulation of the population that flows through misdemeanor courts … the vision of criminal law's social control [in this model] is to sort and regulate people over time. (p. 61)

---

[1] A previous version of this chapter was presented at the virtual workshop "Punishment in Global Peripheries: Contemporary Changes and Historical Continuities" held in April 2021, and organized by the National University of Litoral and Oxford University. The authors want to thank all attendees for their insightful comments and observations, especially to Tim Newburn, Máximo Sozzo, and Paul Hathazy.

Barker (2009) argues that, during the 1970s, New York City became a sort of precursor in new penology and actuarial justice, because the

> managerial penal regime entailed expert-driven policies and practices that sought to regulate and minimize collective risk in the most cost-effective way to preserve limited sources. With an epidemiological model of crime, state officials proposed and carried out policies designed to identify and classify the most threatening risks to public health and isolate and contain those risks. (p. 127)

Initially, these concepts were debated within the Global North. Thereby, the Anglo-Saxon literature established a linkage between actuarial and managerial ideas, where the latter focuses on making the criminal justice system as a whole more cost-effective, efficient, and publicly accountable, while the other refers to risk assessment tools and management of a group of populations to achieve better outcomes.

On the other hand, Brandariz García argues that managerialism, as a global trend in public policy and rooted in New Public Management (NPM), was a driving force in the development of actuarialism. His analysis suggests a strong linkage between them, and the embeddedness of actuarialism in the penal realm cannot be understood without considering a raising advanced liberal governmentality, one of which main features are the diffusion of managerialism in public administration. Specifically, *managerialism* is based on the private business organization that penetrated the criminal justice system, reshaping the functions and practices of police, criminal courts, and prisons (Brandariz García, 2015, pp.120–121, 2016, pp. 111–130).

The impact of this canonic literature in Latin America is very slow. Therefore, this chapter aims to trace how the actuarial and managerial theoretical frameworks have been introduced within the Latin–American scientific debate, trying to understand their operation in our particular cultural context (Melossi et al., 2011, pp. 11–12). This chapter tries to describe both actuarial and managerial theoretical developments and its roads in the Global North, how it travel to the Global South scholarship in crime control and criminal justice, and trace the paths that it took, not only to contrast them but also to map their theoretical and empirical roots.

The travels of criminal questions[2] to Latin America could be traced in criminological theories, crime preventions programs (Sozzo, 2006, 2007a, 2011), or even the introduction of new legislation, practices, or discourses within the criminal justice system (for the introduction of plea bargaining in Argentina, see Langer,

---

[2]Although this concept could not be frequent in the Global North, especially in Anglo-Saxon scholars (Melossi et al., 2011, pp. 1–3), we follow Pitch's idea of *criminal question* as an area constituted by actions, institutions, politics, and discourses with flexible boundaries (Pitch, 2003, p. 100).

2004, 2019, 2020; for new practices or discourses within the criminal courts and its administration, see González Guarda, 2018).

As we will show, the actuarial ideas deployed in our scenarios, due to the rapid translation of Feeley and Simon's (1992) paper *The New Penology* in 1995, were mediated by local adaptations, like the Argentinian example shows where actuarialism was used to understand efficiency in the criminal justice system, marginalizing risk assessment categories. The criminal justice reform processes in Latin America had different backgrounds; transition to democracy, peace processes, or broader public institutions reforms are part of it (see Langer, 2007, pp. 627–659). The latter represents a general trend in Latin America since the 1980s, where state reforms intended to improve and modernize public institutions through management reforms (Ramírez Brouchoud, 2009; Ramos & Milanesi, 2018, pp. 3–7). In this sense, we will focus only on two scenarios Chile and Argentina, not only because of its geographical proximity but also because of its temporal nearness in transition to democracy and neoliberal state reforms.

Del lado de allá: Global North and New Trends in Crime Control: From Actuarialism to Managerialism

Bernard Harcourt and Ernest Burguess (1928) already considered that "predictability is feasible," introducing actuarial tools into the penal realm. Within the United States, the actuarial boost was part of punishment individualization, rooted in continental Europe with Salles' book – *L'individualitasion de la peine* – released in 1898 and presented at a conference in Chicago in 1909. Nevertheless, the actuarial gaze would be more accepted in the last quarter of the 20th century, where even criminal records turned into a fundamental factor for the success/failure prediction of certain institutes such as probation or parole (Harcourt, 2013, pp. 41–54).

Several years after Burguess' work, Malcolm Feeley and Jonathan Simon wrote two milestone papers about new paths in punishment and the criminal justice system, where risk and probability are core features. Feeley and Simon argue that the emergence of a new type of language in the criminal law and criminological realms is moving forward to actuarial consideration of aggregates and techniques to identify, classify, and manage groups labeled as dangerous. In other words, these changes represent *new penology* and involve shifts in three directions: (1) the emergence of new discourses, where the language of risk and probability increasingly replaces previous discourses of clinical diagnosis and retributive judgment; (2) the formation of new objectives in a *systemic* way because of the increasing primacy is given to the efficient control of internal processes in place of the traditional objectives of rehabilitation and crime control; (3) deployment of new techniques that target offenders as an aggregate in place of traditional techniques for individualizing (Feeley & Simon, 1992, p. 450). In a later paper, Feeley and Simon went more deeply into the actuarial feature of the new penology by tracing new practices within the criminal justice system and its intellectual origins. The new practices imply incapacitation – and its intensified element, *selective* incapacitation[3] – as the predominant model of punishment and the management-through-custody of dangerous segments of the population, pre-trial detention decisions that abandon individual basis and operates through aggregate effects, and drug courier profiling in airports. On the other hand, Feeley and Simon (1994) argue that its intellectual origins are rooted in tort law, law and economics narratives, and the application of operations research techniques and approaches that conceive the criminal process as a "system" for purposes of policy analysis, management and integrated goals assigned (pp. 174–190).[4] Later, in a paper entitled *The Forms and Limits of New Penology*, Simon and Feeley (2003, pp. 105–108) argue that new penology failed in providing a crime control narrative, nor providing satisfying cultural representations of crime and control to join in public discourse. The authors nuanced their argument because they

> did not claim, or mean to claim, that [the concepts of new penology and "actuarial justice" were] wholly new or that it had become or even a major paradigm in contemporary criminology. (Simon & Feeley, 2003, p. 77)

The emergence of this new penology and the *actuarial* ideas within the criminal justice system was nuanced by a group of scholars, both theoretically and empirically (see Hannah-Moffat, 2013a, p. 134). Garland argues that the *apparatus* of penal practice is not experiencing any major change of form, although those changes may occur slowly and face a great deal of resistance by its professional groups; moreover, even if Feely and Simon made a valuable contribution, the actuarial ideas are not novel or as extensive as they suggest because "a focus upon the differential risks posed by classes and categories, a notion of criminality as an aggregate phenomenon, and a concern to manage populations were all characteristics of the eugenics movement at the turn of the century, a movement that influenced both criminological discourse and penal policy at that time" (Garland, 2003, p. 65). So, the shifts that occurred over the last quarter of the 20th century may not be reduced to one process or logic due to the coexistence

---

[3]Selective incapacitation is a key element for actuarial penalty. According to Feeley and Simon (1994), "this approach proposes a sentencing scheme in which lengths of sentence depend not upon the nature of the criminal offence or upon an assessment of the character of the offender, but upon risk profiles. Its objects are to identify high-risk offender and to maintain long-term control over them while investing in shorter terms and less intrusive control and surveillance over lower risk offenders" (p. 175).
[4]The concepts related to the emergence of a new penology and actuarial techniques can be traced both on Feeley's and Simon's previous works. Simon already analyzed the role of *actuarial techniques* within legal discourse (1988) or probation in California (1993). Moreover, the key feature of actuarialism for Simon – management and control of a group or population – was inspired by Foucault et al. (2017, p. 17). Feeley, on the other hand, was influenced by tort law and Guido Calabresi's book, *The Cost of Accident* (Feeley, 2010, pp. 43–58, 2016). About the "history" of the Feeley and Simon papers, see Zysman and Sicardi (2019).

of *new penology* of risk assessment and vindictive *old penology* (Garland, 2005, p. 22; for a critical distinction between Garland and Feeley and Simon's work, see Zedner, 2002, pp. 354–358).

Other scholars highlight the role of bureaucratic entities and criminal justice practitioners as part of the limits of actuarial trends. Cavadino and Diggan (2006, pp. 7–8) suggest that all these developments are facets of a continuing process of modernization in line with Weber's analysis related to the development of bureaucracy and legal authority as concomitant with economic change and social modernization, rather than a postmodern penalty. Cheliotis (2006) affirms the importance of considering how "criminal justice professionals oppose subordination to what may be seen as mechanistic logics and practices of governmental power" (p. 321).

Empirical research based on the new penology's framework suggests that those changes in penal policy may not be present at the ground level due to resistance from front-line actors or community-based oppositions. Lynch conducted an ethnography study in a California Department of Corrections parole field office, where she concluded that

> while some of the elements of the new penology model suggested by Feeley and Simon ... continue to flourish at the state and regional management level of parole, the model has not trickled down in a straight and direct path to the front lines, at least in this local site of the agency .... Further, agents in the field actively fought those aspects of the job that pushed toward the model of aggregate risk management suggested by the "new penology." (Lynch, 1998, pp. 861–862)

Bayens et al. (1998, p. 58) conducted research to test new penology claims with a group of officers of intensive supervised probation, and their findings suggest that new penology is more rhetoric than reality. Miller (2001), on the other hand, argues that communities' bonds and power can mitigate the shifts toward actuarial techniques.

Actuarial techniques can take another path as well. Harcourt (2007) narrowed actuarial methods in the criminal justice system "to the use of statistical predictions about the criminality of groups or group traits to determine criminal justice outcomes for particular individuals within those groups" (p. 17). For Harcourt, the distinct feature of actuarial methods is the reliance on statistical correlations, not only on probabilities.[5] Moreover, recent scholarship demonstrated the role of actuarial techniques within the criminal justice system, which are related to

---

[5]Harcourt does not reject actuarial methods at all. In fact, as they act in both policing and sentencing contexts, he suggests that its utilization could be possible only when we can assure that they will achieve law enforcement without imposing undue burden on the profiled groups and without distorting our conceptions of just punishment.

the use of risk assessment tools or techniques – by practitioners and their discretionary decision-making process or assembling other assessment tools (Hannah-Moffat, 2013a, 2013b; Hannah-Moffat & Maurutto, 2006; Hannah-Moffat et al., 2009; Rothschild-Elyassi et al., 2019, pp. 202–203).

The crisis and declination of the welfare state, during the 1970s and 1980s, deployed new trends around public administration in the Global North. The effects of these ideas could be seen in several countries, but they were clearer in the British and US contexts. However, we will suggest that the novel ideas that erode welfare state institutions are clearer in the British context, as its roads to the criminal justice system.

Due to the effects of Thatcher's administration on British society and welfare institutions, its scholars noted the emergency of *managerialism*[6] as a new trend within the public sector. This movement can be seen as an *import* of ideas and concepts from the private sector such as target setting, and performance indicators, among others (Garland, 2016, p. 109). Specifically, the new public management aim is to reshape public bureaucracies, by using management methods from private enterprises and maximize outcomes (Laval & Dardot, 2013, pp. 292–305). Hood argues that the New Public Management (NPM) rise could be linked with four other administrative *megatrends*: (1) attempts to slow down or reverse government growth; (2) shift toward privatization and quasi-privatization and away from core government institutions; (3) development of automation; (4) development of a more international agenda (Hood, 1991, p. 3; for typical features of NPM, see Clarke et al., 2000, p. 6).

Although the UK's NPM incursions on public agencies had different paces, the criminal justice system was the target of a three-pronged strategy around productivity, cost-efficiency, and consumerism (Raine & Willson, 1997, pp. 82–83). Pratt (2007, p. 133) suggests that these methods attempted to make the criminal justice system not only more cost-effective but also efficient and publicly accountable.

Certainly, managerialism introduced several changes within the criminal justice system. For example, the elements of NPM can be seen in policing, with the emergence of performance and quantitative measurement of police activities (Newburn, 2008, p. 103), new types of leadership (Golding & Savage, 2008), and marketization, which implies "the drive to improve cost efficiency and performance effectiveness via the imposition of market disciplines on the police service" (Jones, 2008, p. 706).

---

[6]In this chapter, we acknowledge the distinction between *managerialization* and *managerialism*, presented by Clarke et al. (2000). According to these authors, *managerialization* refers changes to the ways in which other organizational actors are expected to think and behave, how relationships between different organizations are understood and coordinated, and how social policy, politics and service provision are understood. Instead, *managerialism* defines a set of expectations, values and beliefs that works "as a normative system concerning what counts as valuable knowledge, who knows it, and who is empowered to act in what ways as a consequence" (Clarke et al., 2000, p. 9).

In criminal courts, the managerial *shift* not only adopted performance goals but also connected efficiency with the implementation of rapid trial-avoiding conviction mechanisms[7] to thwart unnecessary economic and human resources costs and time reduction as well (Jones, 1993; Raine, 2005; Raine & Willson, 1995). Jordanoska (2017) suggests that the introduction (and expansion) of managerial practices within courtrooms – at least for complex fraud trials – has a contradictory relationship with adversarialism. Managerialism was present in British prison reforms as well (Carlen, 2002), and even merged with new penology ideas and different shades of managerial phases (Liebling & Crewe, 2013).

The theoretical and empirical claims of actuarialism and managerialism in the criminological fields have both common and distinctive features as well. Although they have different approaches and starting points, both narratives converge in the importance of efficiency and effectiveness for the criminal justice systems; however, while actuarialism relies on risk assessment tools, managerialism does it on targets and performance indicators. In the next section, we will discuss deeper these implications and how they were incorporated into the Latin-American criminological realm.

Del lado de acá: Actuarialism and Managerialism in Argentina and Chile

Southern perspectives emerge as a novel trend in the criminological realm. Prompted by a group of scholars that try to introduce new insights within the studies on the criminal question, one of its major claims relies on Connell's idea of *metropolitan thinking*, by which Southern research usually is conducted applying Northern theories of crime, punishment, or policing erasing space, geopolitical and social differences (Carrington et al., 2016, 2018, p. 4). Specifically, Southern criminology

> seeks to introduce a perspective based on the analysis of crime and justice in the global South and of the historical and contemporary relationships linking South and North that have been constitutive of forms of life and thought in both, but which have been obscured by the metropolitan hegemony over criminological knowledge. (Carrington et al., 2018, p. 11)

In relation to this, we will address the travels of actuarial and managerial ideas in Argentina and Chile's criminological realm by using the notions of translations and metamorphosis, developed by Sozzo (2006). Hence, we will suggest that travels of actuarial and managerial theoretical frameworks from the Global North to

---

[7]Despite the specificity of UK's context, we prefer to follow Langer's concept of *trial-avoiding conviction mechanism*, a procedural mechanism that enables reaching a criminal conviction without a trial, including plea bargaining or similar (Langer, 2019, 2020).

our contexts comprise either criminological adoption, rejection, or complementation of ideas and concepts (Sozzo, 2006, pp. 380–381).

In this section, we will address the uses of actuarial and managerial ideas in Latin–American scholarship, and bring into account how they adopt them to inquire into criminal justice studies.[8] Specifically, we will challenge these notions to elucidate whether actuarialism could exist without managerialism or managerialistic theories could be deployed in the absence of actuarial tools; we suggest that the travels of these ideas can be schematized as follows: *pure-actuarial* and *pure-managerial*, which implies the adoption of actuarial/managerial ideas from the Global North in the Global South context, more specifically in Latin America; *actuarial-managerial* by which authors merge one or more features of both managerial and actuarial theories within Latin America criminal justice systems; and *adapted-actuarialism*, that implies the complementation of ideas and concepts from the Global North to the specific features in Latin America.

In Argentina, some authors framed their research through the actuarial lens, albeit with different approaches. Muñiz Oller (2019a, 2019b) drew up her research on policing discourses in the cities of Barcelona (Spain) and Mar del Plata (Argentina), in a merge between actuarial and managerial techniques, where risk assessment plays a key role in situational crime prevention programs, urban segregation and management of risk population groups.

The theoretical frameworks designed by Gutiérrez (2014a) probably reflect the shifts – and travels – from "adapted-actuarialism" to "pure-managerial" ideas to understand the Argentinian criminal courts' reforms waves from the mid-1990s to the present. One of the major claims in Gutierrez's work is that criminal procedure reform toward adversarial systems allows the emergence of risk assessment as a nuclear part of the criminal process. However, the presence of risk assessment tools relies on a displacement of the procedural power from the judge to the victims and defendants. In this idea, the juicio abreviado[9] emerges as an example of actuarial ideas, but the risk is not related to aggregates or populations, instead, it links risk to the outcome and the possibility that the defendants can control the type and amount of the disposition, combined with a series of transformations based on efficiency and cost-benefit logics, close to managerial approaches. In other works, Gutiérrez (2014b, 2016) seems to abandon the idea of actuarial deployment within the Argentinian criminal justice system, especially courts, and move toward penal managerial ideas – in its pure way – where efficiency, celerity, and management techniques play a central role in his object of inquiry.

Ganón (2007) describes the criminal justice reform in the Province of Buenos Aires and suggests that the efficiency narratives and key performance indicators

---

[8] The paper written by Malcolm Feeley and Jonathan Simon, *The New Penology*, was rapidly translated to Spanish by Prof. Máximo Sozzo and published in the Revista Delito y Sociedad in 1995. Nor *Actuarial Justice* or *The forms and limits of the new penology* was translated into Spanish.

[9] Juicio abreviado is the equivalent to plea bargaining in Argentinian criminal procedure codes (Langer, 2004).

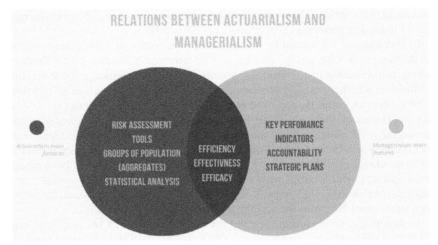

Fig. 8.1. Relationship Between Actuarial and Managerial Techniques.

are related to actuarial ideas of faster dispositions of convictions with lower cost. Castorina (2014), in a similar way, suggests a strong relationship between actuarialism and juicio abreviado in Mar del Plata's criminal courts, a coastal city in the Province of Buenos Aires. Anitua, differently, argues that juicio abreviado emerges as an actuarial technique that would improve efficiency (2001, 2017, pp. 143–170), while organizational reforms such as the Province of Buenos Aires' example are framed within managerialism (2017, pp. 141, 174, 2020, p. 236). Hence, while Ganón and Castorina can be ascribed to what we call adapted-actuarialism ideas, Anitua fits better in the actuarial-managerial group, where actuarialism and managerialism merge in the same context with a different course of action.

Despite the amount of criminological literature framed as actuarial, other research can be classified as framed by *pure managerial*. Ciocchini (2014) shows that, in the Province of Buenos Aires, the criminal justice reform movement took a managerial direction in relation to the problem of court delay, while Sicardi (2020) argues that managerialism is emerging in the District Attorney Office for the City of Buenos Aires and its prosecutors.

Since the transition to democracy in Latin America, Chile has represented the most radical experience in the criminal justice system reform, especially in criminal court organizations (Hersant, 2017, p. 446). Several scholars showed the presence of new public management within criminal justice reform and the tensions between its aims and due process rights (see, e.g., Jiménez et al., 2014, p. 256). Specifically, González Guarda (2015, 2016, 2018) framed his research on criminal court organizational reforms in Chile and Costa Rica through managerial reforms in Latin America. Empirical research suggests that actuarial techniques were deployed in crime control over youth (Chesta Saffiro & Alarcón Bañares,

2018) while policing and crime control discourses are rooted in both managerial and actuarial approaches (Isla, 2017).

Both managerial and actuarial discourses, and narratives, traveled to the Global South but acquired different interpretations. These could be seen, for example, in the metamorphosis of the actuarial approaches to criminal court disposition and plea bargaining in Argentina.

However, as we have shown in Fig. 8.1, actuarialism and managerialism have some common features. Represented by a Venn diagram, efficiency and effectiveness are located at the intersection of two sets.

However, there is not a lineal linkage between procedural reforms to achieve efficacy, efficiency, and effectiveness and the criminal justice system itself. For example, despite the introduction of *juicio abreviado*, the lack of transparency and inefficiency is a common feature among the different criminal courts in Argentina (Binder, 2008). On the other hand, actuarial techniques in policing for some local context scenarios in Argentina seem to collide with the empirical research that highlighted routinary – frequently violent – actions in front-line police officers (Bover & Chaves, 2011, pp. 132–133; Bover, 2019, p. 48), very far of the idea of targeting population as aggregates. The presence of a mixed economy of punishment also clashes with the idea of incapacitation and selective incapacitation as a technique to imprison targeted populations (Sozzo, 2007b, 2009).

Conclusion

The progressive penetration of actuarialism in the penal realm was part of the broader spread of new public management ideas in public institutions and public policies (Brandariz García, 2014b, p. 58), and Latin America was not the exception, especially the criminal justice system (Carvajal Martínez & Guzmán Rincón, 2017; Dezalay & Garth, 2005; Guzmán Rincón, 2011, 2013, pp. 88–99; Martínez Rangel & Soto Reyes Garmendia, 2012).

Argentina and Chile share a common history associated with the spread of neoliberal policies during the 1970s and 1980s by their dictatorships (see, e.g., Klein, 2016, pp. 109–136). However, despite those commonalities, the neoliberal trajectories – in broader terms – diverged; the Chilean case shows that neoliberalism got a deeper penetration than Argentina. In the 1990s, Chilean market reforms had already experienced almost a decade of adaptation, and their social costs were effectively suppressed. In Argentina, on the contrary, marketization was being freshly negotiated between Menem's Peronist administration, unconvinced industrialists, and a strong union movement, so the proposed "adjustments" met with group resistance. Despite these efforts, neoliberal ideas never reached the Chilean levels of deepness, and they were diminished after the 2001 crisis. As for the market and economic orientations, the discursive and symbolic level of neoliberalism related to management is less prominent in Argentinian public institutions (Undurraga, 2014, p. 20, 2015, pp. 269–270, 294).

As neoliberal policies, crime control strategies deployed under those ideas followed the same paths. In other words, Argentina and Chile share a similar pace on their roads to neoliberalism and transitions to democracy, albeit each one took a particular punitive model in crime control strategies (Hathazy, 2013, pp. 13–16, 2016a, 2016b, p. 189), not related to Wacquant's (2010a, 2010b, pp. 211–214) neoliberal penalty thesis (Sozzo, 2018, pp. 674–678; Willenman, 2020; for the Colombian case, see Iturralde, 2019, pp. 484–485). Hence, we argue that actuarial and managerial frameworks in these scenarios were not a mere translation but mediated through national and culturally specific features (Melossi, 2012, p. 418; O'Malley, 2006, p. 229). With a few exceptions that we showed before regarding penal managerialism in specific criminal courts or district attorney offices', the actuarial framework in Argentina deployed as symbolic innovations rather than new practices in the crime control realm (Tonry, 2001, p. 528). As Garland suggests every national pattern is unique, although crime control policies and adaptations can be framed in very specific ways (Garland, 2018, p. 321).

On the other hand, the managerial and actuarial deployments in Argentina and Chile also raise some concerns about the role of the process of travel itself. Put differently, one approach to understand this travel would ask how things change as they move, although this claim is more related to the empirical argument of each theory rather than its core theoretical arguments. In the case of Argentina, a federalized political system like the US, subnational variations could also emerge (Newburn, 2010, pp. 344–350). Policy mobilities scholarship highlights that crime control flow is much more than lineal transfer from one scenario to another, where the application of what is being transferred could diverge between them, but also symbols and rhetorics could also be part of that movement (Jones & Newburn, 2019; Newburn & Sparks, 2004; Newburn et al., 2018).

As Evans and Davies (1999) argue is not only about macro or micro-level analysis, but also meso-level analysis

> which can provide a link between the micro-level of analysis, which deals with the role of interests and levels of government concerning particular policy decisions, and the macro-level of analysis, which is concerned with broader questions concerning the distribution of power within contemporary society. (p. 363)

The travels of the criminal question are not a novel issue among Latin–American scholars. The relationship between the Global North and Global South requires not only that Latin–American scholars not reproduce theories and concepts as a dogma, but also establish a dialogue by situating those theories and concepts in their very context (Sozzo, 2021).

This chapter attempts to understand the travels of actuarial and managerial concepts, narratives, and thesis to the Global South, especially Argentina and Chile. We are aware of the problems and limits of establishing comparisons in different jurisdictions (Nelken, 2012), albeit we could identify different adaptations and mutations of what Global North understands as actuarialism or managerialism and how it travels and was deployed among Latin–American scholars. The differences between those two scenarios also raise two concerns about our aim.

First, strict translation of concepts and theories is hardly possible; as we have seen before, the translations are metamorphoses rather than replications. Second, actuarialism and managerialism thesis within the criminological realm refers to different developments and changes in the criminal justice system; they can be linked by efficacy, efficiency, and effectiveness, but also with the emergence of neoliberalism policies in Western societies, both in developed or under-developed countries. In this regard, we follow Sozzo's approach to suggest that actuarial and managerial theories and practices should be analyzed in specific spatial and temporal coordinates and deals with differences and peculiarities, and recognize the embeddedness of legal punishment in remote and recent past and present of a context (Sozzo, 2018, p. 677). There, even though we put the focus on the *theoretical frameworks*, we should acknowledge another important difference, now regarding the role of the scholars involved in the process of *translation*; unlike his Chilean colleagues, most Argentinean scholars are also – or were – members of the judiciary, mainly through the role of public defenders. We suggest that this should be part of further research analysis, although it posits some questions about their role as "players" or "critical observers" and the metamorphosis of ideas and concepts from the Global North to the Global South across their work as part-time academics at law schools (see Sozzo, 2020).

At least, there is a story to be told regarding the deployment of actuarial and managerial ideas in the crime control field to understand whether or not they had an impact on the criminal justice system both in Argentina and Chile (Jones & Newburn, 2007, p. 147). Empirical research suggests that penal managerialism is more embedded than actuarialism in both scenarios, but the lack of empirical research on the latter, specifically in Argentina, reminds us of the need to develop further research not only at the micro-level analysis but also at the meso-level (Evans & Davies, 1999).

Finally, although incipient and exploratory, one of our implicit aims was to raise some concerns about comparative penology in Latin America. In this regard, this chapter tried to trace some common paths between Argentina and Chile to understand commonalities and discontinuities and their reasons (Cavadino & Diggan, 2006), at least from the perspective of criminological theories receptions.

References

Anitua, G. I. (2001). El juicio penal abreviado como una de las reformas penales de inspiración estadounidense que posibilitan la expansión punitiva. In J. B. J. Maier, & A. Bovino (Eds.), *El procedimiento abreviado* (pp. 137–160). Editores Del Puerto.
Anitua, G. I. (2017). *La justicia penal en cuestión: Aproximación genealógica al poder de juzgar*. Iustel.
Anitua, G. I. (2020). Los peligros de reformar la justicia penal: Actuarialismo, velocidad y deshumanización. In E. Kostenwein (Ed.), *El imperio de castigar: contribuciones desde la sociología de la justicia penal* (pp. 231–268). Editores del Sur.
Barker, V. (2009). *The politics of imprisonment: How the democratic process shapes the way America punishes offenders*. Oxford University Press.

Bayens, G. J., Manske, M. W., & Ortiz Smykla, J. (1998). The impact of the "new penology" on ISP. *Criminal Justice Review*, 23(1), 51–62.
Binder, A. (2008). La Política Judicial de la Democracia Argentina: Vaivenes de la reforma judicial. *Urvio: Revista Latinoamericana de Estudios de Seguridad*, 3, 48–66.
Bover, T. (2019). Destinos y reconocimiento en la Policía Federal Argentina. *Etnografías Contemporáneas*, 5(9), 42–64.
Bover, T., & Chaves, M. (2011). Vivir a los tumbos o vivir (de) uniforme: biografías de jóvenes policías en Argentina. *Última Década*, 19(34), 121–138.
Brandariz-García, J. A. (2014a). *El gobierno de la penalidad: La complejidad de la Política Criminal contemporánea*. Dykinson.
Brandariz-García, J. A. (2014b). Gerencialismo y políticas penales. *Revista de Derecho Penal y Criminología*, IV(8), 51–83.
Brandariz-García, J. A. (2015). Gerencialismo y políticas penales. *Revista Electrónica Direito e Sociedade*, 3(1), 109–138.
Brandariz García, J. A. (2016). *El modelo gerencial-actuarial de penalidad: Eficiencia, riesgo y sistema penal*. Dykinson.
Carlen, P. (2002). Governing the governors: Telling tales of managers, mandarins and mavericks. *Criminal Justice*, 2(1), 27–49.
Carrington, K., Hogg, R., & Sozzo, M. (2016). Southern criminology. *The British Journal of Criminology*, 56(1), 1–20.
Carrington, K., Hogg, R., Scott, J., & Sozzo, M. (2018). Criminology, southern theory and cognitive justice. In K. Carrington, R. Hogg, J. Scott, & M. Sozzo (Eds.), *The Palgrave handbook of criminology and the Global South* (pp. 3–18). Palgrave MacMillan.
Carvajal Martínez, J. E., & Guzmán Rincón, A. M. (2016). Economía de mercado y democracia: Elementos para una crítica al discurso del desarrollo promovido por las instituciones financieras internacionales. *Justicia*, 31, 116–134.
Castorina, A. (2014). *El juicio abreviado: Un análisis socio-jurídico de su utilización en el departamento judicial de Mar del Plata durante el año 2012*. [Unpublished Master's thesis]. Universitat de Barcelona/Universidad Nacional de Mar del Plata.
Cavadino, M., & Diggan, J. (2006). *Penal systems: A comparative approach*. Sage.
Cheliotis, L. K. (2006). How iron is the iron cage of new penology? The role of human agency in the implementation of criminal justice policy. *Punishment & Society*, 8(3), 313–340.
Chesta Saffiro, S., & Alarcón Bañares, P. (2018). Validez preliminar del inventario de evaluación de riesgos criminogénicos YLS/CMI en adolescentes en Chile. *Revista Criminalidad*, 61(2), 25–40.
Christin, A. (2008). *Comparutions immédiates: Enquête sur une pratique judiciaire*. Éditions La Découverte.
Ciocchini, P. (2014). Campaigning to eradicate court delay: Power shifts and new governance in criminal justice in Argentina. *Crime, Law & Social Change*, 61, 61–79.
Clarke, J., Gewirtz, S., & McLaughlin, E. (2000). Reinventing the welfare state. In J. Clarke, S. Gewirtz, & E. McLaughlin (Eds.), *New Managerialism? New Welfare?* (pp. 1–26). Sage.
Cohen, S. (1994). Social control and the politics of reconstruction. In D. Nelken (Ed.), *The futures of criminology* (pp. 63–88). Sage.
Dezalay, Y., & Garth, B. (2005). *La internacionalización de las luchas por el poder: La competencia entre abogados y economistas por transformar los Estados latinoamericanos*. UNAM-ILSA.
Evans, M., & Davies, J. (1999). Understanding policy transfer: A multi-level, multi-disciplinary perspective. *Public Administration*, 77(2), 361–385.

Feeley, M. (2010). Posición 2: Riesgo y delito. *Revista Nova Criminis: Visiones Criminológicas de la Justicia Penal*, *1*, 43–58.
Feeley, M. (2016). Reflexiones sobre los orígenes de la justicia actuarial. *Revista Delito Y Sociedad*, *2*(26), 19–36.
Feeley, M., & Simon, J. (1992). The new penology: Notes on the emerging strategy of corrections and its implications. *Criminology*, *30*, 449–474. https://doi.org/10.1111/j.1745-9125.1992.tb01112.x
Feeley, M., & Simon, J. (1994). Actuarial justice. In D. Nelken (Ed.), *The futures of criminology* (pp. 173–201). Sage.
Fernández Bessa, C., & Bradariz García, J. A. (2016). Transformaciones de la penalidad migratoria en el contexto de la crisis económica: El giro gerencial del dispositivo de deportación. *InDret*, *4*, 1–25.
Foucault, M., Simon, J., & Elden, S. (2017). Danger, crime and rights: A conversation between Michel Foucault and Jonathan Simon. *Theory, Culture & Society*, *34*(1), 3–27.
Ganon, G. (2007). La Macdonalizacion del Sistema de Justicia: nuevo orden o nuevo derecho en la globalidad de la sociedad excluyente. In I. Rivera, H. Silvera, E. Bodelon, & A. Recasens (Eds.), *Contornos y pliegues del Derecho: homenaje al Profesor Roberto Bergalli* (pp. 439–457). Antrophos.
Garland, D. (2003). Penal modernism and postmodernism. In T. Blomberg & S. Cohen (Eds.), *Punishment and social control* (2nd ed., pp. 45–73). Aldine De Gruyter.
Garland, D. (2005). Prefacio a la edición en español. In D. Garland (Ed.), *La Cultura del Control: Crimen y orden social en la sociedad contemporánea* (pp. 19–30). Gedisa.
Garland, D. (2016). *The welfare state: A very short introduction*. Oxford University Press.
Garland, D. (2018). Más allá de la cultura del contro. In M. Sozzo (dir.), *Más allá de la cultura del control? Debates sobre delito, pena y orden social con David Garland* (pp. 299–332). Ad-Hoc.
Golding, B., & Savage, S. (2008). Leadership and performance management. In T. Newburn (Ed.), *Handbook of policing* (2nd ed., pp. 725–759). Willan.
González Guarda, C. (2015). El New Public Management en las reformas al sistema de justicia criminal en Latinoamérica: el caso de Chile. *En Realidades y Perspectivas de jóvenes investigadores. Nuevas Fronteras de Investigación*. Actas Coloquios EchFrancia, Ediciones Ech Francia.
González Guarda, C. (2016). Hacia un modelo organizacional del sistema de justicia penal Latinoamérica: La influencia del management y del gerencialismo en esta reconfiguración. *Nova Criminis*, *7*(11), 135–170.
González Guarda, C. (2018). *Gestión, gerencialismo y sistema penal*. BdeF.
González Guarda, C. (2021). La eficiencia en el sistema penal español: Con especial referencia al modelo de conformidades. *Revista Brasileira de Direito Processual Penal*, *7*(3), 2061–2102. https://doi.org/10.22197/rbdpp.v7i3.538
González-Guarda, C. (2018). *Gestión, gerencialismo y sistema penal*. BdeF.
Gutiérrez, M. H. (2014a). Prácticas y discursos, funciones y disfunciones: El caso de las reformas penales. *Anuario de Derecho Penal y Criminología de la Universidad Nacional de Lomas de Zamora*, *1*(1), 291–312.
Gutiérrez, M. H. (2014b). Acusatorio y Punitivismo: La triste historia de nuestras victorias garantistas (Parte 1). *Revista de Derecho Penal y Criminología*, *IV*(8), 70–84.
Gutiérrez, M. H. (2016). Sobre las ideologías actuales en las reformas penales. *Revista de Derecho Penal y Criminología*, *VI*(5), 154–168.
Guzmán Rincón, A. M. (2011). Tensiones en la estrategia de transformación institucional del Banco Interamericano de Desarrollo en América Latina: Entre el mercado y la gobernabilidad democrática. *Revista Estudios Socio-Jurídicos*, *13*(1), 185–216.
Guzmán Rincón, A. M. (2013). Globalización y reforma del Poder Judicial: Los organismos internacionales y las luchas por la administración de justicia en Colombia. *Pensamiento Jurídico*, *35*, 87–124.

Hannah-Moffat, K. (2013a). Actuarial sentencing: An "unsettled" proposition. *Justice Quarterly*, *30*(2), 270–296.
Hannah-Moffat, K. (2013b). Punishment and risk. In J. Simon, & R. Sparks (Eds.), *The Sage handbook of punishment and society* (pp. 129–151). Sage.
Hannah-Moffat, K., & Amoretto, P. (2006). Assembling risk and the restructuring of penal control. *The British Journal of Criminology*, *46*(3), 438–454.
Hannah-Moffat, K., Maurutto, P., & Turnbull, S. (2009). Negotiated risk: Actuarial illusions and discretion in probation. *Canadian Journal of Law & Society*, *24*(3), 391–409.
Harcourt, B. (2007). *Against prediction: Profiling, policing and punishing in actuarial age*. University of Chicago Press.
Harcourt, B. (2013). Genealogía del actuarialimo penal. In B. Harcourt (Ed.), *Política criminal y gestión de riesgos: Genealogía y crítica* (pp. 39–89). Ad-Hoc.
Hathazy, P. (2013). (Re)shaping the neoliberal leviathans: The politics of penalty and welfare in Argentina, Chile and Peru. *European Review of Latin American and Caribbean Studies/Revista Europa de Estudios Latinoamericanos y del Caribe*, *95*, 5–25.
Hathazy, P. (2016a). Punitivism with a human face: Criminal justice reformers' international and regional strategies and penal-state making in Argentina, Chile and beyond. *Kriminologisches Journal*, *48*, 294–310.
Hathazy, P. (2016b). Remaking the prisons of the market democracies: New experts, old guards and politics in the carceral fields of Argentina and Chile. *Crime, Law and Social Change*, *65*(3), 163–194.
Hersant, J. (2017). Patronage and rationalization: Reform to criminal procedure and the lower courts in Chile. *Law & Social Inquiry*, *42*(2), 423–449.
Hood, C. (1991). A public management for all seasons? *Public Administration*, *69*(1), 3–19.
Isla, P. (2017). Seguridad ciudadana y discursos de control en Chile: análisis de las políticas públicas durante los tres primeros gobiernos posdictadura. *Revista de Estudios de Políticas Públicas*, *3*(2), 40–63.
Iturralde, M. (2019). Neoliberalism and its impact on Latin American crime control fields. *Theoretical Criminology*, *23*(4), 471–490. https://doi.org/10.1177/1362480618756362
Jiménez, M. A., Santos, T., & Gonzalez, P. (2014). *Un nuevo tiempo para la justicia penal: Tensiones, amenazas y desafíos*. Universidad Central–Centro de Investigaciones Criminológica de la Justicia Penal.
Jones, C. (1993). Auditing criminal justice. *The British Journal of Criminology*, *33*(2), 187–202.
Jones, T. (2008). The accountability of policing. In T. Newburn (Ed.), *Handbook of policing* (2nd ed., pp. 693–724). Willan.
Jones, T., & Newburn, T. (2007). *Policy transfer and Criminal Justice: Exploring US influence over British crime control policy*. Open University Press.
Jones, T., & Newburn, T. (2019). Understanding transnational policy flows in security and justice. *Journal of Law and Society*, *46*(S1), S12–S30.
Jordanoska, A. (2017). Case management in complex fraud trials: Actors and strategies in achieving procedural efficiency. *International Journal of Law in Context*, *13*(3), 336–355.
Klein, N. (2016). *La doctrina del shock: El auge del capitalismo del desastre*. Paidós.
Kohler-Hausmann, I. (2018). *Misdemeanorland: Criminal courts and social control in an age of a broken windows policy*. Princeton University Press.
Langer, M. (2004). From legal transplants to legal translations: The globalization of plea bargaining and the Americanization thesis in criminal procedure. *Harvard Law Review*, *45*(1), 1–64.
Langer, M. (2007). Revolution in Latin American criminal procedure: Diffusion of legal ideas from the periphery. *The American Journal of Comparative Law*, *55*(4), 617–676. https://doi.org/10.1093/ajcl/55.4.617.

Langer, M. (2019). Quince años después: Traducciones legales, globalización del plea bargaining y americanización del proceso penal. *Discusiones*, *21*(1), 213–232. https://doi.org/10.52292/j.dsc.2018.2240

Langer, M. (2020). Plea bargaining, trial-avoiding conviction mechanisms, and the global administratization of criminal convictions. *Annual Review of Criminology*, *4*, 377–411 https://doi.org/10.1146/annurev-criminol-032317-092255

Laval, C., & Dardot, P. (2013). *La nueva razón del mundo: ensayo sobre la sociedad neoliberal*. Gedisa.

Liebling, A., & Crewe, B. (2013). Prisons beyond the new penology: The shifting moral foundations of prison management. In J. Simon & R. Sparks (Eds.), *The Sage handbook of punishment and society* (pp. 283–307). Sage.

Lynch, M. (1998). Waste managers? The new penology, crime fighting, and parole agent identity. *Law & Society Review*, *32*(4), 839–870.

Martínez Rangel, R., & Soto Reyes Garmendia, E. (2012). El Consenso de Washington: La instauración de las políticas neoliberales en América Latina. *Política y Cultura*, *37*, 35–64.

Marutto, P., & Hannah-Moffat, K. (2006). Assembling risk and the restructuring of penal control. *The British Journal of Criminology*, *46*(3), 438–454.

McLaughlin, E. (2001a). Actuarialism. In E. McLaughlin & J. Muncie (Eds.), *The Sage dictionary of criminology* (pp. 5–6). Sage.

McLaughlin, E. (2001b). Managerialism. In E. McLaughlin & J. Muncie (Eds.), *The Sage dictionary of criminology* (pp. 169–170). Sage.

Melossi, D. (2012). *Delito, pena y control social: Un enfoque sociológico entre estructura y cultura*. Ad-Hoc.

Melossi, D., Sozzo, M., & Sparks, R. (2011). Introduction: Criminal questions, cultural embeddedness and global mobilities. In D. Melossi, M. Sozzo, & R. Sparks (Eds.), *Travels of the criminal question: Cultural embeddedness and diffusion* (pp. 1–14). Hart.

Miller, L. (2001). Looking for postmodernism in all the wrong places: Implementing a new penology. *The British Journal of Criminology*, *41*(1), 168–184.

Muñiz Oller, M. B. (2019a). *La criminología administrativa/actuarial en la Argentina actual: análisis de los planes de seguridad en el partido de General Pueyrredón en el período 2011–2018* [Unpublished Master's thesis]. Facultat de Dret, Univesitat de Barcelona.

Muñiz Oller, M. B. (2019b). Seguridad urbana y control social: Riesgo y criminología actuarial. *Derecho y Ciencias Sociales (Derecho, ciudad y propiedad)*, *21*, 145–165.

Nelken, D. (2012). Comparing criminal justice. In M. Maguire (Ed.), *The Oxford handbook of criminology* (5th ed.). Oxford University Press.

Newburn, T. (2008). Policing since 1945. In T. Newburn (Ed.), *Handbook of policing* (2nd ed., pp. 90–114). Willan.

Newburn, T. (2010). Diffusion, differentiation and resistance in comparative penalty. *Criminology & Criminal Justice*, *10*(4), 341–352.

Newburn, T., & Sparks, R. (2004). Criminal justice and political cultures. In T. Newburn & R. Sparks (Eds.), *Criminal justice and political cultures: National and international dimensions of crime control* (pp. 1–15). Willan Publishing.

Newburn, T., Jones, T., & J. Blaustein (2018). Policy mobilities and comparative penality. *Theoretical Criminology*, *22*(4), 563–581. https://doi.org/10.1177/1362480617713985

O'Malley, P. (2006). *Riesgo, neoliberalismo y justicia penal*. Ad-Hoc.

Pitch, T. (2003). *Responsabilidades limitadas*. Ad-Hoc.

Pratt, J. (2007). *Penal populism*. Routledge.

Raine, J. (2005). Courts, sentencing and justice in a changing political and managerial context. *Public Money & Management*, *25*(5), 290–298.

Raine, J., & Willson, M. (1995). New public management and criminal justice. *Public Money & Management*, *15*(1), 35–40.

Raine, J., & Willson, M. (1997). Beyond managerialism in criminal justice. *The Howard Journal*, *36*(1), 80–95.

Ramírez Brouchoud, M. F. (2009). Las reformas del Estado y la administración pública en América Latina y los intentos de aplicación del New Public Management. *Estudios Políticos*, *34*, 115–141. Recuperado a partir de. https://revistas.udea.edu.co/index.php/estudiospoliticos/article/view/2810

Ramos, C., & Milanesi, A. (2018). Public management models, Latin America. In A. Farazmand (Ed.), *Global encyclopedia of public administration, public policy, and governance*. Springer. https://doi.org/10.1007/978-3-319-20928-9_2692

Rivera Beiras, I. (2015). Actuarialismo penitenciario: Su recepción en España. *Revista Crítica Penal y Poder*, *9*, 102–144.

Rothschild-Elyassi, G., Koehler, J., & Simon, J. (2019). Actuarial justice. In M. Deflem (Ed.), *The handbook of social control* (pp. 194–206). Wiley-Blackwell.

Sicardi, M. (2020). Reformas del proceso penal en Latinoamérica, gerencialismo y juicio abreviado: Aproximaciones desde la Ciudad de Buenos Aires. In E. Kostenwein (Ed.), *El imperio de castigar: Contribuciones desde la sociología de la justicia penal* (pp. 303–322). Editores del Sur.

Simon, J. (1988). The ideological effects of actuarial practices. *Law & Society Review*, *22*(4), 771–880.

Simon, J. (1993). *Poor discipline: Parole and the social of the underclass, 1890–1900*. University of Chicago Press.

Simon, J., & Feeley, M. (2003). The forms and limits of the new penology. In T. Blomberg & S. Cohen (Eds.), *Punishment and social control* (2nd ed., pp. 75–116). Aldine De Gruyter.

Sozzo, M. (2006). Tradutore traditore': Traducción, importación cultural e historia del presente de la criminología en América Latina. In M. Sozzo (Ed.), *Reconstruyendo las Criminologías Críticas* (pp. 353–431). Ad-Hoc.

Sozzo, M. (2007a). Florencio Varela y el nacimiento del liberalismo penal en la Argentina. *Nueva Doctrina Penal*, *2007*, 635–648.

Sozzo, M. (2007b). Metamorfosis de la prisión? Proyecto normalizador, populismo punitivo y "prisión-depósito" en Argentina. *Urvio Revista Latinoamericana de Seguridad Ciudadana*, *1*, 88–116.

Sozzo, M. (2009). Populismo punitivo, proyecto normalizador y "prisión-depósito" en Argentina. *Sistema Penal & Violência*, *1*(1), 33–65.

Sozzo, M. (2011). Cultural travels and crime prevention in Argentina. In D. Melossi, M. Sozzo, & R. Sparks, R. (Eds.), *Travels of the criminal question: Cultural Embeddedness and Diffusion* (pp. 185–215). Hart.

Sozzo, M. (2018). Beyond the 'neo-liberal penalty thesis'? Punitive turn and political change in South America. In K. Carrington, R. Hogg, J. Scott, & M. Sozzo (Eds.), *The Palgrave handbook of criminology and the Global South* (pp. 659–685). Palgrave MacMillan.

Sozzo, M. (2020). Criminología, mundo del derecho y modos de compromiso público: Exploraciones sobre el caso de Argentina. *Tempo Social*, *32*(3), 109–146. https://doi.org/10.11606/0103-2070.ts.2020.176931

Sozzo, M. (2021, May 4–6). *Criminología crítica y criminología del sur: Pasado y presente* [Conference session]. Jornades 20 anys de l'OSPDH: homenatge a Roberto Bergalli, Barcelona, Spain.

Tonry, M. (2001). Symbol, substance, and severity in Western penal policies. *Punishment & Society*, *3*(4), 517–536.

Undurraga, T. (2014). *Divergencias: Trayectorias del neoliberalismo en Argentina y Chile*. Ediciones Universidad Diego Portales.

Undurraga, T. (2015). Neoliberalism in Argentina and Chile: Common antecedents, divergent paths. *Revista de Sociologia e Política*, *23*(55), 11–34.

Wacquant, L. (2010a). *Castigar a los pobres: el gobierno neoliberal de la inseguridad social.* Gedisa.
Wacquant. L. (2010b). Crafting the Neoliberal state: Workfare, prisonfare and social insecurity. *Sociological Forum*, *25*(2), 197–220.
Willenmann, J. (2020). Neoliberal politics and state modernization in Chilean penal evolution. *Punishment & Society*, *22*(3), 259–280.
Zedner, L. (2002). Dangers of dystopias in penal theory. *Oxford Journal of Legal Studies*, *22*(2), 341–366.
Zysman, D., & Sicardi, M. (2019). Una justicia actuarial: Entrevista a Malcolm Feeley y Jonathan Simon. *Delito Y Sociedad*, *1*(47), 127–152.

Chapter 9

Is Vigilantism an "Extralegal" Phenomenon?

Diego Tuesta

University of Toronto, Canada

Abstract

This chapter makes a critique of contemporary definitions of vigilantism in the social sciences. I demonstrate that many scholarly definitions, especially those that conceptualize vigilantism as an extralegal practice, involve problematic normative assumptions. Such definitions, I argue, often preconceive that state legal classifications are neutral, objective, timeless and universal. The critical question is whether the state is the only possible *locus* of legality. An affirmative response would deny the existence of plural or hybrid legal orders. Furthermore, with respect to vigilantism, extralegality is an external, state-dependent property. Using it as a definitional feature thus comes with the risk of reducing vigilantism to a secondary and subordinated political order vis-á-vis the state. That risk reminds us of the importance of epistemological vigilance in every research operation– especially concept formation. The chapter finally discusses possibilities for a normative-free definition of vigilantism.

Keywords: Legal order; Global South; values; vigilantism; epistemological vigilance; extralegality; hybridization; state-centric vigilantism

Introduction

In 2014, I was working for a government agency in Peru, and I arrived in a remote village on a mission to write a report on coca substitution programs. I got out of the car that took me there and started walking to recognize the terrain. The village, located in one of the country's main drug trafficking regions, was rife with small businesses selling agro-industrial tools. I was wearing sunglasses and casual urban clothing–not the best idea to pass incognito. After three blocks of strolling by the town's central square, a local person on a motorbike appeared out of nowhere and urged me to stop. The man asked me about the purpose of my visit. I was a bit surprised, somewhat scared, for I thought I was doing nothing wrong. He said the area was "under a state of emergency, and I shouldn't wander around." If I wanted to stay, he insisted, I had to introduce myself to the town's mayor or the local organization known as *comité de autodefensa* (self-defense committee). I did as he instructed. I introduced myself to the self-defense committee, a vigilante organization established to counter The Shining Path in the early nineties. Their members were small farmers enraged by the government's plans for crop eradication. I was allowed to stay, and, to my surprise, I got the chance to interview the president of the committee. I never thought this intimidating experience was vigilantism, nor that I would be studying this phenomenon years later.

The word vigilante is of Spanish origin. It shares the same Latin root as the English "vigil" and "vigilance." The expression seems to have traveled into North American English in the 19th century, designating crime control activities by citizens in the rural southwest (Favarel-Garrigues & Gayer, 2016, pp. 13–14). Names such as "vigilance committee," "vigilant societies," "vigilantes," "regulators," and "moderators" spread across growing and economically burgeoning towns. The San Francisco Vigilance Committee, a community-based initiative against theft and murder, was probably one of the first vigilante organizations (Siegel, 2022, p. 5), although other Anglo sources suggest that vigilantism in North America dates to the first Irish settlers of the New World in the 18th century (Pfeifer, 2017, p. 25). Despite lynch laws having disappeared, the idea of vigilante self-help still pervades the sociolegal imaginary in many US jurisdictions, especially in the proclaimed right and culture of firearms ownership (Tonry, 2023, p. 251).

Outside the United States, vigilantism is still common in many societies, especially those where the state is weak, and traditions of people taking the law into their own hands remain pervasive. Jung and Cohen (2020, p. 2) found reports of lynching mob violence in 46 countries between 1976 and 2013 and reports of lynching in more than 100 countries during the same period. Neither dated nor paradigmatic of a bygone era, vigilantism is a global phenomenon that still fascinates scholars across the world.

Interest in the study of vigilantism hearkens to early anthropological and sociological thought. These disciplines shared the quest to unravel an enigmatic "other" and the principles of a given social order. Importantly, social scientists under these traditions have frequently used dualities to capture the specificity of vigilante justice: local versus global; modern versus traditional; legal versus illegal (or extralegal); organized versus disorganized; moderate versus punitive; democratic versus despotic; center versus periphery; normal versus anomalous. My interpretation is that such dualities comprise a dominant pole versus a second one that (by exclusion) presents itself as something mysterious yet indeed marginal and inferior. A given reality, though, can be considered "peripheral" or "aonormal" only if someone speaks on behalf of a "center" of authority – that is, the state and its legal classifications. But it is also true that vigilantism often expresses sentiments (e.g., anger, fear, indignation) that are familiar to crime control experiences in Global North societies, from which it follows that vigilantism puzzles social scientists in light of two contrasting reasons: its reference to an "enigmatic other" and its punitive emotions and values, which scholars viewed as similar in substance – yet dissimilar in form – to those in societies of the Global North (Pfeifer, 2017).[1]

These contrasting sources of inspiration remind us of a knowledge pattern in criminology – and the sociology of crime and crime control. Research within these fields is dominated by the external gaze of scholars from or based in the Global North (Aliverti et al., 2021; Carrington et al., 2016). For example, despite its proliferation in the southern hemisphere, what we know and how we think about vigilantism is shaped by knowledge production in the Global North. However, I do not see this as a problem that justifies the epistemological crusade many critical criminologists seem interested in undertaking. I see it more like a dominant trend that calls for epistemological vigilance. As Bourdieu et al. (1991) describe following the work of Gaston Bachelard, epistemological vigilance aims to filter out biases (cultural, emotional, political) before establishing the study object. Such an exercise is arguably imperative to study practices that – like vigilantism – challenge our normative conceptions, where semantic disagreements are pervasive, and researchers are prone to methodological ethnocentrism.

This chapter is precisely an exercise of critical examination. I will examine some of the most common definitions of vigilantism available in the literature with the aim of identifying normative biases and logical flaws. Against a pervasive trend, I will argue that scholars must be careful when describing vigilantism as an extralegal phenomenon. Most definitions emphasize that vigilantism is extralegal because either it ignores or defies established state rules. I will argue that a priori calling vigilantism extralegal can be a normative intellectual operation. Doing so entails the risk of assuming the state (our Western idea of the state) as a neutral, timeless, and universal principle of classification. But state criminal laws can change, thereby too the spectrum of what is extralegal. Moreover, many informal initiatives of crime control are carried out by individuals who are not thereby vigilantes (Siegel, 2022, p. 9). Extralegality is thus an unreliable quality for definitional purposes. Once vigilantism is defined as extralegal, a second risk is that scholars may ignore analyzing the conception of justice – the political vision – that a vigilante social movement sociologically develops.

Except for two pieces in French, the rest of the studies I will examine are in English. And since many definitions in the literature come from works on African countries, I will inevitably draw from examples in that region. By the mid-20th century, Anglophone scholars and policymakers introduced the term vigilantism to designate how people took the law into their own hands in countries like

---

[1]Examples of this analysis abound; notably, Durkheim ([1899–1900]1973) and Mead (1918) linked punishment sentiments to social solidarity.

Nigeria and South Africa.[2] It is worth mentioning that Latin American scholars have much to learn about studies on vigilante justice in the African context. I am aware that scholars who publish in Spanish rarely use the term *vigilantismo* – despite its linguistic origins and the recurrence of vigilante acts in many Latin American countries. However the notion of extralegality is widely used, and our scholarship is heavily influenced by Anglo sources. Latin America and Africa share quite a few similarities in terms of colonial legacies, state-building, political culture, and importantly, vigilante traditions.

I organize this chapter into five sections. I begin reviewing what could be considered "classic definitions" of vigilantism. Next, I explore definitions from research in the African context and highlight conceptually relevant innovations. The third section examines recent definitional attempts by political scientists who argue that conceptual discord – lack of consensus over a definition – hinders knowledge accumulation and cross-national comparisons (Bateson, 2021; Moncada, 2017). The fourth section discusses definitions that I consider promising for developing rigorous research, and I close this chapter with some final reflections. Throughout the chapter, I will pay attention to how scholars conceptualize the relationship between vigilantism and the state.

Classic Definitions of Vigilantism

In 1974, Rosenbaum and Sederberg (1974, p. 574) defined vigilantism as "establishment violence," which consists of "acts or threats of coercion in violation of the formal boundaries of an established sociopolitical order, which, however, are intended by the violators to defend that order from some form of subversion." The state is here the defining entity of those formal boundaries. Vigilantism is thus the opposite of formality: a phenomenon that violates the rules of state procedure. Even though vigilante violence may target behaviors not enshrined in the criminal code, Rosenbaum and Sederberg (1974) assume that vigilante groups and the state agree on the meaning of criminal offenses. Their definition could be considered an example of normative monism, an ontology – the opposite of pluralism – that reduces all diversity to a single and integrated principle (see Robbins, 2013, p. 100). The state is regarded as the unequivocal principle of integration, from which it follows that vigilantism is a residual category detached from positive and creative meaning.

Decades later, Les Johnson (1996, p. 232) observed that Rosenbaum and Sederberg's (1974) definition might be over-inclusive; for example, grassroots movements and groups with state affiliations can engage in establishment violence in breach of state regulations. To solve this ambiguity, he proposed a narrow definition separating the domains of vigilante justice and state coercion. Vigilantism, Johnston (1996, p. 232) contends, is "a social movement giving rise to premeditated

---

[2]The term experienced semantic variations throughout the decades in line with legal and social transformations. However, as in the United States, vigilante practices precede the nomenclature. African vigilantism dates to colonial times (Fourchard, 2008).

acts of force – or threatened force – by autonomous citizens." This arises, he continues, "as a reaction to the transgression of institutionalized norms by individuals or groups–or to their potential or imputed transgression" (Johnston, 1996, p. 232). Vigilante acts, finally, "are focused upon crime control and/or social control and aim to offer assurances (or 'guarantees') of security both to participants and to other members of a given established order" (Johnston, 1996, p. 232).

This definition first depicts vigilantism as a reaction to defend institutionalized norms – that is, to preserve the social order. The author avoids calling vigilantism legal or extralegal, but the strict separation he proposes between vigilante justice and state coercion is problematic (for reasons I later describe). Johnston (1996) further provides a list of necessary characteristics: vigilantism must involve premeditated, organized actions based on the use of force by autonomous citizens who act privately and voluntarily to provide personal or collective security. Note how Johnston (1996) initially defines vigilantism as a social movement but later states that a participating agent must engage in some preparatory activity "for vigilantism to occur" (p. 222). The author does not rule out the possibility of vigilantism being exercised by an isolated individual, which seems a contradiction with his preliminary notion of vigilantism as a social movement. Moreover, it is unclear if "for vigilantism to occur" refers either to the formation of a vigilante movement or the conditions for one single vigilante act to happen. The notion of a "preparatory activity" in which "the participating agent must engage" (p. 222) is also dubious, as it can either refer to a single act of violence or something more systematic (e.g., a vigilante movement). Conditions explaining the former may not necessarily explain the latter (see Fourchard, 2021).

Another logical flaw can be seen in the notion of private voluntary agency. Johnston (1996) argues that vigilantism involves a private voluntary agent, which leaves the participation of police officers out of the scope of this phenomenon. He agrees that police officers who participate in vigilante justice is puzzling but argues that nothing justifies stretching the concept of vigilantism to cover such instances: "If police officers engage in 'private enterprise,' it is neither as mere private persons nor as mere public police, but as something altogether more complex [...] understanding of that complexity is not assisted by calling it vigilantism" (Johnston, 1996, p. 224). It follows that vigilantism should be used only to designate social movements (or aspects of them) integrated by autonomous individuals without state affiliation or who leave that affiliation aside during vigilante acts. Community policing organizations and private security firms can be autonomous and private but "still function within the legal ambit of the state" (Johnston, 1996, p. 225), falling out of the scope of vigilantism. Private citizens often engage in "community policing," but such designation *ipso facto* entails recognition by the state. Johnston (1996) is concerned about over-inclusiveness, to stretch the concept of vigilantism until it is empty of specificity.

While it is sensible not to disregard or reduce vigilantism to an extralegal phenomenon, Johnston's (1996) definition brings a dubious demarcation. To illustrate, let us consider the case of a police officer who engages in vigilante practices. Such an individual might express pride in performing these simultaneous roles;

moreover, her vigilante affiliation could precede that of a police officer. Johnston (1996) would probably describe this simultaneous identification only as an expression of identity. But we could problematize this interpretation: when acting as a vigilante, does this individual cease to be a police officer? Such interpretation is untenable for under which authority can a researcher, an external observer, deny the status of "vigilante" to a person who identifies as one (see Lemieux, 2014)? I suggest with this example that Johnston's (1996) conceptual demarcation might be artificial, thereby questionable from a theoretical and empirical standpoint.

Unlike Johnston (1996), the anthropologist Ray Abrahams (1996) refuses to separate vigilantism from the state *as an idea*. He understands vigilantism as a collective action that reinforces social values and norms; an ideal type that often "lays claim to the state's own mantle of authority" (Abrahams, 1998, p. 9). This refers to instances where vigilantism and state power converge. Examples of policing in Nigeria, South Africa, and India (Cooper-Knock & Owen, 2015; Fourchard, 2021; Jauregui, 2015; Super, 2020) show that vigilante groups often act in ways that mimic state procedures. This feature allows vigilantism to be differentiated from self-help (e.g., feud, vendetta, or revenge), dispute settlement, and other forms of social control that are unable to speak on behalf of the state as an idea (Abrahams, 1998, p. 9). Participants in those formations rarely act on behalf of ideals that can be generalized as public goods (Boltanski & Thévenot, 2006), the substantive legal aspect common to the state and vigilantism.

Despite this productive theoretical position, Abrahams (1998) posits that vigilantism occupies "an awkward borderland between legality and illegality, and between public and more sectional interests" (p. 7).[3] I see this as a rather normative claim, which reminds us of Ernesto Laclau's (2005) critique of scholars who define this phenomenon in purely negative terms. Abrahams further describes vigilantism as a "frontier phenomenon" due to its occurrence in remote areas "at the margin of the state" (Abrahams, 1998, p. 24). This observation depends on an external and somewhat arbitrary viewpoint. The alleged "borderland nature" of vigilantism reveals the fascination and positionality of an external observer. As previously mentioned, a given reality can only be deemed "peripheral" or "borderland" as relative to some unknown (probably exotic) "other" under the condition of speaking from or on behalf of a "center" of authority. Still, Abrahams's (1998) observation that vigilantism resorts "to the state's own mantle of authority" seems to have paved the way for future studies on the hybridization of many vigilante organizations, as described in the next section.

---

[3] Abrahams (1998, p. 7) further argues that "despite some 'vigilantes attempt to formulate strict constitutions for themselves, the secret and highly personalized nature of much of their activity also helps to make it rather labile. Many of its manifestations are relatively short-lived, and it is always capable of slipping and sliding, in one direction or another. Also, as I noted earlier, vigilantism – like other forms and levels of political activity – is not always what it seems or claims to be. It is typical of vigilantes that they attempt to take the moral high ground, but they may also entertain or covertly develop other agendas."

Vigilantism as a Hybrid Institution

Fieldwork research in Africa has contributed insightful reflections on the relationship between the state and vigilante justice. Based on the empirical observation of vigilante groups transitioning into community policing, for example, scholars have been critical of definitions that draw a clear-cut distinction between these domains. In line with this, Buur and Jensen (2004) propose understanding vigilantism as a "form of everyday policing." This formulation facilitates an inductive analysis of how and why many vigilante groups adopt the conventional language, practices and style of state institutions. The everyday policing perspective depicts vigilantism as a "normal" and recurrent collective practice, which serves too as a conceptual critique. Scholars have been skeptical of media and political discourses that frame vigilantism as necessarily hostile to democracy and the rule of law. The term vigilantism, while it can be treated as a category of analysis, has been the recipient of stereotypical interpretations (Fourchard, 2008; Pratten & Sen, 2007; Super, 2017). Therefore, Pratten and Sen (2007) observe that conceptual construction also involves the critical examination of ideological narratives:

> The definitional issues surrounding vigilantism are many and varied. These persistent questions concern matters of scale, of ethics, and of state complicity among others. These issues raise significant problems in the study of vigilantism. How significant is the organization of violence? Are there analytical distinctions to be drawn between the violence of vigilante organizations and lynch mobs, for instance? Does paying for protection voluntarily or under duress undermine a vigilante ethic? And what does it mean when the state authorizes the use of non-state violence? In retaining flexibility in our own definitions it is equally necessary to account for the ways in which the labelling of vigilantism itself contains a politics of language, and how language is employed to legitimate or oppose vigilante activity. (pp. 7–8)

With respect to the "politics of language," South Africa and Nigeria offer good examples of how the political meaning of vigilantism has shifted throughout the decades. Between the 1970s and 1980s in South Africa, street committees in black townships implemented "popular courts," which the Apartheid government generally tolerated. However, vigilantism was seldom used to name these organizations (Super, 2017). In the 1980s, left-wing social movements used the term "vigilantes" to denote violent and conservative gangs that intended to intimidate, murder, and even kill anti-apartheid activists. Super (2017, p. 519) describes how the words vigilante and mob were counterposed: the former referring to pro-apartheid groupings and the latter used to disqualify anti-apartheid individuals. Only in the aftermath of the Apartheid regime did vigilantism and mob justice come to designate groups dedicated to (non-politically motivated) informal policing and punishment. In Nigeria, the police first introduced the term vigilantism in the mid-1980s to designate corporal punishment practices that dated back to the colonial period (Fourchard, 2008, 2021). The state would sponsor initiatives for community policing among grassroots organizations that evolved from the old hunter-guard system. As Fourchard (2008, p. 16) puts it, vigilantism is "a new name for an old practice."

Scholars have consistently demonstrated transformations in the meaning of vigilantism (Favarel-Garrigues & Gayer, 2016; Fourchard, 2008; Super, 2017), which often correspond to changes in social practices, such as when vigilante organizations adopt the language, practices, and technologies of modern policing institutions. Yet variations in meaning may correspond to changing perceptions over the legitimacy of vigilantism, as when some of its manifestations were derogatorily labeled as "mob violence" or as "community policing" in other contexts (Fourchard, 2021). However, the question remains: how can we establish a conceptual boundary between what is vigilante justice and what is not?

Super (2019, p. 64) argues that vigilantism often operates under the same framework of state punishment in some circumstances, albeit in an unstable and contested manner. Similarly, Lund (2006) and Fourchard (2021) describe how often vigilante groups draw upon the language, resources, and symbols of the state to create legitimacy and exercise authority. These scholars observe that vigilante groups often reveal a degree of *stateness*. For this reason, Lund (2006) defines vigilantism as a "twilight institution." Certainly, almost every institution needs legitimacy to enforce rules of behavior. Such enforcement *ipso facto* involves a claim of legitimacy. Institutions are fragile in a way. They are constantly being tested against the probability of civil disobedience. Lund (2006, p. 693) argues that "it is not useful to see legitimacy as a fixed quality against which actual conduct could be measure" but rather as a process in which a given institution aims to legitimize its actions (see also Lentz, 1998; Moore, 1988). It follows that institutions of public authority (the state included) are never entirely formed. They are in a constant process of formation (Lund, 2006).

Many examples support this thesis. Lineage leaders may often present themselves as chairmen, therefore implying a desire for state recognition; churches borrow from the state's official language by defining themselves as NGOs and hometown associations draw upon formal territorial divisions despite self-declaring their opposition to the state; Nigerian vigilantes would simultaneously decry the state for failing to provide security and still receive funding from high-rank politicians; hunter associations in Burkina Faso, while upholding traditional customs, would advocate meeting state's modern requirement to be recognized as syndicates (Lund, 2006, pp. 687–692). To use Lund's (2006) terminology, these traditional institutions depend on the idea of the state to exercise authority. Similarly, state institutions must frequently resort to the languages and practices of traditional institutions to garner legitimacy and exercise authority at the local level (see Fourchard, 2021; Laryš, 2022; Orock, 2014).

Lund (2006) underscores two mechanisms facilitating hybrid state-vigilante formations: institutional bricolage and leakage of meaning. The former happens, for example, when a vigilante group borrows existing practices and styles associated with state institutions. That is the case with popular courts. Note how, in such instances, vigilantes usually adopt the language of security and even human rights. This *bricolage* outcome is possible because the *underlying meaning* of social practices is fluid (it tends to leak; see also Douglas, 1973, p. 13). Our state-centric notions of security, development, and human rights are subject to being appropriated by institutions that simultaneously speak on the state's behalf and in opposition to it.

Thus far, I have reviewed two sets of definitions. I first analyzed those that may be regarded as "classic definitions." These are extensively cited formulations and relatively early attempts to formalize the concept of vigilantism. Second, I have reviewed conceptual exercises from studies in the African context, where vigilantism is problematized based on the evidence of organizations in a twilight zone. The scholarly tendency has shifted from narrow to more flexible formulations of vigilantism. Johnston (1996) exemplifies the former. Those who understand vigilantism as an "everyday policing" practice exemplify the latter. One implication is that scholars should be aware of the historicity underpinning vigilantism and its relationship to the state – awareness of the transformations and paradoxes in that relationship. Second, since more than one institutional actor can exercise authority over a jurisdiction, analyzing the institutional operations that make hybridization possible is key. What about the extralegality of vigilantism? Does assuming that vigilantism is extralegal and, therefore, separated from the state entail neglecting the processes that Lund (2006) underscores? I will later argue that distinguishing vigilantism from the state is possible, but not under the premise of an extralegal character.

The (North American) Political Science Approach

Despite the theoretical innovations highlighted in the previous section, or perhaps because of them, some scholars argue that research on vigilantism suffers from "conceptual discord" and even "confusion." Bateson (2021) and Moncada (2017) consider that many definitions in the literature either lack clarity or are "too context-specific." They also claim that disagreement over a universal definition, evident in the number of case studies and methodological approaches, hinders operationalization, measurement, cross-national comparisons, and knowledge accumulation:

> Within research on vigilantism, scholars often use varied conceptualisations without explaining how and why their constructs deviate from other variants. This hinders our ability to reconcile findings across studies and, in turn, constrains our ability to advance concerns, including state-society relations, crime and order. And absent explicit understandings of what phenomenon fall under the concept of vigilantism, scholars will be stymied in their efforts to answer emerging calls for more comparative studies of vigilantism. (Moncada, 2017, p. 404)

> Yet although political scientists are increasingly interested in vigilantism, our discipline has never developed a sustained, cumulative

> research agenda on vigilantism. I argue this is largely because existing definitions of vigilantism are contradictory, tautological, and not easily operationalized [...]. (Bateson, 2021, pp. 923–925)

I agree with these authors that comparative research on vigilantism is quite limited.[4] That is the case even with books where the title suggests cross-national comparisons – for example, *Global Vigilantes* (Pratten & Sen, 2007) and *Globalizing Lynching History* (Berg & Wendt, 2011) – but where a careful reading proves otherwise. In this context, Moncada (2017) and Bateson (2021) develop definitions that emphasize the extralegal character of vigilantism and aim to contribute to comparative research.

> I define vigilantism as the collective use or threat of extra-legal violence in response to an alleged criminal act. The social organisation aligns with much extant research that views vigilantism primarily as a group activity. The target is an individual(s) who has allegedly committed a criminal act as defined by the state, defines as an illegal act for which someone can be punished by the government. The repertoire of violence is the extra-legal use or threat of violence, which can be lethal or non-lethal in nature. The justification is the alleged violation of the rule of law. Motivation in this root concept is conceptually aligned with the justification – punishment of the violation of the rule of law – but may diverge to other motivating factors depending on the conceptual strategy used by the researcher. (Moncada, 2017, p. 408)

> Political scientists need a definition of vigilantism that is concise enough to avoid conceptual stretching (Collier & Mahon, 1993), broad enough to allow comparison across time and space, and concrete enough to operationalize. To satisfy these demands, I define vigilantism as the extralegal prevention, investigation, or punishment of offenses. (Bateson, 2021, p. 926)

Moncada (2017) suggests that scholars should consider different dimensions when analyzing vigilantism: social organization (e.g., the degree that a social movement is spontaneous or not), targets, repertoires (e.g., use of lethal or non-lethal violence), justifications and motivations. It is possible to add or reduce the number of dimensions, which, Moncada argues, makes his definition applicable to various contexts. Bateson (2021) also offers many analytical strategies (e.g., taking vigilantism as an "independent" or "dependent" variable). However, as

---

[4]Moncada (2017, p. 407) points that reliance on context-specific definitions "limits our ability to gauge how distinct conceptualisations may vary from a generally accepted understanding of the concept within a particular 'language domain,' defined as a substantive field of study, period of time, location or scholarly discipline."

previously noted with the "classic definitions," these political scientists are adopting a normative standpoint by aprioristically defining vigilantism as extralegal.

Moncada (2017, p. 408) does not explain why vigilantism is extralegal. And against empirical evidence, he restricts vigilantism to offenses enshrined in the criminal code. The author ignores evidence of vigilantes prosecuting behaviors not listed as offenses in the criminal code. For example, some *Rondas Campesinas* (Peruvian vigilante organizations) would whip women accused of having committed adultery,[5] which is not formally criminalized. Meanwhile, some African vigilante groups used to admonish teenagers who played in the streets late at night (Fourchard, 2021, p. 104). By restricting the observation scope to crimes "as defined by the state," Moncada (2017) excludes relevant vigilante practices.

Second, while Bateson (2021) avoids restricting vigilantism to codified offenses, she offers several arguments on the extralegality of vigilantism. The existence of the state, hence of a legal order on its behalf, is the precondition to talk about vigilantism: no state, no vigilantism, she claims bluntly (p. 927). The premise is that *only one* recognized legal order exists: one sanctioned by the state – and by the state only. Bateson (2021) draws upon historical examples like the case of John Chau, an American missionary who intended to step foot on the North Sentinel Island but ended up killed by the islanders. This case does not qualify as vigilantism according to her definition because there was no state – hence no legal order – on that island. But the main example supporting her thesis comes from the 19th century.

George B. Kirk was lynched by the Vigilance Committee of Virginia City, Nevada, in 1871. He was first banished from town by said Committee, but he soon disobeyed the order and decided to go back into town for a walk. After a brief stop at a friend's house, the town's constable – with the support of the Committee – detained Kirk under accusation of assaulting a woman during his walk. Shortly after the arrest, the Committee usurped the state authority and apprehended the alleged offender. Kirk was later conducted to an execution point, where he died strung. This historical narrative, which I directly take from Bateson (2021), consists of three moments. Moment 1: banishment; moment 2: detention and arrest by the constable; and moment 3: apprehension and execution by the Vigilance Committee.

Bateson (2021, p. 929) argues that vigilantism is dynamic. Therefore, incidents like the above can begin legally but "end in vigilantism (or vice versa)." The author describes moment 1 as vigilantism: "when the Vigilance Committee first banished Kirk, this *was vigilantism*, because it was extralegal punishment for an offence" (p. 929). But in moment 2, the Committee "*flipped back to legal behavior*, engaging the police to detain Kirk" (p. 930). Lastly, in moment 3, "the Vigilance Committee overpowered the constable and seized Kirk – very literally usurping the state's authority – they were again *acting* extralegally and engaging in vigilantism" (p. 930).

---

[5]https://www.youtube.com/watch?v=uUgrbxLL5CM

I find Bateson's (2021) narrative quite eclectic as it combines sociological, psychological, and legal vocabulary. The author interchangeably refers to actions, behaviors, and situations. This is not coincidental but an example of failing to establish the object of study. Is the phenomenon under analysis a social movement, a social practice, or a situation? Does the author aim to explain a process or its result? While her definition refers to social practices, Bateson's (2021) supporting arguments include different *explanandums* with terms like "behaviour" and "process."

Instead, I view this case as involving a social movement across three situations. The direction and intensity of the collective action change across these situations. What does not change is its underlying meaning and orientation, which is to punish a probable offender. We thus have a social movement that engages with different normative repertoires and practices: different iterations of the same phenomenon. Bateson (2021) does not provide a detailed account of these iterations, probably because she reduces vigilantism to the state's legal framework.

From the outset, vigilantism is neither defined by the meaning that participants might attach to it – as everyday policing scholars do – nor from the standpoint that external observers would infer. It is neither defined by sociological features (e.g., a collective character) nor by an immanent trait (whether social or political). It is defined through recourse to something external. This external thing is nothing but the state's law, which is contingent and subject to change. Thus, a question that could trouble this reasoning is: what if the state legalizes banishments and lynching by private citizens, then moments 1 and 3 in Bateson's (2021) narrative could not be regarded as vigilantism anymore? This question shows the artificial quality of demarcation based on a normative – non-sociological – conception of legality.

Moncada (2017) and Bateson (2021) introduce a juridical dichotomy (what is legal vs what is not) into the domain of social analysis. From that standpoint, certain practices are beyond legal regulation and should be therefore classified as either illegal or extralegal. The assumption is that a legal classification is neutral, timeless, and universal. From the perspective of disciplines like anthropology or sociology, any human practice is social – regardless of its legal classification. When, instead of distancing herself, a scholar adopts (Eurocentric) legal categories as benchmarks of cognition, there is a risk of epistemological exclusion: practices are characterized not by virtue of their social character but by considering their opposition to legal or political standards. Ultimately, Moncada (2017) and Bateson (2021) adopt a normative definition that is likewise consensual and monist: in their view, the state is the only *locus* of legality.

To what extent does this approach even reproduce colonial thought? What epistemic authority can a social scientist (typically North American or European) claim to sanction what is legal or extralegal? (Fourchard, 2021, p. 104) According to which legal framework is this demarcation being made? Legal classifications are not neutral. They are sociohistorical conventions resulting from valuation practices by individuals or institutions. As Alhaji, an African villager, would put it: "We keep learning strange names such as vigilante for something traditional, but vigilante has been long here. I told you, I did it when I was young"

(Fourchard, 2008, p. 16). This suggests vigilantism is grounded on legal conceptions that can proceed – while later converge – with Western notions of statehood.

Promising Solutions?

From the previous sections, there is a general scholarly consensus that vigilantism involves enforcing norms and establishing moral boundaries. Precisely, Favarel-Garrigues (2016) and Asif and Weenink (2022) formulate definitions that best capture this universal normative dimension. The French authors define vigilantism as "collective coercive practices" which are generally violent, illegal, geared toward maintaining the social order as an exercise of justice on behalf of legal or moral norms:

> [The term] covers a certain number of collective coercive practices by non state actors with the purpose of instilling respect for (social or legal) norms and/or to exercise "justice" – a term that makes reference to the exercise of punishment but that could also evoke – for vigilantes and their public – "a societal ideal." By targeting criminals who are not members of the community but also, frequently, those who are part of the latter, vigilantism engages both in the repression of crime but also on social control. (Favarel-Garrigues & Gayer, 2016, p. 17, translated from French)

Favarel-Garrigues and Gayer's (2016) definition underscores the extralegal character of vigilantism and ignores state actors' possible participation. This constitutes a flaw given the ample evidence of vigilantism working as a "twilight institution," as Lund (2006) would say. But, on the positive side, the definition posits vigilantism as collective actions speaking on behalf of norms. That formulation suggests a connection between actions and norms, paving the ground for analyzing the representations underpinning vigilantism as a form of "everyday policing." The process of "speaking on behalf of norms" is intelligible only by deconstructing the cultural and legal meanings of vigilante actions.

Meanwhile, drawing upon anthropological and sociological theories, Asif and Weenink (2022) develop a cultural understanding of what they call "vigilante violence": "rituals in which participants are mobilized to transform fear and righteous anger into purposive (premeditated or more or less immediate) reactive or preventive unlawful action to punish violations of moral imperatives to restore or uphold the moral community" (p. 3).

Unpacking this definition, the authors define rituals as "repetitive of action sequences, meanings and purposes" (p. 3). So, these rituals work as mechanisms linking the transgression of legal norms, emotions of anger and fear, with the decision to mete out punishment against alleged offenders. Asif and Weenink (2022) describe rituals as interaction scripts – a "know-how" – that guide individuals through the ceremonial of punishment. In Durkheimian fashion, Asif and Weenink (2022) argue that vigilantism tends to restore "moral imperatives" and thus the group's unity. Moral imperatives (another expression for norms) consist of values a community deems sacred and worthy of preservation. This formulation shares with Favarel-Garrigues and Gayer (2016) the idea that vigilantism veers toward producing local justice. But while the French authors ignore the role of rituals, Asif and Weenink (2022) argue that these are necessary mechanisms for vigilantism to happen.

Note that Asif and Weenink's (2022) definition focuses on violent vigilante practices, despite the evidence of coercive vigilante activities excluding the use of violence. Can we treat these outcomes (violent and non-violent) as independent explanatory processes? Explaining the formation of a vigilante movement is one thing but explaining its trajectory (including its violent and non-violent expressions) involves different explanatory arguments. Arguably, the authors overestimate the capacity of a vigilante group or organization to act as a unit. They suggest three conditions for vigilante violence to occur (state legitimacy, people's experience with violence and authorities' encouragement), but seem to uphold the assumption that moral imperatives and participants' will to cooperate are given. But what if that is not the case? What if the alleged transgression does not seriously harm a moral code to make people feel offended? Citizens may agree on the importance of legal norms, yet we cannot directly infer that unity and harmony prevail (Boltanski, 2011). This assumption should not be prescribed but demonstrated as a research outcome.

Overall, the authors in this section are concerned about mechanisms (cultural, social, political) that structure vigilante justice (Garland, 2005), which is likely a contribution. Speaking of mechanisms (in plural) implies accepting empirical variations, that a phenomenon is not given but an outcome of processes which need investigation. By not being too prescriptive, theoretically or ideologically, these definitions are potentially helpful for empirical research.

Concluding Remarks

In *Craft of Sociology*, Bourdieu et al. (1991) describe the role of epistemological vigilance in sociological research. First introduced by Gaston Bachelard, this principle prescribes the need to break with common sense when formulating a research problem and to remain vigilant of biases and preconceptions through every research stage. Somewhat ironically (considering the French origins of epistemological vigilance), Moosavi (2020, p. 347) calls for "Southern scholarship to be subjected to the same epistemological vigilance as Northern scholarship." He argues this might reduce the risk of uncritical translations of Northern theories when studying the Global South, and the "glorification" of knowledge from the peripheries. I could not agree more, and the conceptual issues surrounding vigilantism offer a good example of the importance of epistemological vigilance to avoid normative preconceptions when formulating new definitions or adapting existing ones.

In that sense, when vigilantism is defined as extralegal, there is a risk of reducing the phenomenon to a secondary political order, to something residual regarding the state. Extralegality also means to take the intrusion of a legal criterion into social theory for granted. The object of study is established following an arbitrary ideological demarcation: as if the state would be the only possible *locus* of legality. Legal boundaries are contingent upon cultural and political considerations. Since vigilantism might no longer be extralegal once authorized by the state, extra-legality is neither an objective criterion nor a property inherent to the object under analysis. It refers to something external instead that changes over time: the criminal law – a product of state legislators. Following de Saussure (2013), it is true that semantic contents are the product of opposite meanings. Yet it does not follow that every semantic content should be reduced to opposite relations between symbols. This reminds us of Ernesto Laclau (2005), who noted that scholars frequently defined populism in purely negative terms (as a convoluted ideology, as mere rhetoric, as the opposite of serious politics). Similarly, vigilantism has often been defined negatively as a residual object in its relationship to the state.

In Favarel-Garrigues and Gayer (2016) and Asif and Weenink (2022), the collective orientation toward justice – not extralegality – is leveraged as the main definitional property. I find this to be a productive conceptualization. "Justice" seems to be understood not as a monopoly of the state but of social interactions that vary according to cultural, social, and legal contexts. No state, no vigilantism, claims Bateson (2021). But the correct precondition is no collective orientation toward justice, no vigilantism.[6] These definitions are in line with the pragmatic perspective that understands "justice" as a critical capacity (Boltanski & Thévenot, 1999, 2006), also with the notion of "everyday policing" (Pratten & Sen, 2007), and with Siegel's (2022) recommendation that vigilantism should be understood as bringing to bear "a political perspective on the situations in which they perform their vigilantist acts" (Siegel, 2022, p. 18). All these perspectives, notwithstanding their variations,[7] prescribe conceptualizing "justice" (vigilante justice) in terms of the collective moral reasoning that ordinary citizens mobilize, as a phenomenon that involves people who speak on behalf of norms (Asif & Weenink, 2022; Favarel-Garrigues & Gayer, 2016).

---

[6]This "orientation toward justice" leaves the question of which notion of justice should be considered for analytical purposes. The pragmatic sociology of critique offers a tentative answer. Boltanski and Thévenot (2006) argue that human individuals possess several "critical capacities" – the sense of justice being one of them. So what notion of justice is at stake in vigilantism? Most likely the notion participants express during their activities, which can be captured qualitatively with ethnographic observation and interviews.

[7]That said, scholars should be watchful of definitions that take sociological (and even functionalists) assumptions for granted; for example, depicting vigilantism as if, ipso facto, does "something to preserve the social order" (Rosenbaum & Sederberg, 1974). A similar assumption would see participants of vigilante movements as having some disposition to cooperate and coordinate actions, either because of their free will, attachment to traditions, interest or solidarity (Asif & Weenink, 2022). I suggest these mechanisms should not be established by definition but as an outcome of empirical research.

Indeed, in vigilantism, a person or group always acts on behalf of something – a political vision, Siegel (2022) would claim. Assuming this group of ordinary citizens is doing justice on behalf of the community, that would be the typical expression of vigilantism that comes to our minds. It would be fair to argue that these citizens are speaking on behalf of the community – as an ideal type, this is a penal practice unregulated by the state. Now, when the police arrest an alleged offender (e.g., a robber), one could arguably say that this act is also on behalf of a given community. However, it would be accurate to argue that the police officer *is also acting on behalf of something beyond the realm of community*. That something refers to the framework of state punishment. Super (2020) offers examples of vigilantes who either enforce the state law or whose actions are tolerated by state agencies. However, vigilantism within the state framework does not negate that people are mobilizing moral reasoning drawing upon a community-based notion of punishment – a political vision (Siegel, 2022) that has relative autonomy from state-centric principles of classification.

To conclude, dropping extralegality as a defining feature – highlighting instead the collective orientation toward justice – should not imply a theoretical or moral equivalence between state punishment and vigilante justice. It only means we are being vigilant of preconceptions, thereby paving the way to analyze vigilantism by virtue of its core sociological mechanism: a justice orientation that varies in its degrees of autonomy with respect to the state.

References

Abrahams, R. (1998). *Vigilant citizens: Vigilantism and the state*. Polity Press.
Aliverti, A., Carvalho, H., Chamberlen, A., & Sozzo, M. (2021). Decolonizing the criminal question. *Punishment & Society*, 23(3), 297–316.
Asif, M., & Weenink, D. (2022). Vigilante rituals theory: A cultural explanation of vigilante violence. *European Journal of Criminology*, 19(2), 163–182. https://doi.org/10.1177/1477370819887518
Bateson, R. (2021). The politics of vigilantism. *Comparative Political Studies*, 54(6), 923–955. https://doi.org/10.1177/0010414020957692
Boltanski, L. (2011). *On critique*. Polity Press.
Boltanski, L., & Thévenot, L. (1999). The sociology of critical capacity. *European Journal of Social Theory*, 2(3), 359–377.
Boltanski, L., & Thévenot, L. (2006). *On justification: Economies of worth*. Princeton University Press.
Bourdieu, P., Chambordon, J.-C., & Passeron, J.-C. (1991). *The craft of sociology: Epistemological preliminaries*. Walter de Gruyter & Co.
Buur, L., & Jensen, S. (2004). Introduction: Vigilantism and the policing of everyday life in South Africa. *African Studies*, 63(2), 139–152.
Carrington, K., Hogg, R., & Sozzo, M. (2016). Southern criminology. *British Journal of Criminology*, 56(1), 1–20.
Cooper-Knock, S. J., & Owen, O. (2015). Between vigilantism and bureaucracy: Improving our understanding of police work in Nigeria and South Africa. *Theoretical Criminology*, 19(3), 355–375.
Douglas, M. (1973). *Rules and meanings*. Penguin Education.
Durkheim, E. (1973). Two laws of penal evolution. *Economy and Society*, 2(3), 285–308.

Favarel-Garrigues, G., & Gayer, L. (2016). Violer la loi pour maintenir l'ordre: Le vigilantisme en débat. *Politix, 115*(3), 7.
Fourchard, L. (2008). A new name for an old practice: Vigilantes in South-Western Nigeria. *Africa, 78*(1), 16–40.
Fourchard, L. (2021). *Classify, exclude, police: Urban lives in South Africa and Nigeria*. Wiley.
Garland, D. (2005). Penal excess and surplus meaning: Public torture lynchings in twentieth-century America. *Law & Society Review, 39*(4), 793–834.
Jauregui, B. (2015). Just war. *Conflict and Society, 1*(1), 41–59. doi: 10.3167/arcs.2015.010105
Johnston, L. (1996). What is Vigilantism? *British Journal of Criminology, 36*(2), 220–236. https://doi.org/10.1093/oxfordjournals.bjc.a014083
Jung, D. F., & Cohen, D. K. (2020). *Lynching and local justice*. Cambridge University Press.
Laclau, E. (2005). *On populist reason*. Verso.
Laryš, M. (2022). Far-right vigilantes and crime: Law and order providers or common criminals? The lessons from Greece, Russia, and Ukraine. *Southeast European and Black Sea Studies, 22*(4), 479–502. https://doi.org/10.1080/14683857.2022.2086666
Lemieux, C. (2014). The moral idealism of ordinary people as a sociological challenge: Reflections on the French reception of Luc Boltanski and Laurent Thévenot's on justification. In *The spirit of Luc Boltanski. Essays on the "Pragmatic sociology of critique"* (pp. 153–172). Anthem Press.
Lentz, C. (1998). The chief, the mine captain and the politician: Legitimating power in Northern Ghana. *Africa, 68*(1), 46–65.
Lund, C. (2006). Twilight institutions: Public authority and local politics in Africa. *Development and Change, 37*(4), 685–705.
Mead, G. H. (1918). The psychology of punitive justice. *The American Journal of Sociology, 23*(5), 26.
Moncada, E. (2017). Varieties of vigilantism: Conceptual discord, meaning and strategies. *Global Crime, 18*(4), 403–423.
Moore, S. F. (1988). Legitimation as a process: The expansion of government and party in Tanzania. In *State Formation and Political Legitimacy* (pp. 155–172). Transaction Books.
Moosavi, L. (2020). The decolonial bandwagon and the dangers of intellectual decolonisation. *International Review of Sociology, 30*(2), 332–354.
Orock, R. T. E. (2014). Crime, in/security and mob justice: The micropolitics of sovereignty in Cameroon. *Social Dynamics, 40*(2), 408–428.
Pfeifer, M. (2017). *Global lynching and collective violence*. University of Illinois Press.
Pratten, D., & Sen, A. (2007). *Global vigilantes: Perspectives on justice and violence*. Hurst Publishers.
Robbins, J. (2013). Monism, pluralism, and the structure of value relations: A Dumontian contribution to the contemporary study of value. *Journal of Ethnographic Theory, 3*(1), 99.
Rosenbaum, J. H., & Sederberg, C. (1974). Vigilantism: An analysis of establishment violence. *Comparative Politics, 6*(4), 541–570.
de Saussure, F. (2013). *Course in general linguistics*. Bloomsbury Academic.
Siegel, S. (2022). Vigilantism and political vision. *Washington University Review of Philosophy, 2*, 1–42.
Super, G. (2017). What's in a name and why it matters: A historical analysis of the relationship between state authority, vigilantism and penal power in South Africa. *Theoretical Criminology, 21*(4), 512–531.
Super, G. (2020). 'Three warnings and you're out': Banishment and precarious penality in South Africa's informal settlements. *Punishment & Society, 22*(1), 48–69. doi: 10.1177/1462474518822485.
Tonry, M. (2023). Why Americans are a people of exceptional violence. *Crime and Justice, 52*, 233–264.

Chapter 10

Southern Green Victimology: A Look at the Cycle of Environmental Harms, Resistance and Over-criminalisation

Valeria Vegh Weis

Konstanz University, Germany

Abstract

Building upon the working notion of Southern green victimology, the presentation explores the case of Andalgalá, Province of Catamarca, Argentina, where international corporations have been trying to develop a mining project that would affect the environment and the health of the local population. Facing the lack of support from the state, the organised local community tried to prevent their actual environmental victimisation and they committed to stop this damaging undertaking. Following these intents, the Argentinean criminal justice system acted to the detriment of these local actors (over-criminalisation) and favour mining corporations that can cause irreparable damage to the local water and air resources (under-criminalisation). In short, the case study will shed light on the common features of Southern green victimisation: (1) attempts to consolidate corporate investments involving extensive environmental harms in forms already banned in the Global North, (2) a committed resistance by the local environmental groups, (3) the harsh selectivity of the criminal justice system, and (4). immunity of corporate environmental harms/crimes.

Keywords: Southern; green victimology; environmental harms; resistance; Argentina; criminalisation

The burgeoning research of green criminology in/from/on the Global South builds upon Southern perspectives within criminological research (Carrington et al., 2016, 2019; Travers, 2019), and it seeks to expand Northern perspectives on environmental harms and environmental criminalisation. In particular, this literature looks at geopolitical inequalities and highlights the scope of Global Northern exploitation in the Global South (e.g. Northern actors taking resources on a scale that threatens local food security, the transfer of waste from North to South, or fracking investments).

Following this perspective, it is possible to argue that environmental/green victimisation is not only targeting specific populations but also entire parts of the globe located in the South. In this regard, environmental/green victims have been defined as 'those of past, present, or future generations who are injured as a consequence of change to the chemical, physical, microbiological, or psychosocial environment, brought about by deliberate or reckless, individual or collective, human act or omission' (Williams, 1996, p. 35). However, to this shall be added that environmental victimisation is often shaped by what might be referred as 'environmental selectivity', that is, how race, ethnicity, gender, class, and religious membership but also glocalisation play a relevant role in conditioning whose wellbeing is more likely to be affected by environmental hazards (more on selectivity in Vegh Weis, 2017).

To this is added that the usual environmental victims do not only face structural marginalisation and specific green crimes/harms but, on top, they are usually ignored within scholar and public policy work. Indeed, 'the most notable absentees from the vast majority of work carried out in relation to environmental victimisation so far are the voices of environmental victims themselves' (Hall, 2014b, pp. 139–140). As a result, 'almost no empirical research has been carried out which takes into account the perspective of environmental victims themselves' (Hall, 2014b, p. 135), undermining the development of political and policy strategies from below. In particular, 'poor people are usually excluded from the environmental decision-making process, and once a policy is made, they are usually powerless to change it' (Lee, 2022, pp. 3–4).

Against this background, critical scholars call academics to 'take a stand' and embrace research as praxis, putting knowledge at the disposal of activism. This position involves, following the lessons of left realism, understanding that victims' rights are not the exclusive incumbency of right-wing representatives. Moreover, taking a stand also means going beyond the focus on individual environmental victims and helping develop victims' movements and engaging with workers, the poor, and indigenous peoples in the management and defense of high-value natural resources (Brisman & South, 2013). From a Southern perspective, the literature supports this call and aims to raise (resistant) Southern voices, including those of local populations (Goyes, 2020; Natali, 2014), radical environmentalists (O'Brien, 2016), environmental groups taking action both online and offline (Ronco & Allen-Robertson, 2021), feminists (Massé et al., 2021), and Indigenous groups (Puerta Peña, 2021).

Following this call, and linking the contributions from Southern criminology, green criminology and environmental/green victimology, this chapter explores a *Southern green victimology* perspective that can shed light on the specific features of environmental victimisation, resistance and criminalisation in the Global South, with a focus on the experiences of those engaged in resistance strategies. In this regard, a Southern perspective within environmental/green victimology can help avoid the danger of treating green/environmental victims as if they were a uniform group and acknowledging, instead, different crime impacts and reactions in different parts of the globe (Hall, 2014b) based on actually listening and analysing their experiences and actions.

Moreover, following this logic, a Southern perspective can contribute to highlighting the fact that actors in the South are more affected by environmental harms and have, nevertheless, fewer possibilities to confront and overcome the consequences of environmental disasters in the global debate. To exemplify, the 1992 UN Framework Convention on Climate Change (FCCC) recognises that climate change does not have a geographical even impact but that particularly vulnerable are the 'low-lying and other small island countries, countries with low-lying coastal, arid and semi-arid areas or areas liable to floods, drought and desertification, and developing countries with fragile mountainous ecosystems' (Hall, 2014b). However, Global North countries along with national and international NGOs are the ones directing the environmental global efforts. Moreover, local NGOs in the South may be increasingly influenced by state and corporate funders from the North and therefore may have a difficult time challenging practices that go against the Northern agenda (Stretesky & Knight, 2013).

A Southern perspective within environmental/green victimology can also shed light on the resistance movements that spread throughout the South to face both corporate harms/crime and the lack of response (or even complicity) of state agents and international organisations. Moreover, a Southern perspective can also point out how, when victims resort to protest to confront the spread of impunity, the criminal justice system reacts especially hard, including the use of deadly force and the over-criminalisation of those exercising the constitutionally granted right to protest. In this vein, the excessive (and even deadly) use of force by law enforcement in relation to environmental protest is a common feature in large parts of the Global South. In Brazil, 71 leaders and members of social movements were killed in 2017 alone (Lacerda & Rolemberg, 2021). In South Africa, the residents of the township of Mpumalanga resisted an initiative to install a flat rate for their water services which would have led to the privatisation of the access to this basic right. As a response, the government called the military to intervene, the protests were banned and police fire was employed (Pauw, 2003). In Bolivia, similar protests against the privatisation of access to water culminated in an eight-day blockade and state of siege in April 2000, during which at least six people were killed (White, 2003).

Building upon this working notion of *Southern green victimology* and the specific features described above, this chapter explores the case of Andalgalá, Province of Catamarca, Argentina, where international corporations have been trying to develop a mining project that would affect the environment and the health of the local population. Facing the lack of support from the state, the organised local community tried to prevent their actual environmental victimisation and they committed to stop this damaging undertaking. Following these intents, the Argentinean criminal justice system acted to the detriment of these local actors (over-criminalisation) and favour mining corporations that can cause irreparable damage to the local water and air resources (under-criminalisation). In short, the case study will shed light on the common features of Southern green victimisation: (1) attempts to consolidate corporate investments involving extensive environmental harms in forms already banned in the Global North, (2) a committed resistance by the local environmental groups, (3) the harsh selectivity of the criminal justice system, and (4) immunity of corporate environmental harms/crimes.

Open-Pit Mining and Environmental Victimisation

About 2.7 million square kilometres in Argentina have mineral deposits. Reservoirs of lead, zinc, tin and silver are located along the 4,500 kilometres of extension of the Andes Mountains, whereas the South region is known for borates, lithium and potassium salts, and to the West is rich in copper, gold and silver. Catamarca, a province in north-western Argentina located 245 kilometres from the provincial capital city, is known for its copper, molybdenum, gold and silver resources. Andalgalá, the third-largest city in Catamarca, has the largest gold and copper mine in the country and one of the most important in the world (Coria, 2007).

Andalgalá' resources were identified by the Argentine State in 1970 when the Dirección de Fabricaciones Militares (Directorate of Military Fabrications) carried out the so-called Plan Cordillerano Norte (Northern Cordillera Plan) intending to identify the existing mineral resources in the extreme north of the Argentine mountain range.[1] The information gathered was sent to the Secretaría Nacional de Minería (National Mining Secretariat) and then passed on to transnational companies interested in investing in the extraction of national mining resources (Cornejo Torino, 2003). Through a contract signed on 3 March 1972, the state authorised the US company Cities Service International to exploit the mining *Mi Vida* (My Life, today known as Agua Rica, Rich Water) for 50 years in exchange for a payment of 2 million dollars, free of taxes and with full freedom to transfer remittances abroad (Pastoriza, 2008). The Australian company BHP and the Canadian transnational Northern Orion completed a feasibility study to start the exploitation of the mine. However, because of the low international price of copper, no progress was made on the project (el Ancasti, 2005, 2016).

In 1997, the mining corporation Bajo La Alumbrera was finally established in the region with a construction cost of 1,200 million dollars. The consortium, conformed by Xstrata (Switzerland, 50%), Goldcorp (Canada, 37.5%) and Yamana Gold (Canada, 12.5%), is one of the world's top 10 copper mines and one of the top 15 gold mines and has an annual turnover of 680 million dollars. Locally, it decided to develop a three-stage extraction process (prospecting,

---

[1] See http://www.alumbrera.com.ar/institucional.asp and http://www.atlas.catamarca.gov.ar/PDF/unidades%20tematicas/territorio%20y%20medio%20ambiente/division%20politica/departamentos/Andalgala/andalgala.pdf.

exploration and exploitation) (Lamalice & Klein, 2016). This mega-project was the first large-scale transnational strip-mining project in the country. Exploration and exploitation rights were held by Yacimientos Mineros de Agua de Dionisio, which included the Government of Catamarca (60%), the National University of Tucumán (20%) and the national government (20%) (Berea, 2013).

The residents of the towns of Andalgalá, as well as those of Belén and Santa María, expressed their opposition, denounced the false promises of economic and social progress, and made explicit the negative impact that the mining process would have on the region's natural and cultural assets (Gallego Zapata, 2018). This was not an isolated reaction: throughout Latin America, mega-mining projects are often confronted by local communities generating a total of 209 social conflicts by 2014, according to the Latin–American Mining Conflict Observatory. Only in Argentina, there are 26 social conflicts within the 157 mining planned projects, 42 of which have already started.[2]

The first mining conflict in the country was in the province of Chubut in the Patagonia region. The local community of Esquel organised a referendum and 81% of the population voted against the project. The outcomes were not limited to stopping the project but also a law was passed banning any future open-pit mining project. Following this model, environmental social movements in eight other provinces engaged in legal battles to pass similar laws banning mining projects when they included the use of leaching methods and chemicals (Marin, 2009). These provinces were Río Negro (2005 but nullified in 2011); Mendoza (2007); La Rioja (2007 but nullified in 2008); Tucumán (2007); La Pampa (2007); Córdoba (2008); San Luis (2008) and Tierra del Fuego (2011).

The overall consequences of the extractive model and, specifically of the open-pit mining system, were made public through the documentary film *Las Fuentes del Jardín de tus Arterias* by German Ciarí,[3] in which the environmental liabilities, social conflict and environmental destruction were exposed. Indeed, in line with the analysis of the film, Bajo La Alumbrera destroys an average of 340,000 tonnes of rock per day to obtain, for each ton, approximately six grams of gold and six kilograms of copper. The destruction of the mountains alters the geology and can cause subsequent landslides and avalanches. In addition, the process involves the use of 66,000 litres of water per minute (la Vaca, 2007) and tons of chemicals that remain partly in a tailings dam – a dam that stores the remaining solids from the ore processing – as well as in the atmosphere – as part of the suspended dust generated by the rock explosions. In turn, the tailings dam sits on the Vis-Vis River basin, contaminating the water (Möhle, 2018). Community members denounced that their homes are located 2 kilometres downstream of the dam where polluting material is discharged and they argued that 'the quality of the water caused stomach pains, diarrhoea, diarrhoea with fever and vomiting' and that 'the animals, mainly goats, died'.[4]

---

[2]See https://www.ocmal.org/.
[3]See https://www.youtube.com/watch?v=SDDYbAe_DFU.
[4]See Conflicto Minero: Bajo Bajo La Alumbrera acusada de contaminación, https://mapa.conflictosmineros.net/ocmal_db-v2/conflicto/view/20.

Environmental Victims Resistance

The first milestone in the resistance to mining took place in September 2006, when residents and socio-environmental organisations began a protest in front of the municipal sports centre. As soon as the demonstration began, the protestors were repressed by the provincial police and the Gendarmerie. Many were beaten, shot with rubber bullets, and gassed, while some were arrested. In other words, repression was accompanied by the environmental over-criminalising of those resisting the mining project. The community filed criminal complaints about the repression before the Prosecutor's Office of the 2nd District of Andalgalá, but environmental under-criminalisation of the repressive actions of the security forces was the solo response they obtained. None of the law enforcement agents was charged for their actions.

Years later, the situation intensified when a threatening official document was disclosed: it stated that the corporation Billington had the right to move the whole city of Andalgalá:

> The area of the mine practically covers the city of Andalgalá, a situation that is normal and commonplace, since according to the Mining Code the two properties can coexist, both the mining and surface properties can coexist, the mining, in this case, being for Prospecting and Exploration purposes, which in the case of exploitation, has the greater public interest and the state must prioritise its development. (Christel & Gutiérrez, 2017)

Protests escalated since then. In December 2009, a resident and lawyer of Andalgalá, Sergio Martínez and his friend Aldo Flores went together trying to disrupt traffic on the road El Potrero in Chaquiago, which is the road that leads to the Agua Rica deposit. The goal was to prevent the supply of mining inputs. The radio spread the word and community members started to gather to support the initiative. That day la Asamblea El Algarrobo (The Carob Tree Assembly) was formed. The name was chosen in honour of the carob tree that gave them shade on the side of the road during the hot summer days. Simultaneously, on 2 January 2010, the community organised the first of the more than 600 weekly Caminatas por la Vida (Walks for Life), a non-violent protest that gathers thousands of families in the main town of the city. Eduardo, an Andalgalá resident, explains his motivation to take part in the Saturday demonstrations:

> Just as there are people who go to Mass on Sundays, I go to the walk on Saturdays ... I want my children to continue living here, that they can learn the things I have learned, that they can see the magic of planting a seed and seeing the plant grow. That is why I walk. Because I feel worthy when I walk. (Tierra Viva, 2021)

From then on, the community started a double strategy. On the one hand, they engaged in a legal struggle with the support of activist lawyers from the community, such as Sergio Martínez, and with lawyers from the human rights organisation Servicio Paz y Justicia, SERPAJ (Service Peace and Justice).[5] One of the first legal battles started as soon as January 2010 when the recently confirmed assembly presented a constitutional complaint against the corporation Agua Rica and its subsidiary Yamana Gold and LLC. They demanded the immediate suspension of all the work in progress aimed at preparing for the exploitation of the mine. They argued that the mining project will violate the rights to a healthy and balanced environment, the right to health, the right to life, the protection of their physical integrity and the property of the inhabitants of the region (Christel & Gutiérrez, 2017). On the other hand, the blockade and the weekly walking became two permanent features of the city. For the blockade, neighbours organised themselves into shifts and guards so that there would always be someone on-site, preventing the corporation from accessing the mining camp with heavy machinery. The local civil tribunal dismissed the constitutional complaint arguing that the case demanded a broader discussion on the provided evidence. As a response, the community lawyers presented an appeal before the Supreme Court of Justice, with the hope that a non-local tribunal might show a less biased performance when evaluating the actual harms associated with the mining project.

The Harsh Selectivity of the Criminal Justice System: Over-criminalisation of Peaceful Local Resistance and Under-criminalisation of the Violent Repression by Law Enforcement Agencies

Meanwhile, the local criminal court did engage in the conflict, now for the second time, in a strategy of environmental over-criminalisation: the attorney general opened a criminal case against four community members for the crime of hindering the operation of land transport (art. 194 of the Criminal Code). The statute of limitations prevented the case to progress, but the judge delayed the dismissal of the proceedings and left the case open. This exposes how, even when

---

[5]SERPAJ was created in 1974 as part of a continental Christia-ecumenical non-violent movement committed to liberation theology and the principles of civil disobedience developed earlier by Gandhi and Martin Luther King Jr that met in Medellin, Colombia. The common grounds were commitment to the oppressed peoples and a non-violent orientation. In 1975, as a response to the increasing violence of the Triple A, right-wing squads acting with the support of the democratic government, SERPAJ initiated a campaign to disseminate the Universal Declaration of Human Rights and habeas corpus templates. SERPAJ's goals are the promotion of peace, non-violence and a culture based upon human rights. Its leader is Adolfo Perez Esquivel, who was a victim himself, detained and tortured during the dictatorship. Perez Esquivel was awarded the Nobel Prize in 1980. After the transition to democracy in 1983, SERPAJ started to also intensively collaborate with communities fighting against environmental harms and particularly with Indigenous Peoples (Author's interview with Adolfo Perez Esquivel, SERPAJ offices, 10/7/19).

the criminal procedure rules are there to protect the constitutional rights of the defendants, the selective criminal justice system can manipulate the cases to prolong the subjection of the community members to the detriment of their constitutional rights.[6]

Less than two months later, the judge intervening in the case issued two simultaneous rulings, reinforcing the under-criminalisation of the heads of the mining corporation and the over-criminalisation of the community members. On the one hand, he rejected a precautionary measure[7] that would stop the mining company's actions. He did so based on a formal argument (Asamblea El Algarrobo, 2010d; el Trece, 2010) that was so weak that it would later be revoked by the Supreme Court of Justice. On the other hand, the judge accepted the request issued by the Agua Rica corporation and the attorney general office to evict the road where El Algarrobo Assembly was located.[8] The operation was led by a special and militarised law enforcement group (Grupo Kuntur) that belongs to the Catamarca police force. They were armed as a combat force and fired rubber bullets at those who were peacefully demonstrating on this rural road, thus guaranteeing that the company could pass machinery to its camp.[9]

Notably, the judge ordered the police to clear the area, even though violence was likely to take place because of the features of this law enforcement group, which is specially trained to intervene in highly conflicting situations, pre-under-criminalising the violence through the judicial authorities to act. The state-corporate symbiosis in the case was clear in the fact that this judge was the former Director of Yacimiento de Agua in Dionisio. The violence occurred, and, in response, community members filed a complaint against the mayor, the attorney general, the judge and the police personnel.[10] However, in another example of environmental under-criminalisation, the facts were never investigated and the judge in charge dismissed the case (McEvoy, 2019). In contrast, the criminal justice system did intervene but did so by fostering the environmental over-criminalisation of the community members, charging them for damaging public property during the protest. Once again, exposing the state-corporate symbiosis, the charges originated in a complaint filed by a local businessman who was providing supplies to the Agua Rica mining company and an active promoter of the mining industry in the region.[11]

---

[6]Exp. 03/2010 s/simple threats, minor injuries and damage in ideal competition.
[7]The 'precautionary measure' is a precautionary decision taken by the judge to avoid irreparable damage being caused during the judicial process. The 'medida de no innovar' refers to not moving forward in the mining process until the final judicial decision is taken.
[8]Expte. No. 23/10 s/ilícito penal -Chaquiago Andalgalá.
[9]Expte. No. 19/10 s/ilícito penal -Chaquiago Andalgalá.
[10]Exp. No. 40 s/instigators of damage and aggravated theft.
[11]The optional referendum is a mechanism for direct public consultation so that the population can vote directly on a specific issue of great relevance, in this case on mining.

In turn, trying to dispute the charges presented against them within the environmental over-criminalisation process, community members once again engaged with activist lawyers and together they devised a creative and peaceful strategy. They agreed upon refusing to be notified of the criminal charges against them, arguing that the summons did not comply with articles 173 and 175 of the provincial Criminal Procedure Code, which state that these notifications must contain the object and/or motive of the judicial process and the full name of the person to be notified. This strategy was disseminated in the community through the radio program of El Algarrobo Assembly so all members would be aware of how they could better defend their right to due process. Interestingly, this experience shows that the selective functioning of the criminal justice system forced ordinary citizens who oppose the mining industry to learn about Criminal Procedure provisions to avoid being over-criminalised.[12]

A month later, following grassroots pressure from the population of the town, the government called for an optional referendum (Asamblea El Algarrobo, 2010a). The citizens of Andalgalá would be entitled to vote if they wanted or not mega-mining developments in their hometown. However, the attorney general challenged the constitutionality of the referendum and called for the democratic consultation process to be suspended. A group of residents decided to gather anyway in the main square on the day of the referendum to demonstrate against the suspension of the referendum.

In this context, one of the community members approached a local bar, where he found the aforementioned judge sitting with his family. A group of neighbours then approached the bar to peacefully repudiate the judge's presence in the area. The state response was further environmental over-criminalisation: disregarding the right to dissent and the freedom of expression that all citizens should enjoy on a constitutional basis, the attorney general filed a criminal complaint about the crime of threat against the person who noticed the presence of the judge in the bar (Meganoticias, 2010). In the absence of evidence of a threat, the case could not proceed. However, the courts again resorted to the strategy of leaving the case open and delaying the dismissal.

Months later, in July 2010, the residents of Andalgalá issued an ultimatum: 'Agua Rica must leave on the first week of September because the people do not want to continue bearing the eternal delays of the justice system and the government' (Asamblea El Algarrobo, 2010c). From August onwards, a group of assembly members set up a tent where they began a collective fast to reinforce and make visible the seriousness of the ultimatum.[13] Moreover, a procession of all faiths and religions took place to unite wills and overcome ideological differences under the slogan 'Peace, respect and love for life' (Lamalice & Klein, 2016).

In response to the ultimatum, more police were sent to protect the mining company, escalating the tension. During one of the Walks for Life, protesters

---

[12]Exp. 133/10 s/coercion.
[13]Exp. No. 205/10 s/aggravated damage, illegal deprivation of personal liberty and coercion.

denounced that the streets adjacent to the mining company's headquarters were fenced off and inaccessible, even if there was no legal authorisation to do so. However, instead of applying sanctions against the mining company for having fenced off a public road, the security forces proceeded to over-criminalise twenty-three neighbours for the crime of aggravated damage and attack on authority, alleging that they had tried to dismantle the installed physical barriers. Once again, the justice system was not able to gather evidence for these accusations and the charges against the community members were finally dismissed.

In the same month, August 2010, a group of members of the El Algarrobo Assembly held a demonstration at the door of the City Council during a session devoted to the discussion on glaciers and periglacial environments. Unsurprisingly, the action ended with criminal charges being brought against five members of the El Algarrobo Assembly for the crimes of damage and unlawful deprivation of liberty (due to the situation of the members of the Deliberative Council who 'could not leave' the Council and go home) in a new instance of environmental over-criminalisation. Again, the lack of evidence was clear, and the charges did not go forward, but the case has not yet been closed (Carrizo et al., 2012).

Interestingly, women represent two-thirds of those over-criminalised in the protests against mega-mining initiatives in the province of Catamarca (Lamalice & Klein, 2016) and they became, as in many other places, a central pillar of the struggle (Carrizo et al., 2012). In Andalgalá, a group of female community members decided to create the group Mujeres del Silencio (Women of Silence). In mid-September, this group carried out a new form of demonstration to make visible the over-criminalisation of the right to protest and the extensive violence deployed by law enforcement. Every Wednesday, these women began to walk silently, walking from the square, passing by the town hall, the judiciary and the attorney general office, to end up before the headquarters of Agua Rica and its bigger supplier, Mafap. The women stopped for a few minutes before each place, in silence, with their mouths covered, their hands tied and holding signs saying that they were defending the Aconquija, their 'Nature Sanctuary'. The banners stated: 'We are daughters and mothers of Andalgalá, is this also a crime?' (Veneranda, 2012).

In turn, teenagers from the community also organised themselves under the name Los Nuevos Defensores (The New Defenders). They give talks on environmental issues in schools to raise awareness among their peers. Likewise, a meeting of the Unión de Asambleas Ciudadanas (Union of Citizen Assemblies) was held in Andalgalá to exchange, articulate and strengthen links among assemblies from all over the country (Asamblea El Algarrobo, 2010b). Following these efforts, several socio-environmental assemblies began to protest along with Indigenous communities in the province at the beginning of 2012. Altogether, they carried out blockades to obstacle the transport of mining supplies to the Bajo La Alumbrera corporation (Asamblea El Algarrobo, 2012). The response was, once again, repression followed by the under-criminalisation of this excessive use of force by police agents and the over-criminalisation of community members under fake allegations of threat and damage to private property.

In the town of Tinogasta in Catamarca, the repression included the deployment of rubber bullets and dogs that caused serious severe injuries to the protesters. In the town Amaicha del Valle in the province of Tucuman, the police repressed and besieged protesters on a plot of land without a warrant. In Belén in Catamarca, protesters were arrested and charged with offences under the Anti-Terrorism Law (Indymedia, 2012). By then, 44 members of the El Algarrobo Assembly have been prosecuted under criminal charges.[14] All these cases ended up being dismissed after long periods of distress for those accused. The trick deployed by the judges to maintain the cases open for a long time in this opportunity was to argue that, as it was a small town, they had personal links with the accused, which allowed them to self-inhibit from issuing a decision and to transfer the case to another judge in a vicious circle.

In turn, the state protection of the mining corporations continued. Agua Rica was benefitted from an extension of the original concession[15] and plans were drawn up to open another mining site known as Bajo el Durazno (Under the Peach) next to Bajo La Alumbrera. Meanwhile, the provincial Secretariat of Mining approved the Environmental Impact Report for the exploration of another project known as Cerro Atajo, presented by the mining corporation CAMYEN SE, associated with Yamana Gold (Catamarca Actual, 2016). All of this was done without complying with the existing legal obligation that establishes the duty to allow local citizens to express their opinion on the acceptance or rejection of mining exploitation projects in their hometown.

Immunity of Corporate Environmental Harms/Crimes

Meanwhile, the appeal which had been filed by the residents of Andalgalá back in 2010 against the mining corporations and which was supposed to be resolved by the Supreme Court was still pending. In November 2014, the community members decided to stop waiting passively and raised funds to travel to the capital city of the country, Buenos Aires, where the Supreme Court is located. Once there, they set up a camp in Plaza Tribunales, in front of the Supreme Court and a few blocks from the attorney general's office. The action was supported by national social and human rights organisations, among them SERPAJ, the Sindicato de Trabajadores del Estado (the Union of State Workers), the social organisation Conciencia Solidaria (Solidary Consciousness), public intellectuals, individual citizens, and students' networks such as Visión Sostenible (Sustainable Vision). These organisations offered cultural activities to the public and the turnout

---

[14]Exp. No. 273/12 for aggravated damage in ideal concurrence and real concurrence with aggravated minor injuries as co-perpetrators and Exp. No. 54/13 for a double aggravated attack on authority in ideal concurrence with damage and real concurrence with aggravated minor injuries as co-perpetrators.
[15]Interlocutory Ruling No. 1/2015, Fs. 345 in case No. 271/08 'Minera Agua Rica s/Minera El Portezuelo, Dpto. Andalgalá'.

increased. Press conferences were held, documentaries were screened, and political representatives and prominent personalities were received in the tent settled by Andalgalá community members. In addition, the Walks for Life were now held around the courthouse, while holding a long Argentinean flag (Resumen Latinoamericano, 2016).

The neighbours of Andalgalá were able to meet with public servants from the attorney general office. The attorney general ended up ruling in favour of the people of Andalgalá, stating that 'the defendants (Yamana Gold and the Provincial State) would be in a position to carry out operations or actions that could result in damage to the environment and health that, due to their magnitude and the factual circumstances, would be irreversible'. Furthermore, the attorney also argued that 'the Judiciary of Catamarca (Court of Guarantee, Court of Appeals and Court of Justice) did not act on the basis of the existing law', since 'the judges violated the constitutional rights of the residents of Andalgalá (...)'.[16] The attorney highlighted that art. 41 of the Constitution, indicates that 'the issues under debate involve the human right of all inhabitants to enjoy a healthy, balanced environment, suitable for human development and that productive activities must satisfy current needs but without compromising those of future generations'.[17]

This statement was sent to the Supreme Court, which incurred new delays. El Algarrobo Assembly decided to organise a campsite for the second time in the same place. This time the slogan was 'Sentencia YA' (Sentencing now). Finally, on 2 March 2016, the Supreme Court of Justice ruled on the case, upholding the community's claim and deciding that the constitutional complaint was an appropriate remedy because the authorisation to operate that was granted to the mining company was likely to produce a level of environmental damage that, due to its magnitude and factual circumstances, could be late, insufficient or impossible to repair at a later date. Furthermore, the Supreme Court stated that:

> in environmental matters, when the protection of a collective good is under discussion, the prevention of future damage is the absolute priority ... carrying out an environmental impact study before the start of activities does not mean that the commencement of the mining activities will be prohibited, but rather an instance of reflexive analysis on a scientific basis and with citizen participation is needed.[18]

---

[16]PGN, Opinion of 03 December 2014, exp. No. 1314/2012 T° 48 Letras M, titled 'Sergio Martínez y Otros c/Minera Agua Rica LLC Suc. Argentina y su propietaria Yamana Gold Inc. y otro s/acción de amparo'.
[17]PGN, Opinion of 03 December 2014, exp. No. 1314/2012 T° 48 Letras M, titled 'Sergio Martínez y Otros c/Minera Agua Rica LLC Suc. Argentina y su propietaria Yamana Gold Inc. y otro s/acción de amparo'.
[18]CSJN. Judgment of 2 March 2016, Case 1314/12 entitled 'Recurso de Hecho. Sergio Martínez y otros c/Minera Agua Rica LLC Sucursal Argentina y su propietaria Yamana Gold Inc. y otros s/acción de amparo'. The full ruling can be retrieved at http://esdocs.com/doc/1798669/archivofallocompletosobremineraaguarica.

This was the first legal victory in favour of the community and the environment. However, the case went back to the local judge who supported the arguments of the community members and prohibited any further mining activity in the region. In June 2016, the corporation announced the closure of Bajo La Alumbrera mining project and on 8 September, the Municipal Ordinance 029/2016 was passed, prohibiting metalliferous and nuclear mineral (uranium, thorium, etc.) mining activities in any form, whether through open pit or galleries, in deposits discovered or to be discovered, in all its stages, in the entire upper basin of the Andalgalá River (Aranda, 2016; Diario Judicial, 2020; Marcha, 2016). The ordinance is being challenged by the Agua Rica company and the Government of the Province of Catamarca, to which the Assembly responded by intervening as an interested third party.[19]

Contrary to the provisions of the injunction, the mining company did try to enter machinery into the Agua Rica deposit in December 2016. In response, a group of neighbours presented charges against the company's managers and the CEO for judicial disobedience against the ordinance prohibiting mining activity. Furthermore, the community members also presented charges against the Secretariat of Mining for breach of duty about the lack of compliance with its obligations of protecting the environment. To investigate the case, the general attorney ordered an inspection of the mining site. The forensic experts hired by the mining company stated that there was no activity while those hired by the community members argued that there was. In 2019, the court dismissed the case against the company managers, the CEO and the Secretariat of Mining, in a new instance of environmental under-criminalisation.

Finally, in mid-August 2019, a network of social organisations linked *to El Algarrobo Assembly became aware of the fact that Agua Rica and Bajo Bajo La Alumbrera* were going to merge into one and that this was being discussed at the National University of Tucumán, given that the university was a shareholder of another related company, Yacimiento de Agua Dionisio. Community members demanded access to public information and asked the university representatives to visit Andalgalá to show them that the exploitation of the Agua Rica deposit was environmentally, socially and economically unviable. A commission from the university visited Andalgalá and issued a report in which they stated that:

> The town of Andalgalá presents itself as a society split in two and a burden of anguish is verifiable by direct observation (…). A high level of social stress is observed, which is at least partially linked to the project.[20]

---

[19] Exp. 133/2016. Gobierno de Catamarca c/Municipalidad de Andalgalá s/Acción de Inconstitucionalidad and Exp. 143/2016, Minera Agua Rica LLC c/Municipalidad de Andalgalá s/Acción de Inconstitucionalidad.

[20] Adm. Exp. 1091-19 on Formal Offer on Integrated Project Minera Agua Rica and Resolution 2372/2019.

Based on this document, a unanimous vote was taken to reject the merge of Agua Rica and Bajo La Alumbrera. The dispute is ongoing.

Conclusions

This chapter puts forward the working notion of *Southern green victimology* to shed light on the particularities of environmental victimisation in the Global South. *Southern green victimology* identifies the particularities of environmental/ green victimology in the Global South, highlights the limited capacity of Southern actors in terms of shaping environmental governance regulations at a global scale, and is attentive to the experiences of those grassroots actors engaged in resistance strategies. Concerning the latter, *Southern green victimology* sheds light on the vicious circle in which resistance movements that spread throughout the South to face both corporate harms/crime face the lack of response (or even complicity) of state agents, how they must resort to protest to stop the environmental-threatening investments, and how the criminal justice system reacts especially hardly, including the use of deadly force and the over-criminalisation of those exercising the constitutionally granted right to protest while ensuring corporate immunity.

Looking at these features, the chapter analysed the case of Andalgalá in Argentina. The case shows how environmental under-criminalisation protects corporations, even when they cause irreparable environmental damage and systematically break the law. In this vein, it has been shown how courts, particularly at the local level, tend to dismiss the most severe social harms caused by mining corporations against the environment and under-criminalise corporate representatives, even when they fail to follow specific rulings. Environmental under-criminalisation also protects law enforcement agencies, who are not subjected to criminal prosecution even though their actions are harmful and can affect the physical integrity of unarmed residents exercising their constitutional right to protest. This means that, particularly at the local level, the criminal justice system tends to under-criminalise law enforcement agencies even when they engage in excessive use of force against non-violent protesters. Finally, environmental under-criminalisation also benefits those members of the judiciary who act in symbiosis with corporations and to the detriment of the environment and the rights of the citizens that they should protect, with the result that no charges were brought against them. On the other hand, the case study exposes that environmental over-criminalisation displays against those who demand the respect of their fundamental rights through non-violent means. Moreover, local prosecutors were unable to gather sufficient evidence against the community members in all the criminal cases filed against them. Nevertheless, these processes were not dismissed immediately but remained open, distressing the defendants entitled to a due and expedited process. Interestingly, this phenomenon also exposes that environmental over-criminalisation occurs particularly at the level of law enforcement actions while charges are unlikely to be sustained due to the lack of evidence when the cases are already in court.

Overall, the case study allows to shed light on the fact that those communities resisting environmental damage are doubly affected by the process of criminal selectivity: they are over-criminalised for their direct protest actions against the corporations and later re-victimised on a triple basis: when the courts reject, in the vast majority of the cases, their legal petitions aimed at stopping the environmental damage caused by corporations; when the courts dismissed the cases against law enforcement agents who attacked to the community members' physical integrity; and when judges and prosecutors remain unpunished despite their collusive collaboration with the corporations.

Finally, the chapter also sought to expose that the process of bottom-up resistance through non-violent protest and the legal tools deployed by lawyers who belong and are daily engaged in the grassroots organisation became a unique tool to confront state-supported mining activity. As Hall (2014a) points out, given the relevance of political activism, it is essential to look at what works and what does not in terms of resistance to environmental harms. The experience of Andalgalá shows that success was due to the commitment and consistency of the vast majority of the community members acting united and involved in cooperation networks with committed lawyers as well as with members of other towns struggling against mining as well as with national social and human rights organisations. The combination of legal strategies with protest and blockades both in their hometown, where the mining corporation was located, as well as in the capital city, where the highest court functions, was proven to be a successful strategy. Moreover, peaceful, and creative protest strategies such as the women of the community marching in silence and the framing of clear and catching slogans became a crucial component of the struggle. As it is written on banners throughout the town of Andalgalá, the message of the community is clear: 'Drinking water gives us life. Awareness-raising gives us water and that is why the Aconquija snow-capped mountains are not to be touched!'

Acknowledgements

I want to thank Mariana Katz and Sergio Martinez, lawyers and activists in the region, with whom I wrote the first version of this chapter published in 'El Povo Organizado. El Caso Andalgalá'. *Introdução à criminologia verde: Perspectivas críticas, descoloniais e do Sul*, edited by Marilia Budó Marília de Nardín Budó, David Rodríguez Goyes, Lorenzo Natali, Ragnhild Sollund, Avi Brisman, Tirant Le Blanch, 2022.

References

Aranda, D. (2016, September 12). *Un Stop a La Megaminería*. Sociedad, Página. https://www.pagina12.com.ar/diario/sociedad/3-309169-2016-09-12.html
Asamblea El Algarrobo. (2010a, July 29). *Comunicado de Prensa*.
Asamblea El Algarrobo. (2010b, November 14). *Comunicado de Prensa*.

Asamblea El Algarrobo. (2010c, August 20). *Comunicado de Prensa.* http://catamarcacontaminada.blogspot.com/2010/08/comunicado-de-prensa-asamblea-el.html.

Asamblea El Algarrobo. (2010d). *Represión En ANDALGALÁ (1° Parte) 1/5* [YouTube]. https://www.youtube.com/watch?v=3iAZykq0ai0

Asamblea El Algarrobo. (2012). *Pantalla Para Los Pueblos (Corte Final)* [YouTube]. https://www.youtube.com/watch?v=X8zbZVlnZ0o

Berea, J. (2013). Andalgalá: Entre Bajo de La Alumbrera y Agua Rica. La Minería de Gran Escala En La Construcción Del(Os) Lugar(Es). Síntesis 4. https://revistas.unc.edu.ar/index.php/sintesis/article/view/12226

Brisman, A., & South, N. (2013). A green-cultural criminology: An exploratory outline. *Crime, Media, Culture: An International Journal, 9*(2), 115–135.

Carrington, K., Hogg, R., & Sozzo, M. (2016). Southern criminology. *The British Journal of Criminology, 56*(1), 1–20.

Carrington, K., Hogg, R., & Sozzo, M. (2019). Southern criminology. In W. S. DeKeseredy & M. Dragiewicz (Eds.), *Routledge handbook of critical criminology* (pp. 57–73). Routledge. https://doi.org/10.4324/9781315622040-6

Carrizo, B., Monte, M. E., & Saccucci, E. (2012). Desposesión y Resistencias: Una Mirada de Género Sobre La Particularidad de La Participación de Mujeres En Los Movimientos Sociales y Políticos de Chilecito y Famatina. In M. A. Ciuffolini (Ed.), *Por El Oro y El Moro: Explotación Minera y Resistencias En Catamarca, Córdoba y La Rioja* (pp. 167–189). Ediciones El Colectivo.

Catamarca Actual. (2016, October 17). *Cerro Atajo: Que La Comunidad Conozca.* https://www.catamarcactual.com.ar/politica/2016/10/17/cerro-atajo-que-comunidad-conozca-122708.html

Christel, L. G., & Gutiérrez, R. A. (2017). Making rights come alive: Environmental rights and modes of participation in Argentina. *Journal of Environment and Development, 26*(3), 322–347.https://doi.org/10.1177/1070496517701248

Coria, L. G. (2007). *Desarrollo Local y Actividad Minera En La Provincia de Catamarca.* Oidles. https://www.eumed.net/rev/oidles/00/Coria-resum.htm

Cornejo Torino, M. (2003). *Dirección de Fabricaciones Militares: Un Pilar Industrial Del País.* Universidad Católica de Salta.

Diario Judicial. (2020, January 21). *Impacto Ambiental Profundo.* https://www.diariojudicial.com/nota/74630

el Ancasti. (2005, August 15). *La Historia Del Emprendimiento: Vaivenes En Un Siglo de Vida de La Mina.* https://ri.conicet.gov.ar/handle/11336/110300

el Ancasti. (2016, March 3). *Agua Rica: La Corte Suprema, a Favor de Vecinos de Andalgalá.* https://www.elancasti.com.ar/politica-economia/2016/3/3/agua-rica-corte-suprema-favor-vecinos-andalgala-290324.html

el Trece. (2010). *Andalgalá de Pie, Un Pueblo Que Dijo ¡basta! Primera Parte [1/2] 23 y 24 de Febrero* [YouTube]. https://www.youtube.com/watch?v=wUYGl8b0xoA

Goyes, D. R. (2020). Little development, few economic opportunities and many difficulties: Climate change from a local perspective. *International Journal for Crime, Justice and Social Democracy, 9*(2), 170–182 https://doi.org/10.5204/IJCJSD.V9I2.1132

Hall, M. (2014a). The roles and use of law in green criminology. *International Journal for Crime, Justice and Social Democracy, 3*(2), 96–110.

Hall, M. (2014b). Environmental harm and environmental victims: Scoping out a 'green victimology.' *International Review of Victimology, 20*(1), 129–143. https://doi.org/10.1177/0269758013508682

Indymedia. (2012, February 10). *Imágenes de La Represión Sucedida Hace Pocas Horas En Tinogasta, Catamarca.* https://archivo.argentina.indymedia.org/news/2012/02/808215.php

la Vaca. (2007, December 29). *La Mina de Andalgalá, En Catamarca: El Agujero Negro.* https://lavaca.org/notas/la-mina-de-andalgala-en-catamarca/

Gallego Zapata, M. (2018, December 13). La Comisión de La Verdad y Las Mujeres. *El Espectador.* https://www.elespectador.com/colombia-20/analistas/la-comision-de-la-verdad-y-las-mujeres-article/

Lacerda, P., & Rolemberg, I. (2021). Violence and violations of rights against leaderships in the Brazilian Amazon. In W. Valeria Vegh (Ed.), *Criminalization of activism: Historical, present and future perspectives* (pp. 180–190). Routledge.

Lamalice, A., & Klein, J. L. (2016, December 6). Efectos Socio-Territoriales de La Mega-Minería y Reacción Social: El Caso de Minera Alumbrera En La Provincia de Catamarca, Argentina. *Revista Geográfica Norte Grande.* https://www.scielo.cl/scielo.php?pid=S0718-34022016000300008&script=sci_abstract&tlng=es

Lee, T. -P. (2022, December 22). *A welfare approach to mitigating environmental injustice: Exploring needs of pollution victims.* Umdcipe.Org. https://www.academia.edu/1315429/A_Welfare_Approach_to_Mitigating_Environmental_Injustice_Exploring_Needs_of_Pollution_Victims

Marcha. (2016). *Megaminería: Sabemos Que Agua Rica Se Va.* https://www.marcha.org.ar/megamineria-sabemos-que-agua-rica-se-va/

Marin, M. (2009). El No de Esquel Como Acontecimiento: Otro Mundo Posible'. In S. Maristella & A. Mirta (Eds.), *Trasnacional, Narrativas Del Desarrollo y Resistencias Sociales* (pp. 181–203). Biblos.

Massé, F., Givá, N., & Lunstrum, E. (2021). A feminist political ecology of wildlife crime: The gendered dimensions of a poaching economy and its impacts in Southern Africa. *Geoforum, 126*(11, November). 205–214. https://doi.org/10.1016/j.geoforum.2021.07.031

McEvoy, K. (2019). Cause lawyers, political violence, and professionalism in conflict. *Journal of Law and Society, 46*(4), 529–558.

Meganoticias. (2010). Se Levanto La Carpa Ambientalista: Continua El Ayuno. *Radio Mega 91.5 MHz, Andalgalá, Catamarca, Argentina.* http://andalgalamega.blogspot.com/2010/08/se-levanto-la-carpa-con-el-ayuno.html

Möhle, E. (2018). *Who decides over the territory? Governance of mining conflicts: The cases of Andalgalá in Catamarca and Famatina in La Rioja (2005–2016).* Faculty of the Graduate School of Arts and Sciences of Georgetown University.

Natali, L. (2014). Green criminology, victimización medioambiental y social harm. El Caso de Huelva (España). *Crítica Penal y Poderi, 7,* https://revistes.ub.edu/index.php/CriticaPenalPoder/article/view/10459.

O'Brien, T. (2016). Radical environmentalism: Nature, identity and more-than-human agency. *Social Movement Studies, 15*(5), 540–541. http://doi.org/10.1080/14742837.2016.1149463

Pastoriza, E. A. (2008). *El Gran Despojo.* Editorial Diógenes.

Pauw, J. (2003). The politics of underdevelopment: Metered to death—How a water experiment caused riots and a cholera epidemic. *International Journal of Health Services, 33*(4), 819–830.

Puerta Peña, S./P. A. (2021). Notes from the Field II: The judicial persecution in the Amazonian indigenous struggle—"El Baguazo"—Amazonas-Peru. In V. Vegh Weis (Ed.), *Criminalization of activism: Historical, present and future perspectives* (pp. 201–205). Routledge.

Resumen Latinoamericano. (2016, February 7). *Segundo Acampe de Los Vecinos de Andalgalá Frente a Tribunales: ¡Por La Sanción Definitiva Del Amparo Ambiental Contra La Minera a Cielo Abierto de La Alumbrera!.* https://www.resumenlatinoamericano.org/2016/02/07/segundo-acampe-de-los-vecinos-de-andalgala-frente-a-tribunales-por-la-sancion-definitiva-del-amparo-ambiental-contra-la-minera-a-cielo-abierto-de-la-alumbrera/

Ronco, A., & Allen-Robertson, J. (2021). Representations of environmental protest on the ground and in the cloud: The NOTAP protests in activist practice and social visual media. *Crime, Media, Culture, 17*(3), 375–399. http://doi.org/10.1177/1741659020953889

Stretesky, P. B., & Knight, O. (2013). The uneven geography of environmental enforcement INGOs. In W. Reece, D. W. Solomon, & W. Tanya (Eds.), *Emerging issues in green criminology* (pp. 173–196). Palgrave Macmillan. http://doi.org/10.1057/9781137273994_10

Tierra Viva. (2021, August 5). *Andalgalá, La Autodeterminación y 600 Caminatas Por La Vida*. https://agenciatierraviva.com.ar/andalgala-la-autodeterminacion-y-600-caminatas-por-la-vida/

Travers, M. (2019). The idea of a southern criminology. *International Journal of Comparative and Applied Criminal Justice, 43*(1), 1–12. https://doi.org/10.1080/01924036.2017.1394337

Vegh Weis, V. (2017). *Marxism and criminology: A history of criminal selectivity*. Brill and Haymarket Books.

Veneranda, M. (2012, February 18). *Las Mujeres Del Silencio Avivan La Guerra a La Minería*. La Nación. https://www.lanacion.com.ar/politica/las-mujeres-del-silencio-avivan-la-guerra-a-la-mineria-nid1449810/

White, R. (2003). Environmental issues and the criminological imagination. *Theoretical Criminology, 7*(4), 483–506.

Williams, C. (1996). Environmental victims. *Social Justice, 23*(4), 1–6.

Index

Abbreviated justice, 77
Abbreviated procedure, 64–67
Abolition of slavery, 31
Absolutism, 23
Accusatorial/adversarial model, 60, 62, 65, 67n12
Activists, 62–63
Actuarial justice, 3, 165
Actuarial methods, 135, 167n4, 168
Actuarial-managerial ideas, 171
Actuarialism, 164–165
    in Argentina and Chile, 170–173
Adapted-actuarialism, 171
Adjudicative model of criminal law, 164
Afonsinas Ordinances, 23
Agricultural penal colony, 31
Aljube Jail, 26
Americanization, 63–64, 75
Andean Community of Nations, 41
Andean Trade Preference Act (ATPA), 41, 45–46
Andean Trade Promotion and Drug Eradication (ATPDE), 41
Andean Trade Promotion and Drug Eradication Agreement (ATPDEA), 46
Anti-drug policies, 119
Argentina, 60, 204
    actuarialism and managerialism in, 170–173
    criminal justice reform, 60–64
    "effectiveness and efficiency" and "abbreviated procedure", 64–67, 81
    dominant and legitimized mode of sentencing, 70–77
    insecurity, 80

Province of Santa Fe, 78–79
    translation and "weak" Americanization in "law on the books", 67–70
Argentinean criminal justice system, 204
Aryan culture, 32
Assessment instruments, 134–136
Atlas-ti programme, 93
Authority, 102

Bajo el Durazno, 211
Body, 146
Brazil, 20
Brazilian colonial formation, 23–24
Brazilian elites, 35
Brazilian naturalism, 29–33
Brazilian penitentiary system, 20
    Brazilwood, 21–22
    considerations, 33–35
    discipline in Brazilian colonial formation, 28–29
    labor problem and punitive practices, 22–25
    post-abolition, 29–33
    slave quarters to first jails, 25–27
Brazilian social thought, 33
Brazilian Welfare State, 33
Brazilwood, 21–22
Bricolage, 191
Bureaucratic entities, 168

Capital accumulation, 23
Capital creation, 24
Capital Jail, 25–26
Capital punishment, 152
Capoeiras, 32
Carceral anthropology perspective, 146
Cartagena Declaration, 45

Casa Grande e Senzala ("The Masters and the Slaves"), 33
Cattle farming, 25
Celerity, 66n9
Cerro Atajo, 211
Chile
  actuarialism and managerialism in, 170–173
  prison management in, 94–96
Chilean prison service (*Gendarmería de Chile*), 91, 93–94
Chilean prison system, 91
Circular causality, 110
Citizen security, 6
City Council, 210
Civil war, 20
Civilisation, 9
Closed-circuit television (CCTV), 98
Coffee farmers, 31
Colombia, 41, 46
Colonial dungeons, 27
Colonial knowledge, 5
Colonial punitive practices, 23
Colonialism, 4, 33
Coloniality of penality, 9
Colonised subjects, 5
Community policing, 190
  organizations, 187
Conciencia Solidaria (Solidary Consciousness), 211
Confiscations, 98
Continental law, 155
Control, 92, 98
Coordination, 122–123
Corporal punishment, 21, 23, 150–151
  of enslaved people, 28n3
Corporate environmental harms/crimes, immunity of, 211–214
Correctional model, 10
Counter-reformist, 62
Court House of Correction, 30
Crime, 135
Crime control, 44
  Global North and new trends in, 166–170
Criminal Code of the Empire, 23
Criminal dangerousness, 140

Criminal justice, 9–10
  actors, 80–81
  harsh selectivity of, 207–211
  policy, 97
  practitioners, 168
  system, 32, 164
Criminal justice reform, 60–64
  processes, 166
  in Province of Buenos Aires, 171–172
Criminal policies, 40
Criminal Procedure Code (Law 12734), 64–65, 209
Criminal question, 4–5, 7, 11
Criminalisation, 203
Criminogenic factors, 136
Criminological positivism, 34
Criminological research, 40
Criminologists, 7
Criminology, 4, 6
Critical thought, 11
Culebras, 116
Cultural analysis of death penalty, 152
Cultural hegemony, 5
Cultural values, 44
Culturalism, 29–33

Dangerousness, 133, 138
Death, 152
Death penalty, 23, 152
Del lado de acá, 170–173
Del lado de allá, 166–170
Deliberative Council, 210
Democratic justice, 65, 72
Department of Justice, 63
Department of State, 63
Dependency, 4
Diagnostic tools, 133–136
Disadvantaged social groups, 110
Disciplinary power, 21, 28, 35
Discipline in Brazilian colonial formation, 28–29
Dissemination, 4
"Dos por uno" (two for one) policy, 51
Drug trafficking, 45, 80
Drug-enforcement, 48–52
Drug-related crimes, 52

Drugs, 43, 45, 111, 119
Dungeon prisons, 25–26

Economic Commission for Latin America and the Caribbean (ECLAC), 51
Economic volatility, 44
Ecuador, 40
　criminalization processes, 41
Ecuadorian penal real, 41
　punitive imperialism, 48–52
　punitive repression particularities in Ecuador, 44–48
　punitive turn, 42–43
Ecuadorian politics, 44
"Effectiveness and efficiency", 64–67, 81
El Algarrobo Assembly, 210
Empirical criminology, 138
England, 24
Environmental harms, 202
Environmental selectivity, 202
Environmental victimisation, 202, 204–205
Environmental victims resistance, 206–207
Environmental/green victimology, 202–203
Epistemological vigilance, 185
Eugenics, 32
Eurocentrism, 150
European immigration, 31
European theoretical models, 23
Evidence-based policy, 135
Exclusion, 110–111
Extralegal, 184
Extralegality, 185

Failed punishment, 146
Failed states, 146
Families, 110–111
Family networks, 116–117
Female poverty, 51
Feminization of poverty, 51
Foucauldian thesis of carceral archipelago, 119
Free Africans, 27

Free labor force, 24
Free trade, 30
Free Trade Agreements, 46

Gangs, 80, 113
Gendarmería, 94–95, 97, 102
Global North, 20, 34, 110, 132, 152, 165, 203
　and new trends in crime control, 166–170
Global peripheries, 2
Global South, 6–7, 20, 41, 132, 196
Gold and mining cycle, 25
Green criminology, 202–203

Historical contexts, 44
Holland, 24
Human resources, 139
Humanization of punishment, 150
Hybrid state-vigilante formations, 190
Hybridization, 188

Ideological relations and processes, 5
Illegal economies, 111
Imperialism, 4
Importation, 112
Imprisonment, 24
Inca's two bodies, 147–151
Incarceration rates, 43
Incentives, 31
Infanticide, 52
Informality, 10
Innovation, 7
Inquisitorial model, 60, 62, 67*n*12
Insecurity, 80
Insecurity crisis, 61
Institutional bricolage, 190
Institutional frailty, 44
Institutionalisation, 5–7
Instrument users, evaluations by, 139–140
Intangible' aspects of prison policy, 132
Integrity principle, 134
Inter-American Development Bank (IDB), 137–138

Internalisation of colonial mentality, 5
International organization, 60n1
Irmaos (brothers), 120

Jails, 25
Jesuits, 28–29
Judge, 69
Juicio abreviado, 173
Justice system, 23

Knowledge production and exchange, 4–8

La Modelo (Bogotá), 146
Labor problem and punitive practices, 22–25
Labor shortage, 23
Latin America, 40, 112
 criminal justice reform processes in, 62
 criminology, 4
 modern' penality in, 9
 penal dynamic, institutions and practices in, 3
 prison condition in, 151–156
 slum, 112–123
Latin American penality, 8
Latin American prison systems, 137
Law 108, 49–50, 52
Law in action, 64
Law in books, 64
"Law on the books", 67–70
Leakage of meaning, 190
Left-wing social movements, 189
Legal discourse, 149, 151
Legal order, 193
Legal reform, 63, 68
Legal transplant, 67
Liberal discourse, 147–151
Liberal penal discourses, 149
Los Nuevos Defensores, 210

"Managerial justice" program, 61, 65, 66n10
Managerial practices within courtrooms, 170

Managerialism, 95n17, 164–165, 169, 169n6
 in Argentina and Chile, 170–173
Managerialization, 169n6
Manual labor, 29
Marginal criminological realism, 7
Marginal position, 11
Marginalisation, 8, 11
Marketization, 169
Marxist thought, 20
Mass incarceration, 111
"Master and slave" mentality, 35
Matricide, 52
Mental colonialism, 5
Metamorphosis of theoretical vocabularies, 7, 9
Metropolitan thinking, 170
Military format, 94
Miscegenation, 32–33
Mixed economy, 10
Mixed model, 65
Mob violence, 190
"Modern and civilized" penitentiary project, 22
'Modern' penality, 9
Modernity, 9
Modernization, 71
Moral imperatives, 195–196
Moral reform, 29

National Criminal Procedure Code, 65
National Institute of Rehabilitation (INR), 132, 137
National Offender Management Service (NOMS), 135
National Rehabilitation Institute (INR), 95n15
Neighborhood, 111
Neo-liberal penality thesis, 41
Neoliberal ethos, 61
Neoliberal logic, 44
Neoliberal model, 41
Neoliberal policies, 51, 95n16
Neoliberalism, 40, 44
"Neopositivist" approach, 134
Neutralization of violence, 151

New management, 95n17
New penology, 133, 165
New Penology, The, 166–167
New Public Management (NPM), 165, 169
Nigerian vigilantes, 190
North American Political Science Approach, 191–195
Northern theories, 4–5, 8
Nuda vida (bare life), 153

Offender Assessment System (OASys), 132, 135–136, 139
    adoption process, coverage, and use of information, 138–139
Open-pit mining, 204–205
Optional referendum, 208n11
Order, management of, 91–93
Ordinances, 23
Organisational dynamics, 99
Original colonialism, 9
Over-criminalisation of peaceful local resistance, 207–211

Penal Enlightenment, 20–21
Penal imperialism, 41, 47
Penal outcomes, 77
Penal policy, 40, 168
Penal power, 47
Penal reform
    between Brazilian naturalism and culturalism, 29–33
    discourse, 21
Peripheral, 11
    penality, 9
    punishment, 8–11
Peripherality, 3
Peru, 3, 45, 120
Philippine Ordinances, 23
Physical violence, 147
Pink Tide wave, 43
"Pink tide" movement, 132
Plan Cordillerano Norte, 204
Plea bargaining, 67, 70
Policy, 40, 45
Policy transfer, 48

Political instability, 44
Political scientists, 192
Politics of language, 189
Popular illegalisms, 20
Positivist criminology, 7, 32
Post-abolition, 29–33
Post-release support, 94
Postgraduate degrees, 6
Power, 21
"Pragmatic" legitimization, 73
"Pre-modern" traits of Brazilian society, 33
Precautionary measure, 208n7
Preparatory activity, 187
Presigangas, 26
Primacy of economic rationality, 134
Primitive accumulation, 24
Prison, 3, 6, 9, 90, 145–146
    condition in Latin America, 151–156
    culture, 91n2
    economy, 116
    experience in Latin America, 152–153
    history, 20
    Inca's two bodies and liberal discourse, 147–151
    intelligence, 98
    interactions, 110
    officials, 98
    policy, 132
    prison-form, 21
    prison-slum continuum, 112
    punishment, 149
    as punishment, 24
    reform, 28, 131–132
    social order, 90
    staff, 103
    systems, 137
    violence, 151
Prison gangs, 110, 113
    prison gang-form, 111
Prison Gendarmería Corps, 94
Prison management, 91, 131–132
    in Chile, 94–96
    considerations, 103–104

findings on daily life in prisons, 97–99
management of order, 91–93
methodology, 93
operationalising prison order, 96–97
rewards and punishment, 99–103
Private citizens, 187
Private security firms, 187
Private voluntary agency, 187
Pro-convicts, 102
Problematisation of prison order, 92
Professional discretion principle, 134
Profits, 24
Protestantism, 21
Province of Buenos Aires, 171–172
Province of Santa Fe, 78–79
Public defender (PD), 73, 75n25
Public Defense Service, 65
Public management principles, 95n17
Public Ministry for the Prosecution, 65, 68
Public security, 6
Punishment, 1–3, 28–29, 41, 44, 99–103, 146, 166
knowledge production and exchange, 4–8
peripheral punishment, 8–11
Punishment and society', 2–3
Punitive imperialism, 41, 48–52
Punitive power, 146
Punitive repression particularities in Ecuador, 44–48
Punitive swamps, 10
Punitive turn, 40–43
Pure accusatory model, 65
Pure-actuarial ideas, 171
Pure-managerial ideas, 171
Purity, 79

Questione meridionale, 34

Racial democracy, 33
Racial homogeneity, 111
Racial pride, 33
Racial purification, 33
Racism, 32
Radicality, 79
Raids, 98
Rasphuis, 21–22
Recife House of Detention, 30
Reform processes, 61–62
Reformers, 62–63
Regeneration, 30
Regional Prosecutor, 67
Rehabilitation, 137–138
Repression, 44
Reputation, 115
Resistance, 203
Revolution of 1930, 33
Rewards, 99–103
"Rights-based" justice, 60–61, 65, 72
Risk, 92, 98
Risk assessment tools, 136
Risk model, 131, 133
and use of diagnostic tools, 133–136
Risk paradigm, 132, 134
Risk-Need-Responsiveness (RNR) model, 132–134
adoption of RNR model by Uruguayan prison system, 137–140
Romanticization, 150
Roraima (Brazil), 146

San Antonio Texas Anti-Drug Summit, 45
San Francisco Vigilance Committee, 184
San Miguel (Chile), 146
Secondary prisonization, 116
Segregation measures, 28–29
Selective incapacitation, 167n3
Self-defense committee (*comité de autodefensa*), 184
Self-government, 34
Sentencing, dominant and legitimized mode of, 70–77
Service Peace and Justice (SERPAJ), 207
Sexual violence, 135
Simplicity, 150
Simplification, 66n9

Skyrocketing prison population, 111
Slave, 23
  labor, 25
  quarters to first jails, 25–27
  trade, 30
Slavery, 4, 31, 33
Slum, 112
  continuous flow of incarcerated population, 113–114
  coordination, 122–123
  discipline, 119–120
  economies, 117–119
  expectations, 114–115
  family networks, 116–117
  prison shapes, 119
  regulation, 121–122
  trajectories, 115–116
Social differentiation, 111
Social networks, 115–116
Social order, 110
Social reintegration, 100, 102
Social relations, 92n4
Social sciences, 7
Societal norms, 44
Societal transformations in Western societies, 42
Society scholarship, 1–3
Socio-economic model, 40
Sociological studies, 90
Sociologies of punitive turn, 40
Sociopolitical order, 186
South American context, 41
Southern criminology, 202–203
Southern green victimology, 203
Spinhuis, 21
State coercion, 186–187
State-corporate symbiosis, 208
Structured "second generation" instruments, 135
Structured clinical judgment, 135
Subalternity, 4

Technical staff, evaluations by, 139–140
Topo Chico (Mexico), 146
Transfers, 98
Translation and "weak" Americanization in "law on the books", 67–70
Transparency, 71
Trial-avoiding conviction mechanism, 170n7
Tutchhuis, 21
Twilight institution, 190

UN Framework Convention on Climate Change (FCCC), 203
Under-criminalisation of violent repression, 207–211
Uruguay, 131
  adoption of RNR model by Uruguayan prison system, 137–140
  methodological strategy, 136–137
  prison management in, 131–132
  risk model and use of diagnostic tools, 133–136
US agenda of the War on Drugs, 119
Utilitarianism, 20–21

Vagrants, 32
Values, 185
Venezuela, 110, 115
Vigilante acts, 187
Vigilante groups, 188
Vigilante justice, 186–187
Vigilante violence, 195
Vigilantism, 3, 184
  classic definitions, 186–188
  as hybrid institution, 189–191
  North American Political Science Approach, 191–195
  promising solutions, 195–196
Violations of public order, 32
Violence, 92, 153
Visión Sostenible (Sustainable Vision), 211

White Aryans, 31
Whitening process, 31
Workhouses, 24

Printed and bound by CPI Group (UK) Ltd, Croydon, CR0 4YY
05/02/2025
14638643-0001